Perspectives on Postal Service Issues

A Conference Sponsored by the
American Enterprise Institute for Public Policy Research

Perspectives on Postal Service Issues

Edited by Roger Sherman

American Enterprise Institute for Public Policy Research
Washington, D.C.

Library of Congress Cataloging in Publication Data

Main entry under title:

Perspectives on Postal Service issues.

  (AEI symposium ; 79J)
  1. United States Postal Service—Congresses.
2. Postal service—United States—Congresses.
I. Sherman, Roger, 1930–   II. American Enterprise
Institute for Public Policy Research.   III. Series:
American Enterprise Institute for Public Policy
Research.   AEI symposia ; 79J.
HE6371.P47   383'.4973   80-12071
ISBN 0-8447-2173-5
ISBN 0-8447-2174-3 (pbk.)

AEI Symposium 79 J

Contributors

Douglas K. Adie
Ohio University

William J. Baroody, Jr.
American Enterprise Institute

James I. Campbell, Jr.
DHL Corporation

Michael A. Crew
Rutgers University

Clyde S. DuPont
Chairman, Postal Rate Commission

Melvyn A. Fuss
University of Toronto

Charles L. Jackson
Staff, U.S. House of Representatives, Subcommittee on
Communications

Leland L. Johnson
National Telecommunication and Information Administration

Timothy J. May
Patton, Boggs, and Blow

Leonard Merewitz
National Transportation Policy Study Commission

James C. Miller III
American Enterprise Institute

Bridger M. Mitchell
The Rand Corporation
and
International Institute of Management

Roy A. Nierenberg
Council on Wage and Price Stability

Contents

Foreword

It is hardly necessary to defend the calling of a conference on Postal Service issues. While complaints about the federal bureaucracy are standard political rhetoric, the Postal Service is perhaps the only federal bureaucracy that reaches the vast majority of people in this country every day—and certainly one of only a few that touch people in tangible, direct, and visible ways. To put it simply, people can see what they are getting for their money from the Postal Service in a way that they cannot with most other federal services. Thus, the public's experience with the Postal Service may significantly influence its general notions about the efficiency, competence, and reliability of federal employees and services. As poll after poll confirms, the public does not like what it is getting. Despite price increases totaling 150 percent over the last eight years for first-class mail—compared with a 60 percent increase in the consumer price index during the same period—people complain more about the *quality* of postal service than the price!

But if the visibility of postal operations makes them especially important in the crystallization of public attitudes toward government, postal inefficiencies produce a variety of invisible effects that are far from negligible. Postal prices represent an inescapable cost of doing business in this country—and in some cases a particularly crucial cost. For the struggling literary journal or small-circulation opinion magazine, for the unknown political challengers seeking to spread their messages to all the homes in their districts, for the small entrepreneur with a clever new product and a determination to reach just the right market through careful mailings—for all these, a postal rate increase can make the difference between success and failure. If postal policy does not rank among the most glamorous issues on the public agenda today, it may still be among the most important.

The Post Office Department was one of the first federal agencies established after the ratification of the Constitution, and it ranked as the largest federal employer until well into the present century. Amos Kendall, President Andrew Jackson's postmaster general, is credited in all the old history texts with being the principal founder of the spoils system in national politics. Noting that Kendall sought to rationalize and centralize federal administrative procedures, a new school of revisionist historians now argues that Kendall should be viewed instead as a conscientious reformer. I leave it to the professional historians to reconcile these competing interpretations of Kendall's legacy. But though this conference concerns recent postal policies and operations, politics and administrative reform have long been entangled in discussions of postal services.

In 1970 Congress passed the Postal Reorganization Act, which transformed the old Post Office Department into a new, semiautonomous public corporation—our present-day U.S. Postal Service. A principal aim of this legislation was to free the Post Office once and for all from politics. In that endeavor, the legislation has not fully succeeded—though in this day and age it is hard to see how any public service of great size and importance could be, or perhaps even should be, entirely insulated from political influences. Yet, if the Postal Service is ever to meet public expectations, there is an urgent need for closer attention to economic constraints and opportunities and for more refined methods of calculating costs and prices in postal operations. In this respect, too, postal reform has an importance that transcends the immediate focus of this conference. An obstinate inflation rate, a growing demand for tax reductions, and a variety of other fiscal pressures have made almost every politician and policy maker aware of the need for more cost-effective management of public programs, as compared with the easy spending of a decade ago.

The prestige of modern techniques of economic analysis has in some respects never been greater. But even economists, as they have been drawn deeper into actual policy making, have come to appreciate that their analytical techniques—however refined—will never resolve basic policy questions if they ignore political factors. For better or worse, this is a fundamental fact about the way government works. The experience of the last decade indicates that, even in the best of circumstances, economic calculations must be tempered by political prudence just as political enthusiasms must be restrained by economic realities. With this in mind, the American Enterprise Institute has broadened its research programs to include not only economists and technical specialists but also political scientists and a variety of people with practical experience in government programs.

The subject of the present conference is particularly appropriate to the kind of sober public inquiry we try to foster at AEI. Those participating—both on the panels and in the audience—are well qualified and no doubt will present a variety of views. Such is in the spirit of AEI's motto: "Competition of ideas is fundamental to a free society."

WILLIAM J. BAROODY, JR.
President, American Enterprise Institute

1

Introduction

Roger Sherman

We all send and receive mail. Yet we know very little about the U.S. Postal Service, the federal government enterprise that delivers our mail. Beyond the corner mailbox that swallows our letters and the routine appearance in our mailboxes of incoming mail, just how the Postal Service operates remains for most of us something of a mystery. The U.S. Postal Service is certainly an enormous enterprise, spending nearly $20 billion a year and employing more than 600,000 persons. The rates it charges for mail services can be hard to understand; only the post office window clerks who kindly (if slowly) answer our queries seem to know them. Many of us also have our private horror stories about bad mail service (my own is a letter that took two months to go seventy miles). But we tend consistently to expect our letters to be reliably delivered.

Mail is a basic service provided by governments all over the world. How it is provided, how it is priced, and who, if anyone, receives favored or unfavored treatment are important matters. Not only are the possible economic effects in the United States enormous, running into billions of dollars, but questions of public literacy and general knowledge as well as political community and rights of privacy also may be at stake. So perhaps we should know more about the Postal Service than we do, about how it is controlled, how efficiently it runs, whom it benefits, and whether those benefits are justified.

As William Baroody, Jr., indicated in the Foreword, the purpose of AEI's Conference on Postal Service Issues, as well as of this volume of papers from the conference, is to illuminate important current postal issues and to speculate about the future of the Postal Service. Judge Seymour Wenner, the first chief administrative law judge at the Postal Rate Commission and author of influential initial decisions, chaired the morning sessions presented in Part One of this book. Stanley Besen, on leave from his position as professor of economics at Rice University to serve as codirector of the Network Inquiry Special Staff at the Federal

1

Communications Commission, chaired the afternoon sessions that make up Part Three. The participants (both formal contributors and speakers from the audience) know well the issues they tackle, and the reader should be able to see postal issues more clearly as a result of their stimulating discussions.

Postal service is about as old as our country. The U.S. Constitution gave Congress the power "to establish Post Offices." In the nineteenth century, the department of the federal government that was created for that purpose, the U.S. Post Office, expanded dramatically, easily raising revenues to cover the costs of its services. As the nation expanded, however, delivery costs to the South and West raised average postal costs nationally. Rates set to cover those higher average costs attracted competitors in eastern cities, where costs were much lower. To prevent competition from private express services, the Postal Act of 1845 was passed, the so-called private express statutes, forbidding competition in letter mail. That legislation established what is referred to today as the postal monopoly. Unlike the public perception of most monopolies, however, the major postal service issues do not revolve around monopoly profits but are concerned with rate relationships (Are some users being subsidized and, if so, by whom?), excessive costs, subsidy requirements, service quality, innovation, and threats from potential competition.

When the private express statutes were passed in 1845, mail traveled the vast majority of miles by stagecoach and horseback. It then cost five cents per ounce to send a letter up to 300 miles, and ten cents per ounce to send a letter any farther. The extraordinary expansion of railroads, however, brought revolutionary economies to transportation, and with them reductions of postal costs and rates. In 1851 rates were reduced to three cents per ounce within 300 miles and five cents per ounce for up to 3,000 miles. In 1855 the rate was set uniformly at three cents per ounce for distances up to 3,000 miles. Postage stamps had been introduced by then, and specialized mail cars made their appearance in railroad trains. The United States was developing one of the largest and most efficient mail services in the world, and the three-cent letter rate would last into the lifetimes of many people alive today.

Postal developments in the twentieth century have not been so auspicious, and the 1960s were especially troubled times for the Post Office Department. Large financial deficits and serious service problems arose. More and more messages were being transmitted by telephone, gradually eroding the power of the postal monopoly. Despite changing circumstances, the Post Office Department appeared unresponsive and was charged with poor management and unfair cross-subsidization among the mail services. In 1970 the U.S. Postal Service was formed as an independent government enterprise rather than a department of the federal government as its predecessor had been. The new enterprise was to be operated with sound management methods, and postal services were to be made self-supporting. A Postal Rate Commission was also created to enforce statutory requirements governing postal rates—in essence, to regulate postal rates.

Part One of this volume considers the recent past and reviews experience with the U.S. Postal Service since it was created in 1970. In Chapter 2 Leonard Waverman reviews pricing principles developed by economists for public enterprises and relates them to Postal Service practices. In Chapter 3 Melvyn Fuss describes principles for determining costs, including recent developments that may make it possible to ascertain costs for public enterprises with more accuracy than previously. Both authors find considerable scope for improvement in current U.S. Postal Service pricing and costing practices.

Chapters 4 and 5 examine the experience of mailers and workers under the Reorganization Act of 1970. First, James Miller and I examine the mailers' experiences. We find that inequities in the pre-1970 postal rates seem to have persisted well into the 1970s. Repeated findings by the Court of Appeals of the District of Columbia have been needed to move the Postal Rate Commission toward enforcing requirements of the 1970 act. Then Douglas Adie shows that workers have fared handsomely under the act and argues that compared with wages in similar private-sector jobs postal workers are now considerably overpaid.

In Chapter 6, which constitutes Part Two of this volume, the Honorable Clyde S. DuPont, chairman of the Postal Rate Commission, assesses the present situation of the commission. In particular, he reviews efforts by the commission to acquire better data on postal costs, to refine its conceptual framework for rate making, and to streamline its procedures for deciding rate cases.

Future postal issues are examined in Part Three. There Charles Jackson sketches rather dramatically the new technologies that will affect postal service in the future. Since these technologies may alter a market's role in controlling the Postal Service's economic behavior, it is appropriate that Robert Willig then describes the potential for that role. He draws on recent work that defines natural monopoly and describes ways to control it. These matters have a bearing on current postal practices and decisions, for the kind of postal service we have in the future depends very much on actions taken today.

Because new technologies can be expected to produce new opportunities, the major institutions that affect those opportunities also need to be examined. In Chapter 9 Kenneth Robinson considers how much change can be accommodated within the present law. He examines in particular the legal issues that will be raised if the Postal Service enters the electronic communications industry, and he makes suggestions for how we might proceed. In Chapter 10 James Campbell describes the major political forces and anticipates their development, perhaps illuminating the headlines of the future.

Thus, this volume assesses postal reorganization since 1970. It also describes future technical opportunities and the expected economic, legal, and political responses.

Part
One

The Past: Postal Reorganization
Since 1970

2

Pricing Principles:
How Should Postal Rates Be Set?

Leonard Waverman

The post office is properly a mercantile project. The government advances the expense of establishing the different offices and of buying or hiring the necessary horses or carriages and is repaid with a large profit by the duties upon what is carried.

Adam Smith, *The Wealth of Nations*

Since 1945 the United States Post Office (the United States Postal Service since 1971) has not fulfilled Adam Smith's dictum that the carrying of mail would be a mercantile project. Instead, the postal service has been plagued by large and, in certain periods, growing deficits, increased competition for various classes of mail, challenges in the courts to the rates that were set, and continued labor strife. Since the passage of the Postal Reorganization Act,[1] which was heralded as opening a new era for the Post Office, the profitability of postal service has not improved. The reorganization, which was intended to end the purely political nature of many Post Office operations, has not had that effect. Dividing the authority to establish rates between the Postal Service and the independent Postal Rate Commission has perhaps intensified the political nature of rate setting.

The question of how postal services should be priced is unanswerable unless there is agreement on a set of noncontradictory objectives for these prices. In fact, however, there is not broad agreement on the objectives that prices for postal services should embody. Instead, the objectives written in the Postal Reorganization Act are self-contradictory. There are, in my mind, four possible objectives for prices generally. The first is economic efficiency; the second, equity; the third, external or social considerations; and the fourth, political considera-

---

[1] Postal Reorganization Act of 1970, 84 Stat. 719 (1970), 39 *U.S. Code.*

7

tions. Economically efficient prices would generally lead to the greatest output from any set of inputs. Equity considerations may require an adjustment of prices from the efficient set in order to make the distribution of income more equitable. Adjusting efficient prices for external social reasons recognizes considerations that the marketplace does not take account of in setting prices based on private costs. Political objectives of pricing principles require changes in efficient prices in response to the political realities of powerful interest groups. It should be obvious that these objectives are contradictory, or at least that the last may contradict the first two. If politically advantaged groups such as the powerful and the rich are able to use political lobbying to adjust efficient prices to suit their own purposes, then the resulting deviations from efficient pricing will clearly not be equitable. The politically dominant group may argue that equity considerations are behind their lobbying; they may even give social, external reasons for changing prices. The resulting prices, however, act to redistribute wealth toward the politically powerful.

The objectives of the Postal Reorganization Act are ambiguous and contradictory because they attempt to meet a number of conflicting objectives. According to section 3622, rates and fees shall be "fair and equitable" (subsection 1); "they shall bear the direct and indirect postal costs attributable to that class of type, plus that portion of all other costs of the postal service reasonably assignable to such class or type" (subsection 3); they shall bear some relationship to the "value of the mail service" actually provided each class (subsection 2); the fees should consider "the available alternative means of sending and receiving" (subsection 5); the "educational, cultural, scientific and informational value to the recipient of mail matter" should be considered (8) and "such other factors as the Commission deems appropriate" (9). Moreover, section 403(c) requires that "the Postal Service shall not, except as specifically authorized in this title, make any undue or unreasonable discrimination among users of the mails." And above all, the basic function of the Postal Service as stated in section 101 is "the obligation to provide postal services to bind the nation together."

Although we may all have different objectives for the price of apples, haircuts, and Cadillacs, we do not argue forever about what the prices for these goods should be. But we have worried about and debated postal rates since time immemorial because of the production characteristics of the Postal Service and the way in which it is organized as distinct from the production of our markets for apples or Cadillacs. First, since the Postal Service is organized as a "public service," the conflicts between objectives of equity and efficiency and intrusions of political considerations are much protracted. Second, it is felt by some that postal services involve public aspects that apples and haircuts do not—binding the nation together and disseminating material of educational, cultural, scientific, and informational value.

Third, for the most part, postal service is offered by a monopoly rather than a competitive market. Prices are set not by market forces but by regulators who must mediate among the various interests that appear before them. Furthermore, the Postal Service sells a number of joint services that utilize common costs and capital. Because of this joint production, it is difficult, if not impossible, to ascertain the cost of each service offered.

Finally, the large and continued deficits of the Postal Service indicate another difference from goods and services such as apples and haircuts provided by competitive markets. No privately organized market would allow twenty-three years of continual losses. The large deficits indicate that taxpayers generally are subsidizing mail users. Moreover, given the conflicting objectives and political elements implicit in rate making, the presence of a deficit probably indicates that specific groups are receiving this subsidy.

To decide how postal rates should be set, it is necessary to agree first on the *absolute level* of postal prices; that is, should the Postal Service as a whole or postal services in total cover the cost of operation? Second, having determined the absolute level of postal prices, we must agree on the *relative prices* of the various classes of service offered. In the following sections, I examine how prices are set by the Postal Service and the Postal Rate Commission and then I discuss how the characteristics of organization and production enumerated above affect decisions on absolute and relative prices and enable price discrimination and subsidization.

How Postal Prices Are Set

Rates are determined in order to cover the cost of postal service, given the objectives of the act, the nature of competitive forces, and the explicit subsidies for certain classes of mail. First-class mail consists of five categories: letters and sealed parcels, postal and private cards, domestic airmail, domestic air parcel post, and business reply mail. First-class mail may be deposited in letter boxes or at the post office and is delivered to the home or business.

Whereas the present price for the first ounce of a letter mailed anywhere in the country is fifteen cents, in an act of 1792 Congress established this set of prices: "for every single letter [that is, one folded sheet of paper] conveyed 30 miles, 6¢; over 30 miles and not exceeding 60 miles, 8¢; over 60 miles and not exceeding 100 miles, 10¢; . . . over

450 miles, 25¢." It was not until 1863 that Congress introduced a uniform rate for first-class mail, independent of distance and independent of the number of sheets carried.

Since the Constitutional Post was set up in 1775 giving Congress "the sole and exclusive right and power of . . . establishing and regulating post offices from one State to another, throughout all the United States exacting such postage on the papers passing through the same as may be requisite to defray the expenses of the said office" (Article 9, paragraph 4), competitive carriers for first-class mail have been discouraged. Throughout the nineteenth century, prohibitions against private express were extended.[2] The 1968 report of the President's Commission on Postal Organization concluded that the postal monopoly provided by the private express statutes should be preserved. Competition in the future for first-class mail is likely to come, however, not from private express companies but from the change in technology to electronic funds transfer. Rather than many pieces of paper being passed via the Postal Service, accounts will be debited and credited via telecommunication lines.

Second-class mail consists of magazines, newspapers, and other periodicals. There are five categories of second-class mail: regular-rate mail, within-county mail, nonprofit mail, classroom publications, and transient mail. Except for publications mailed at the transient rate, second-class mail must be bulk-delivered to the post office. No statute prevents competitors from carrying this class of mail. For example, it is obvious that within a city newspapers are delivered by carriers or sold on the street and not delivered by the post.[3] Certain users of this rate are experimenting with private delivery services.[4]

Fourth-class mail consists of four subcategories: parcels weighing over one pound and under seventy pounds; catalogs; a special rate for books, films, and sound recordings; and a library mail rate for materials mailed to and from schools, libraries, and certain specified nonprofit organizations. For these classes of mail, the Postal Service is but one of many competitors.

Third-class mail is really a catchall for mail that weighs less than

---

[2] George L. Priest, "The History of the Postal Monopoly in the United States," *Journal of Law and Economics*, vol. 13 (1973); M. S. Baratz, *Economics of the Postal Service* (Washington, D.C.: Public Affairs Press, 1962).

[3] "In fact 67 per cent of all American magazines are delivered through the post. A vicious circle has thus been created. The newsagent cannot exist because his delivery costs would exceed the postage charges; postage charges cannot be raised to economic levels because the absence of a cheap alternative method of distribution enables publishers to claim that such an increase would ruin them." J. K. Horsefield, "British and American Postal Services," in R. Turvey, ed., *Public Enterprise* (Baltimore: Penguin Books, 1968).

[4] See U.S. Postal Rate Commission, Docket R77–1, p. 378.

one pound but does not qualify for special second-class rates. The differences in the per piece and per pound rate for second-class regular-rate mail and third-class mail are quite substantially in favor of second-class mail.

To follow the procedure by which the Postal Service and the Postal Rate Commission set prices is not an easy task.[5] First, the costs are determined for some future test year. In the decision in Postal Rate Commission Docket R77–1 (May 12, 1978), a March 1978 to March 1979 forward test year was used. The Postal Service and the commission must determine what costs are to be in that year. Included in costs are escalations for labor, a 4 percent contingency fee, and a recoupment of prior year losses ($2.3 billion since 1971). In R77–1 the revenue requirement is estimated to be some $17.6 billion, from which is deducted $920 million representing the public service appropriation to the Postal Service from the United States government. This $920 million represents the cost of maintaining rural postal facilities, which are considered to be in the public interest. A second deduction from the revenue requirement involves the continuing appropriations for losses on special classes of mail, principally subclasses of second-class mail. In R77–1 this is estimated to be $242 million. After further deductions for investment and other income, the revenue recoverable from mailers is estimated to be $16.2 billion, and this represents the absolute level of prices which must be exacted from all users of the Postal Service. The establishment of relative prices determines the degree to which various classes will contribute to this absolute level of the revenue requirement. Not all classes make identical contributions to revenues (nor should they). The problem of course is how to allocate or attribute common costs to each service. The "cost separations" game is played constantly. Separating nonseparable costs is the modern version of alchemy—a consultant appears with a black box, and out of one end, like magic, come the "correct" average costs of service. The only thing that turns to gold, however, is the consultant's pocket.

Court proceedings in the past several years have disapproved of some of the rate-making and costing methodology used in the two previous decisions of the Postal Rate Commission, namely, Dockets R74–1 and R76–1.[6] Before these appeals, the Postal Service with the approval

[5] See Rodney E. Stevenson, "The Pricing of Postal Services," in Harry M. Trebbing, ed., *New Dimensions in Public Utility Pricing* (East Lansing: Michigan State University Press, 1976).

[6] *National Association of Greeting Card Publishers* v. *U.S. Postal Service*, 569 F.2d 570 (D.C. Cir., December 28, 1976), no. 75–105b et al. (*NAGCP* 1); *National Association of Greeting Card Publishers* v. *U.S. Postal Service* (D.C. Cir., July 8, 1976), no. 76–1611 (*NAGCP* 2).

of the Postal Rate Commission had attributed approximately 50 percent of total costs as causally related to specific users of the mail. Institutional costs that were not so attributable were apportioned to rate classes by the inverse elasticity rule, according to which the Postal Service charged proportionally more institutional costs to those services with inelastic demands. These pricing and costing principles were used because they were thought to be grounded both in economic theory and in the act, and they were considered fair and equitable. I will have more to say about all three reasons.

The 1976 decision (*NAGCP* 1) required further attribution of causally related costs and therefore a minimization of the allocation of institutional cost elements in order, in the court's view, to minimize "discrimination." The district court also disapproved of the inverse elasticity rule. Therefore, in the latest Postal Rate Commission decision some 70 percent of total costs are classified as attributable or assignable, and the use of the inverse elasticity rule has become implicit rather than explicit.

M. S. Baratz estimated that in 1961 first-class mail covered 100 percent of its expenditures, airmail 113 percent of its expenditures, second-class mail 23 percent of its expenditures, controlled-circulation mail 64 percent, third-class 66 percent, fourth-class 83 percent, and all classes 83 percent of expenditures.[7] Ignoring the amount recoverable for prior year losses, the Rate Commission expects that if the Postal Service reaches the objectives of R77–1, the Postal Service as a whole would cover some 93 percent of total expenditures. All classes are expected to meet 100 percent of the attributable and assignable costs. First-class letters and sealed parcels will contribute 124 percent of attributable and assignable costs. For second-class mail, revenue will bring in only 100.2 percent of directly attributable and assignable costs (R77–1, p. 302). Three subcategories of second-class mail—within-county mail, nonprofit mail, and classroom publications—only bring in revenues equal to their attributable costs. For third-class mail, the Rate Commission approves a 104 percent cost coverage ratio. Finally, for fourth-class service, the commission recommends rates that bring in 104 percent of attributable and assignable costs. Thus, ignoring the real issue of how costs are considered assignable, the commission apportions 23 percent of costs (93 − 70) by the degree of competition facing that service. First-class mail covers most of these nonassignable costs because of the pricing factor used (124 percent of assignable and attributable costs) and the size of the class (50 percent of total revenue).

---

[7] Baratz, *Economics of the Postal Service.*

LEONARD WAVERMAN

Five Propositions on Subsidies

Earlier I discussed the elements in the organization and nature of production that complicate the setting of rates and the analysis of the principles behind such rates—monopoly elements, joint services produced with common inputs, the presence of external or public good aspects, and the ambiguity of equity considerations. As shown below, these elements also aid the establishment, disguise, and maintenance of subsidies.

The Impact of Providing Services through a Monopoly. The fact that part of the services offered by the Postal Service are provided under monopoly restrictions complicates the pricing principles. If the Postal Service did not have a monopoly but had in fact to compete in competitive markets with a number of other firms for each of the various classes of mail, then rate setting could be left to the marketplace. Economic theory suggests that where there are not increasing returns to production, the competitive market will lead to the Pareto-optimal allocation of resources, that is, the highest rate of output for any given set of inputs.[8] Some critics of the Postal Service have therefore suggested that the obvious answer is to remove the restrictions against private express.[9] By allowing competition, it is argued, the invisible hand will set the correct prices, thus eliminating the need for postal rate commissions (or even for this paper itself). The call for a market solution may be a voice in the dark for two reasons. First, it has not convincingly been proven that the Postal Service does not enjoy increasing returns to scale. Melvyn Fuss (Chapter 3 herein) will go over the evidence, which indicates that there may be decreasing returns to scale when the operations of large offices are compared with medium-sized offices. To examine the operations of individual post offices is but one facet of the evaluation of the benefits of single-firm control. Recent advances in the theoretical literature indicate that examination of whether average and marginal costs are falling or increasing today is an inappropriate way of determining whether in fact a natural monopoly exists.[10] The essence of that literature indicates that where decreasing returns to scale are evident it is still possible for competition to decrease social welfare and increase social costs.

---

[8] Assuming that there are no externalities, and so on; see J. M. Henderson and R. E. Quandt, *Microeconomic Theory: A Mathematical Approach* (New York: McGraw-Hill, 1971), pp. 255–64.

[9] John Haldi, *Postal Monopoly: An Assessment of the Private Express Statutes* (Washington, D.C.: American Enterprise Institute, 1974).

[10] John C. Panzar and Robert D. Willig, "Free Entry and the Sustainability of Natural Monopoly," *Bell Journal of Economics,* vol. 8 (Spring 1977).

Although the examination of the Postal Service as a natural monopoly has engaged and will continue to engage consultants and academicans, whether postal production has monopoly attributes in production is really ancillary to whether postal rates will be regulated. There are many instances in the economy where prices are not set by the market, even where market prices would be efficient (agriculture and telecommunications, for example). Because the Post Office has been organized as a monopoly in first-class mail since 1775, irrespective of any evidence as to the monopoly characteristics of production, it is obvious to some members of society that a monopoly is necessary for improvements in welfare. These improvements may be based on reasons of externality or equity; they may with equal probability be welfare improvements for some specific group, at the expense of society generally.

The organization of the Postal Service with a monopoly over certain services does give greater weight to objectives other than efficiency, especially redistribution (cross-subsidization). The first of five unproven propositions is as follows: the organization of enfranchised monopolies, either public or private, affects the redistribution of income toward specific groups. Without this enfranchisement, it would be impossible for the monopoly to maintain losses in markets. Enfranchised monopolies then are characterized by long-run continual losses in some markets they serve, that is, cross-subsidization of various classes of service.[11] No private, unregulated firm, monopolistic or competitive, will lose money in a market for a long time. The "deep pockets" theory of predatory pricing holds no coins. The ability to lose money is not one of the better management techniques taught at the Harvard Business School. Some specific postal markets that are subsidized are examined later in this paper.

Joint Services and Common Costs. If the Postal Service offered only one kind of service to a homogeneous group of buyers, then I would argue that in all likelihood all buyers would be charged the same price—that is, none would be subsidized. The second proposition is that the offering of heterogeneous services within one public firm makes it easier to charge prices that are unrelated to costs. The second proposition is tied in with the third: the existence of common costs also makes it easier to charge prices to some groups that do not reflect the full long-run marginal costs of service.

The second proposition, I think, is fairly obvious. When all cus-

---

[11] Cross-subsidization is not unique to the Postal Service but is a common feature of most regulated utilities.

tomers are identical—that is, of the same size and sophistication—and purchase the identical service, then if the price varies among customers it is obvious that some person is being discriminated against, for the costs of serving each must be the same. However, where the enfranchised monopoly offers a wide variety of services to different classes of buyers, ranging from small residential consumers to large industrial firms, then the simple comparison of prices will not lead to any obvious feeling of discrimination since the costs of providing these different services will vary.

The third proposition can be highlighted with the following example. Assume that the enfranchised hypothetical monopoly offers three services; each of them is produced in a distinct plant in three different regions of the country. The services are produced so distinctly that customers can compare the costs of production for each of the three services or, at least, ask the enfranchised monopoly to make such a comparison. The hypothetical monopoly would have little discretionary power in determining either the fully allocated average costs or the long-run incremental costs for each of these three services. If the example is changed so that all three services are produced in the same plant, however, monopolistic price discrimination is made easier. The existence of common costs (capital, labor, and materials used in common by two or more of the services) makes the calculation of the costs of production for any one of the three services difficult for outsiders.

There is in fact no way to allocate common costs (although incremental costs are always measurable). As Fuss indicates in Chapter 3, any formula that attempts to allocate common costs is arbitrary and merely reflects the objectives of the rate maker. Cost apportionment cannot be used to ascertain the correct prices for the services of an enfranchised monopoly. Cost allocation and attribution lead only to the prices that one has in mind before one makes the allocations. Thus, the third proposition follows.

Public Goods and Externalities. The existence of externalities is often used to justify a differential between the costs of service to the firm and the price actually charged. In the case of telecommunications and the Postal Service, rural users of these services are subsidized, for it is suggested that society is more stable, literate, and aware when all members of the community, no matter their location, are connected to the center. The fourth proposition is that positive externalities can always be used to justify subsidizing some group. Such justifications are, however, not necessarily consistent. Few of these calculations of the importance of externalities examine the equity of the subsidy; that is, no attempt is made to examine the ability to pay of these groups (or their

15

income). Subsidization for externality purposes may then turn out to be inequitable and inconsistent with efficiency.

Efficiency versus Equity. The Postal Service code requires rates to be "just and equitable." Definitions of fairness and equity are not something all reasonable men would agree on. Can prices be fair and equitable and also bear a fair representation to costs? The prices set by competitive markets (equal to long-run marginal cost) can be considered in one light to be fair and equitable. No customer is subjected to economic discrimination. Because all prices equal long-run marginal costs (the costs of serving that particular customer), all customers would be bearing their fair share of costs. When all commodities, goods, and services, including the services of inputs such as labor, are sold at their marginal cost, the resulting allocation of resources is efficient, but the resulting distribution of income may be inequitable. By "inequitable," I mean that some substantial portion of the citizenry would prefer to see a more equal distribution of income. What, however, do we mean by fair and equitable postal rates? The amount spent on postal services for any single residential household is small. Although the cost of mailing magazines and newspapers and third-class mail may be a substantial proportion of the cost of producing such services, the total expenditures on postal services as a percentage of gross national product (GNP) is still small. By just and equitable postal rates, we therefore cannot mean that altering postal rates can greatly affect the distribution of income in the country. Congress, in setting uniform rates for first-class mail, directly subsidizes many rural postal users and also indirectly subsidizes newspapers and magazines through second-class mail rates. There is therefore an assumption that the efficient prices as set by a cost-minimizing or profit-maximizing firm would be unjust or inequitable.

Justice and equity therefore here represent price discrimination; in other words, prices are set to favor those in distant and small communities so as not to discriminate against these inhabitants because of their location. This is done, however, not because of considerations of the equality of income but because of arguments on the external advantages of a nationwide postal system. The system should be not only nationwide but uniform in price. Equity then refers to equal treatment. I would argue that "fair and equitable" refers not to income distribution but to quality of treatment. The Postal Rate Commission has used the term "fair and equitable" in many different ways in determining rates, including the use of the inverse elasticity rule. For example, the commission in R77–1 used the term "fair and equitable" to reflect "the high value of the controlled circulation classification to the public" (p. 363). The same term is also used to determine splits between rate categories within a given subclassification, such as the difference between piece and pound rates for regular second-class mail (p. 351). Proposition five is as follows: equity, like beauty, is in the eyes of the beholder and can be used to rationalize any act.

An Evaluation of the U.S. Postal Service's Pricing Philosophy

In the previous sections I developed five propositions, each of which would tend to complicate the application of a single pricing philosophy to the services offered by a firm. All five propositions apply to the U.S. Postal Service. First-class mail representing some 50 percent of the revenue of the Postal Service is protected from competition via monopoly restrictions. The Postal Service offers four classes of service, but within each of these there are various subcategories. Moreover, the rate schedules applying to second-, third-, and fourth-class mail are extremely complex. For example, for regular-rate second-class mail there are piece rates and varying poundage rates depending on the percentage of editorial content within a newspaper or magazine. This range of services is offered under the umbrella of joint production; that is, certain elements of inputs are used in common to provide a variety of services. The arguments for the positive externalities of the postal system and for the public good of mail in general have led to demands for subsidies for specific groups. The criteria of efficiency in pricing has been subverted by a call for fair and equitable pricing.

It is of course difficult, if not impossible, to disentangle the effects that any one of these five propositions has had on the actual pricing practices for postal services. Below, I critically examine several elements of pricing philosophy practiced in the United States and then make a number of recommendations.

The Rural Station Subsidy and the Uniform Pricing Rule. After the closing of many rural post offices created an outcry from small communities, Congress decided to provide a direct subsidy to the Postal Service to maintain a large number of rural post offices. The subsidy represents a transfer from taxpayers generally to users of rural post offices. Closing the post offices would not have meant the end of mail service for these communities, however. There would have been collection boxes and the same rate of delivery as before, but the residents would have had to travel farther to purchase stamps and to undertake other transactions at a post office. Users of first-class mail pay a uniform rate for delivery of a piece of mail under one ounce anywhere within the country but do not pay for or directly use the services of a single postal substation. The fact that some post offices may therefore be uneconomic simply reflects the volume of transactions in that community rather than the community's explicit desire for its own post office. Since the price of mailing a letter is uniform and independent of distance and density of population in both the receiving and sending points, users of the first-class postal system are unaware and unconcerned about the profitability of any single substation. Certain stations, therefore, in large cities may generate large "profits" while certain stations in small communities generate "losses." Because of the uniform pricing rule, however, these "profits" and "losses" do *not* indicate the social value of any single post office. An example will help clarify this issue.

Consider a single substation in a large metropolis and a post office in a rural community in northern Wyoming. Those in the metropolis wishing to send a letter to Wyoming are indifferent as to whether a post office is physically located in this northern community; they care only that the letter be delivered. Those living in the Wyoming community are worse off if there is no post office there, however, because they have to travel farther to undertake certain transactions. If a nonuniform price were charged for delivering first-class mail so that the price reflected the cost of delivery, a letter sent to a distant nonurban location would cost more than one sent to a nearby urban center. The costs and benefits of any single substation could be analyzed from its revenues and costs under a nonuniform pricing system. If under this nonuniform pricing system the post office in the northern Wyoming community did not make a profit, then it should be closed. Because of the uniform pricing system, however, one cannot compare the revenues and costs that apply to any single substation, since these revenues do not reflect what people would in essence bid for the right to that service in a competitive market. Given a system of uniform pricing for first-class mail, one cannot then justify closing small rural offices because they are uneconomic.

To deviate from the uniform pricing philosophy would require a complete rethinking of three principles of postal rate making—equality, externalities, and transactions costs. It would challenge the principle that users of the first-class system should not be penalized—that is, pay the true costs of a service—simply because they live in communities that are more expensive to service (equality and externalities). Moving to a nonuniform pricing system might also require a change in accounting and be so disruptive to consumers that the costs would exceed the benefits (transactions costs). In my view the equity argument is misguided. I can see no equity considerations that would justify price discrimination in favor of those who live in communities that are more expensive to serve. The externality argument that mail binds the nation together may have been true in 1775, but it is questionable whether it is still true today. No one has seriously argued that telecommunications rates be independent of distance in order to bind the nation together. Since 80 percent of first-class mail is business use, it is not clear how invoices, statements, and checks serve national unity. Newspapers, which, it is argued, tend to bind the nation together (or perhaps divide it), fall under rate class two, where zone rates differentiate prices by distance.

I am not seriously recommending disbanding the uniform pricing system for first-class mail.[12] I am, however, trying to indicate three issues. First, since the postal system is a network, one pricing philosophy such as a uniform rate for first-class mail makes other decisions difficult to undertake or estimate. Second, the pricing philosophy behind a uniform rate may be unimportant in today's society. Third, the example attempted to show that because of common inputs providing a network of services it is difficult to analyze the efficiency of one distinct piece.

Cost Apportionment Rules and the Inverse Elasticity Rule. In 1974 the U.S. Postal Rate Commission found that 50 percent of the total costs of the Postal Service were directly apportionable to some class of customers. In 1976 this apportionment rose to 60 percent of total costs. In the recent rate case for 1977 pushed by the *NAGCP* 1 decision, the commission found apportionable costs to be some 70 percent of total costs. That 20 percent of total costs changed from being fixed to variable within three years is mystifying. Fuss's paper goes into details on the apportionment procedures, but I do not think that they stand the light of day. Nor does the inverse elasticity rule as used to allocate the unallocable costs to the various classes stand up to the full light of analysis.

The inverse elasticity rule as discovered by Frank Ramsey in 1927 and rediscovered by W. J. Baumol and D. F. Bradford in 1970 suggests that, for services which are independently demanded and where pricing at marginal cost will not cover total costs because of downward-sloping marginal and average cost curves (a natural monopoly), the relative markups for each service over marginal costs should be proportional to the inverse of the elasticity of demand.[13] Consider a natural monopoly offering three products. Pricing each at marginal cost would involve heavy losses, which the public purse would not pay. How then should

---

[12] The major reason to keep a uniform pricing scheme, in my opinion, is the transactions costs issue. Before mailing any letter, a complex chart would have to be examined. Would rates change as density changed, and so on?

[13] Frank P. Ramsey, "A Contribution to the Theory of Taxation," *Economic Journal*, vol. 37 (March 1927), pp. 47–61; William J. Baumol and David F. Bradford, "Optimal Departures from Marginal Cost Pricing," *American Economic Review*, June 1970, pp. 265–83.

this hypothetical natural monopoly price so as to break even? Raising prices above marginal cost will generate losses in welfare for consumers; these losses are proportional to the elasticity of demand. Therefore, to minimize the deadweight loss or the loss in welfare from deviations in marginal cost pricing, prices should be raised proportionally more where demand is less elastic. In the specific hypothetical example, were one of the three services totally inelastic in demand, the entire loss of the firm would be recouped by raising price above marginal cost in this one market and leaving price at marginal cost in the other two markets.

Note three important distinctions between this theoretical rule and the way it was used by the U.S. Postal Service. First, the rule holds only for commodities that are independently demanded. Yet in rate hearings, evidence is presented that there is some cross-elasticity of demand between services.[14] Where this cross-elasticity of demand is nonzero, the Ramsey rule—pricing according to the inverse elasticity of demand—does not hold; it is not the correct rule to minimize welfare distortions. Second, the rule suggests that deviations of prices from marginal costs should be proportional to inverse elasticities of demand; the rule does not suggest that the *difference* between fixed costs and variable costs should be apportioned by the inverse elasticity of demand. Third, the rule does not contemplate a firm that has one monopoly service and competes with other firms in its other services.

Not only has the inverse elasticity rule been used incorrectly by the Postal Service, it also has been used for the wrong purposes. The inverse elasticity rule is a rule for the efficient pricing of services for a natural monopoly. The rule also implies an equity judgment in that, by maximizing aggregate consumers' surplus, all individuals are weighted equally. The Postal Service and the Rate Commission justify the use of this rule to exact less contributions from some services *because* these services are deserving of a subsidy. The Ramsey rule that efficiency in pricing implies an equal weighting of consumers is used to provide unequal contributions because consumers deserve different weights. This is incorrect. Several papers by M. S. Feldstein of Harvard show how the Ramsey rule for efficient pricing should be altered when distributional equity considerations are included—that is, when there is an unequal weighting of consumers to reflect a priori views on "needs."[15] In one such paper, which examines the sale of a number of products

---

[14] In Docket R77–1, p. 239 (third class will shift to postcards if rates for cards are lowered); p. 360 (diversion from second-class regular to controlled circulation); p. 380 (diversion of controlled circulation to third-class catalogs); p. 404 (diversion of special rate fourth class to parcel post).

[15] Martin S. Feldstein, "Distributional Equity and the Optimal Structure of Public Prices," *American Economic Review,* March 1972; "The Pricing of Public Intermediate Goods," *Journal of Public Economics,* April 1972; "Equity and Efficiency in Public Sector Pricing: The Optimal Two Part Tariff," *Quarterly Journal of Economics,* May 1972.

to households, Feldstein concludes, "the more that the consumption of the good is concentrated in low income families, the lower should be the relative price of that good."[16] If the consumption of first-class mail is more concentrated in low-income families than the consumption of second-class mail, equity considerations of the type that Feldstein postulates would require a lowering of the price of first-class mail relative to second-class mail, reversing the effects of the inverse elasticity rule. Since 80 percent of first-class mail is business use, the Feldstein rule does not directly apply; however, if the Postal Service and the Rate Commission are really concerned about equity in terms of the distribution of income, then the inverse elasticity rule (whether explicit as in R76–1 or implicit as in R77–1) must be modified.

Subsidies to Second-Class Mail. Second-class mail has been subsidized since the first rates were set for carrying mail within the United States.[17] The reasons for these subsidies are twofold: first, the "educational, cultural, and scientific value" of second-class mail (newspapers and magazines); second, the "externality" effects of having a wide variety of opinions flowing to all regions of the country. In 1775 or 1863, when the mail was the fastest or the only means of communication between central points and distant points, the subsidy may have served some underlying social purpose. The dissemination of news is important not only for the public but also for the government, for what is news to one is propaganda to another.[18] Clearly, efforts to build the nation or to wage war require broad public consent. Carrying the government's voice to all the people may help create such consent.

But why continue the subsidy today? Newspapers and magazines are but one form of multidimensional media. No one subsidizes the transmission or reception of radio and television waves by those living in distant rural communities in order that they may receive the national news. Yet these media compete with newspapers and magazines in both editorial content and advertising. If we are to subsidize certain classes of mail because of their educational, cultural, scientific, and informational value to the recipient, why do we not subsidize all educational, cultural, scientific, and informational transmissions? The subsidy to print publishers benefits either the consumers of these publications who pay a lower price or the shareholders of the publications who enjoy higher profits or the managers, suppliers of capital, or laborers at these publishing institutions. Are these the groups we wish, *today,* to subsidize for equity purposes?

---

[16] Feldstein, "Distributional Equity," p. 34.
[17] Priest, "Postal Monopoly," p. 56.
[18] Ibid., pp. 51–52.

The subsidy comes about in two ways. First, certain subclasses of second-class mail receive direct appropriations from Congress to cover part of the costs of service. Second, it is likely that the revenue from most second-class mail does not cover the true cost of service. Baratz estimated that in 1961 second-class mail covered only 23 percent of its expenditures.[19] Although second-class mail offers some cost savings to the Postal Service, it must be presorted and ZIP-coded; the revenue concessions probably more than make up for these cost reductions. For example, under the latest rates (May 29, 1978), a six-ounce sealed, presorted, first-class parcel would cost seventy-eight cents to mail anywhere in the country, if at least 500 pieces were shipped.[20] If the parcel were classified as second-class mail and consisted of half advertising and half editorial content, and if it were sent to the farthest zone outside the county of publication, the per piece charge would be 15.42 cents.[21]

Second-class-mail users suggest that the costs attributable to the services provided to them are far lower than for first-class-mail users, primarily because weekly or monthly magazines do not need daily delivery and can be sorted and delivered in off-peak periods. While for these publications, six-day-a-week delivery may not indeed be necessary, the attributable costs depend upon the load that the magazine or newspaper places on the entire system, not just on delivery. If the number of pieces is significantly large and if the Postal Service feels that they must be delivered as soon as possible, these second-class-mail publications may create significant peaks. In the example used above a representative piece of second-class mail travels at a price some 80 percent lower than a first-class piece of equivalent weight.[22]

In 1977 the *Wall Street Journal* (published five days a week in various parts of the country) accounted for 300 million second-class-mail pieces and 130 million pounds of mail (R77–1, p. 288). The *Journal* requires speedy, five-day-a-week delivery and may not therefore generate substantial cost savings compared with first-class mail. Yet it is carried at less than one-seventh of the price of an equivalent first-class

---

[19] Baratz, *Economics of the Postal Service,* p. 36.

[20] The discount for presorting is only available on payment of a thirty-dollar annual fee. If less than 500 pieces were shipped, the per piece charges would be eighty cents (with no annual fee payable).

[21] Arrived at as follows: three ounces of advertising at 13.8 cents a pound, 5.96 cents; three ounces of editorial at 13.1 cents a pound, 2.46 cents; per piece rate, mixed states level of presort, 7.0 cents; total, 15.42 cents per piece. Note that if the mail is presorted by carrier route, the per piece charge drops to 12.82 cents. The calculation in the text minimizes the comparison of differences in rates between first-class and second-class mail. The per pound rate for the advertising portion ranges from 31.8 cents per pound to zone 8 down to 17.5 cents per pound to zones 1 and 2.

[22] An "average" piece of second-class mail weighed 6.1 ounces according to the Postal Service (Docket R77–1, pp. 286–89).

piece.[23] Do we really wish to subsidize the readers of the *Wall Street Journal*? Are they the politically and economically disadvantaged? How about the owners of the *Journal*? Do we wish to grant them a subsidy? Voices will be raised that it is the small publications with volumes of under 5,000 pieces per mailing that would be hurt by reducing or eliminating the subsidy. Should publications exist whose customers are not willing to pay the full costs of these publications? Who reads the small specialized publications, the poor or the wealthy? We have little empirical evidence to judge the need of the recipients for these subsidies. If we are really interested as a social objective in increasing or maintaining a large number of independent publications, then let us directly subsidize publications, not the costs of mailing them, and let us subsidize only those that are small, unprofitable, and below efficient scale. A critical examination of other subsidies in first class (rural communities), third class, and fourth class (books, publications for the blind) is also warranted.

Competition and the U.S. Postal Service. In Dockets R74–1 and R76–1 the Postal Rate Commission used the inverse elasticity rule as a surrogate for the degree of competition facing the Postal Service in that rate category. In R77–1 the commission no longer utilizes the inverse elasticity rule to calculate markups over apportionable costs: instead, the commission examines the degree of competition directly but cursorily. The low cost coverage or markup over attributable and allocable costs for second-class mail is explained by the Postal Service as being due to the "augmented threat of private delivery of such matter at the higher full rates that must be proposed."[24] The commission concludes that "we believe that the availability and variety of private delivery services has diminished somewhat the value of service associated with the regular rate mail" (R77–1, p. 302). Intervenors had objected to Postal Service rate design that would have greatly increased the rates for second-class mail. The commission has not attributed institutional or common cost to second-class mail because of the threat of potential private delivery systems. In fact, the commission could have reversed policy by raising the rates of second-class mail so as to encourage the formation of private delivery systems. Unless it can be shown that the Postal Service has natural monopoly aspects and that there is subad-

---

[23] Calculated as follows: assume that because of publication procedures the *Journal*, which weighs six ounces on average, is shipped to no more than four zones, that it is presorted to carrier route, and that it contains 75 percent editorial and 25 percent advertising. The postal cost per piece is then 10.2 cents versus 78 cents via first class.

[24] McCaffrey, Testimony, Docket R77–1, Exh. USPS–T–76, p. 13.

ditivity of the cost function,[25] the commission should welcome losing second-class-mail customers to private services, since every second-class-mail customer involves a direct loss. Who but a regulated, enfranchised monopoly could justify the setting of prices below costs so as not to lose business?

The commission also uses the threat of competition to conclude for third-class mail that "a cost coverage below first class properly reflects the criteria of Section 3622(B). The existence of competition from television, radio, newspapers, magazines, etc., plus the lower value of service resulting from the absence of free forwarding and return and the lower service standards for third class mail are of substantially greater weight in determining the cost coverage for third class regular rate." Note the incongruity in the argument. Already having set the rates for carrying second-class mail (newspapers and magazines) below the cost of service, the commission now uses the existence of those rates to justify a lower cost coverage for third-class than first-class mail. Also in Docket R77–1, the commission in setting rates for parcel post or fourth-class mail states "a cost coverage of 102.7% is consistent with parcel post's relatively low value of service."

The Postal Rate Commission has not dropped the inverse elasticity rule. Utilizing the words "competition" or "value of service," the commission sets rates above attributable costs in the same fashion as in the past: first-class mail bears the great percentage of institutional costs. Yet it is clearly first-class mail that faces the greatest potential competition. Electronic funds transfer may, within the decade, substantially lessen the number of first-class pieces carried by the Postal Service. The loss of this traffic will destroy the elaborate house of cards on which the Postal Service and the commission have erected their rate structure. Without first-class mail to carry most of the common costs, rates will have to be increased for the other categories of mail. Intense pressure from the lobbying groups who benefit from the present discriminatory rate structure will, I suggest, mean increased deficits for the Postal Service. These deficits are a product of the pricing principles used by the Postal Service and the five propositions I have attempted to outline in this paper. Neither the absolute level nor the relative ratio of prices charged for postal service reflects efficiency considerations. In my mind they do not represent equity considerations either. Considerations of the appropriateness of the distribution of income are redundant when one considers the small percentage of GNP that is reflected in postal costs. While many rates may appear under the guise of externalities, public good, and definitions of equality or universal coverage, I suggest

---

[25] See Melvyn Fuss, Chapter 3 herein.

that the true reason for their existence is the redistribution of income toward some specific group. George Stigler in 1971 stated that regulation exists for the benefit of the industry. [26] Richard Posner in that same year suggested that the benefits of regulation are to provide more services at a lower price than would be provided by the competitive market. [27] I feel that the Postal Service, while not a traditional rate base utility, is a classic example of the Stigler/Posner firm—classic because it shows that where lobbying is intense, and without competition to prevent discrimination, particular groups are subsidized.

Summary and Recommendations

I have attempted to show that the setting of postal rates depends on the objectives one has in mind for these prices. The postal code contains four conflicting objectives: rates should be fairly representative of costs; rates should be fair and equitable; rates should consider the educational, cultural, and scientific value of the material transmitted; rates should not cover the full costs of certain services. No one can design rates to meet all these objectives simultaneously. To rationalize the pricing philosophy for the Postal Service and to eliminate the continuing deficits, we have to agree on a consistent set of objectives. As an economist, my first suggestion is that the overriding concern for the Postal Service be economic efficiency. While I would of course consider objectives that include social or equity values to be equally as valid as efficiency criteria, my cynical bias as an economist makes me believe that these other objectives involve redistribution toward some specific group rather than some broad social value.

My second recommendation would be to analyze correctly the costs of postal service. The present methods used by the Postal Service to apportion some costs and allocate others are archaic and not well-grounded in economic theory. These costing methods are really pricing methods, for they lead to the prices that regulators wish to set. A correct ascertainment of the long-run incremental costs for each class of service can be undertaken. Such an incremental cost study would indicate the presence or absence of systemic economies of scale and economies of scope and could be used to calculate socially efficient prices.

My third recommendation is that the Postal Service and the commission realize that efficiency and equity are not necessarily the same. The inverse elasticity rule, if used correctly (and I do not think they

---

[26] George L. Stigler, "An Economic Theory of Regulation," *Bell Journal of Economics,* vol. 2 (Spring 1971).

[27] Richard A. Posner, "Taxation by Regulation," *Bell Journal of Economics,* vol. 2 (Spring 1971).

use it correctly), would determine the efficient but not necessarily the equitable set of prices. If the commission wishes to consider distributional equity, let it do so directly rather than through the rubric of elasticity of demand or competition considerations.

Fourth, I suggest determining the groups that receive the subsidies. What group in society receives the subsidy for rural post offices—are they the poor or the wealthy? Who receives the subsidies (explicit and implicit) for the carriage of newspapers and magazines and other second-class rates—the publishers, the shareholders, or the customers? If customers receive these subsidies, who are they—the rich or the poor? A subsidy may be good in theory to promote universality or bind the nation together, but we should be concerned with its use in reality and the true equity of the subsidy. If these subsidies go to the rich, let us end them.

Fifth, I would price postal services to earn a positive return on investment. Long-run incremental costs of service would be used to calculate relative prices, but the absolute price level would be high enough to end all further losses. Economists generally approve of the efficiency principle for setting prices. We may therefore be biased, but at least we are unambiguous. If all these suggestions fail to arouse any sympathy, then I would appreciate consideration by the Postal Service as a nonprofit institution worthy of the lowest mail rates.

Commentary

Michael Visscher

Leonard Waverman presents a grim but no doubt accurate picture of the pricing policies of the U.S. Postal Service (USPS). He suggests that goals of economic efficiency (with external effects considered) and equity may have been sacrificed for the sake of political interests because costs have not been carefully measured or allocated and pricing rules have been incorrectly used. The Waverman evidence is compelling, and I will but briefly add some further considerations in rectifying the existing, potentially suboptimal, rate structure.

Economic efficiency is a defensible goal in this instance. The principal users of mail service are businesses for whom the mail is an input or intermediate good in a production process. The benefits and costs of movement to efficient prices would therefore be spread over the many customers of these firms, and the list of ultimate winners and losers spans a broad cross section of socioeconomic strata with the benefits being concentrated among no particular group. Expenditures on nonbusiness mail per capita are small relative to income. In sum, the distributional impact of efficient prices is not obviously pernicious, and postal prices do not seem an expeditious means of redistributing wealth.

It would appear that efficient prices are more easily described than computed, and more easily computed than established. The static welfare ideal is, of course, to set prices equal to marginal social costs of services. Thus, obtaining good cost estimates is clearly important. The correct question to ask is, What is the incremental cost of expanding a particular service on a particular class of mail? If distance traveled, weight, size, priority, and type of delivery influence that incremental cost, then the private schedule should not be uniform; rather, the spectrum of mail classes should expand to reflect those factors.

If, because of technology, ideal marginal cost prices will not cover total costs, we are almost surely in a world of second best, because the ideal policy is not feasible. One possibility might be subsidization. However, subsidies must be covered by taxes, which have their own distor-

27

tions; furthermore, costs might rise if monitoring is difficult, and if it is easy for the Postal Service to go to the public till. The alternative is to require the Postal Service to recover its costs, meaning that USPS would have to deviate from marginal cost prices, and this should be done in the least harmful way. Ramsey-rule prices accomplish this goal by distorting least the consumption patterns of mail users. If marginal cost prices yield an ideal consumption pattern, raising price above marginal cost most where demand is most inelastic deflects the fewest customers and keeps consumption nearest the ideal. Ramsey prices have the additional advantage of sometimes avoiding the entry in a natural monopoly situation that would destroy scale economies (if indeed USPS is a natural monopoly) where other prices would not.

Waverman offers caution in the use of Ramsey prices. The source of demand elasticity for one type of service may be the specter of competition. The Ramsey rule is still satisfactory for choosing prices. We want prices lower, other things being equal, where demand elasticity is higher. Prices less than short-run marginal cost might even be appropriate if, say, keeping customers using that postal product is crucial to achieving scale economies in service as a whole, or if different postal products are strong complements. Arbitrary assignments of common costs, however, designed to make variable costs appear least where demand for whatever reason is most elastic are not justified and deprive the Ramsey rule of content. A further warning is that Ramsey-rule prices must be adjusted for the presence of uncertainty. With an unexpected surge in demand, we would prefer higher, market-clearing prices so that price would serve to ration service to those who value it most if capacity is scarce. But price cannot be adjusted on the spur of the moment, so prices slightly above Ramsey prices must be set in advance to hedge against the possibility of increased demand.[1]

As it turns out, scarce capacity has not been much of a problem according to Rodney Stevenson, who claims USPS has overbuilt.[2] To assure uniform reliability of service throughout the year, USPS has provided excess capacity that lies idle most of the year. The efficient alternative is to make do with less capacity and use peak-load prices when demand pushes against the capacity constraint. It is the marginal user in such peak periods who requires capacity expansion; that user should value service enough to help pay for the additional capacity if expansion is worthwhile. The postal user who adds his demand for service to many others during the end-of-the-year holidays can pay extra

[1] Roger Sherman and Michael Visscher, "Second Best Pricing with Stochastic Demand," *American Economic Review*, vol. 68 (March 1978), pp. 41–53.
[2] Rodney E. Stevenson, "The Pricing of Postal Services," in Harry M. Trebing, ed., *New Dimensions in Public Utility Pricing* (East Lansing: Michigan State University Press, 1976).

for the additional capacity he makes necessary. Another advantage of correct pricing is that it gives correct signals for investment in plant and machinery. These investment signals are not being generated with prices as they are set now.

How prices should be adjusted for the presence of external effects is a thorny issue. There may be positive net external benefits to society in movement of population from urban to rural areas. Postal subsidies to rural areas are one conceivable way of promoting that migration. Alternatively, we could directly subsidize rural living and not attempt the correction through postal prices. Perhaps the correction is administratively cheaper to make through USPS prices than through the tax system, but that is not obvious. The other externality often cited as justification for subsidized postal prices is the informational value of printed material. Some would argue that reading should be subsidized because of the social benefits of having an informed populace. There is probably something to the alleged desirability of a well-read citizenry, although it is not clear that postal pricing policy has served this end. Mail subsidies for printed matter may have fostered the growth of, say, the Book-of-the-Month Club at the expense of, say, the local bookstore. Conceivably, the literacy of the country is better served when people spend more time browsing in more numerous corner bookstores. There are many ways to promote printed material, such as direct subsidies for the purchase of books, or publishers, or even authors. Subsidizing postal usage is not obviously superior to any of these.

Much is known about the principles of efficient pricing. The difficulty, of course, is getting price setters, whose interests will not in general coincide with those of the public at large, to use those principles faithfully. The present USPS price structure is testament to that difficulty. Designing regulatory institutions that ameliorate the difficulty may require permitting market alternatives, the careful measurement and allocation of costs, and construction of new incentives within the Postal Service.

Editor's note: In February 1980, after an illness of only three months, Michael Visscher died of cancer. Besides being very bright he was always cheerful, and his premature death at the age of thirty-one is a great loss to all of us. It is fortunate he was able to learn much in his short life, for no one could gain more sheer pleasure from new ideas than he did.

3

Cost Allocation:
How Can the Costs of Postal Services
Be Determined?

Melvyn A. Fuss

The supply of postal services is a classic example of the production of more than one output through the use of common production facilities. For example, the provision of the various classes of letter and parcel services utilizes the same sorting plant, delivery vehicles, and manpower to operate these components of capital equipment. Common production facilities give rise to common costs of production, which create great difficulties in determining the cost structure, the allocation of costs among the different outputs, and the structure of rates to be charged. The lengthy deliberations of the Postal Rate Commission and regulatory commissions in industries such as telecommunications and railroads attest to the practical difficulties of determining optimal resource allocation for industries dominated by multiproduct firms. The main purpose of this paper is to review some recent advances in economic theory and econometrics literature dealing with the multiproduct firm and to explore the ways in which these new ideas may be of some use in the determination of cost allocation for postal services. I will argue that the propositions derived from the new theoretical literature render a detailed knowledge of the cost structure even more important than was previously recognized. This knowledge is necessary for the determination of whether the postal service industry constitutes a natural monopoly and for the administrative allocation of costs when the natural monopoly hypothesis is maintained.[1] I will also argue, however, that when cost allocation is desired, complete cost allocation (that is, full distribution of costs) cannot be accomplished from a knowledge of the cost structure alone.

---

[1] It seems useful to call cost separation, as practiced by the Postal Rate Commission and regulatory commissions, "administered" cost allocation. Multiproduct firms with common costs of production also exist in more competitive industries. Cost separation controversies do not arise in these industries because the marketplace in effect allocates costs.

In the presence of common costs of production, complete cost allocation and rate setting are simultaneous activities. It is an error to assume that the causal chain runs from cost allocation to rate setting; the reverse is closer to the truth. Hence, it will not be possible to separate our discussion of cost allocation from that of rate setting. In fact, all the issues of efficiency and equity usually associated with rate setting also properly belong in any discussion of complete cost allocation.

Analysis of both the natural monopoly question and cost allocation requires such a detailed knowledge of the cost structure that the technology of postal services must be estimated by methods that do not impose a priori restrictive assumptions on that technology. Recent advances in the econometrics literature inspired by the pioneering work of W. E. Diewert have made possible the estimation of cost functions that can represent, with minimal a priori restrictions, general multiproduct technologies.[2] The estimation of multiproduct generalized cost functions could provide an important econometric supplement to the current methods of cost allocation in future hearings before the Postal Rate Commission. Cost functions of the type to be discussed have recently been applied to railroads by Randall Brown, Douglas Caves, and Laurits Christensen and to telecommunications by Melvyn Fuss and Leonard Waverman.[3]

The second part of this paper presents a summary of the theoretical considerations underlying the natural monopoly issue, after which I evaluate cost allocation procedures as currently practiced by the Postal Service. An analysis of the econometric cost function approach to the determination of the cost structure and the allocation of costs follows. Finally, I suggest how both traditional cost allocation and econometric cost allocation could be used as inputs for an appropriate determination of the rate structure.

The Importance of Determining the Cost Structure

In a series of theoretical articles, W. J. Baumol; W. J. Baumol, E. E. Bailey, and R. D. Willig; and J. C. Panzar and R. D. Willig have

---

[2] W. E. Diewert, "An Application of the Shephard Duality Theorem: A Generalized Leontief Production Function," *Journal of Political Economy,* May/June 1971, pp. 481–507.

[3] Randall Brown, Douglas Caves, and Laurits Christensen, "Estimating Marginal Costs for Multi-Product Regulated Firms," Social Science Research Institute Working Paper no. 7609 (Madison: University of Wisconsin, July 1976); Melvyn Fuss and Leonard Waverman, "Multi-Product, Multi-Input Cost Functions for a Regulated Utility: The Case of Telecommunications in Canada," Paper presented at the National Bureau of Economic Research Conference on Public Regulation (Washington, D.C., December 1977), forthcoming in G. Fromm, ed., *Papers and Proceedings of the Conference on Public Regulation.*

established the importance of a detailed knowledge of the cost structure of a multiproduct monopolist subject to external regulation.[4] Baumol has refined the definition of a natural monopolist and shown that the basic requirement is that the cost function be "subadditive." A firm's cost function is subadditive if it can produce any configuration of outputs at a lower cost than that attained by multifirm production. Baumol shows that a firm may exhibit diseconomies of large-scale production and still be a natural monopolist under the subadditivity definition or, conversely, may exhibit increasing returns to scale and still not be a natural monopolist. Hence, the preoccupation with economies of scale to the exclusion of other characteristics of the cost structure for the multiproduct firm is misplaced.

An additional concept that needs to be considered is that of economies of scope. A production technology exhibits economies of scope when, for any configuration of multiple outputs, these outputs can be produced at less cost by a firm that operates a multiproduct technology than by a number of firms each operating a single-product technology. Although the necessary conditions for subadditivity have yet to be established, Baumol demonstrates that the simultaneous existence of economies of scale and economies of scope are sufficient to ensure subadditivity. Panzar and Willig have shown that a natural monopolist (defined in terms of a subadditive cost function) may not be sustainable in the face of competitive entry in one of the multiproduct monopolist's markets. A monopolist's pricing strategy is said to be sustainable if it can find a set of stationary product and quantity prices that does not attract rivals into the industry. Panzar and Willig describe conditions under which the natural monopoly is sustainable. Their paper is important for an analysis of the Postal Service because it is often alleged that repeal of the private express statutes would render the "natural monopolist" post office nonsustainable in the face of entry in the dense population markets. The Baumol, Bailey, and Willig paper is particularly important in the context of cost allocation and rate setting. They demonstrate that a natural monopolist (again defined as a multiproduct firm with a subadditive cost function) is sustainable if it chooses the Ramsey-optimal rate structure. The Ramsey-optimal rate structure is equivalent to the inverse elasticity rule for allocating total costs when

[4] William J. Baumol, "On the Proper Cost Tests for Natural Monopoly in a Multiproduct Industry," *American Economic Review*, December 1977, pp. 809–22; William J. Baumol, Elizabeth E. Bailey, and Robert D. Willig, "Weak Invisible Hand Theorems on the Sustainability of Prices in a Multiproduct Natural Monopoly," *American Economic Review*, vol. 67 (June 1977), pp. 350–65; John C. Panzar, and Robert D. Willig, "Free Entry and the Sustainability of Natural Monopoly," *Bell Journal of Economics*, vol. 8 (Spring 1977), pp. 1–22.

the cross-price elasticities of demand for the multiproduct firm's outputs are zero.[5]

The importance of the Baumol, Bailey, and Willig paper for our purposes is that it demonstrates how subtleties in the production technology of a multiproduct monopolist such as the Postal Service can have an important bearing on public policy decision making. According to the theorems proved in this paper, a monopolist whose production technology yields a cost function that exhibits both economies of scale and economies of scope can sustain itself against competitive entry if it chooses the Ramsey-optimal rate structure. Hence, if we accept the value judgments inherent in the Ramsey-optimal rate structure, the monopolist need not be protected from competitive entry by such government regulations as the private express statutes. Furthermore, competitive entry will act somewhat like Adam Smith's invisible hand, forcing the firm to adopt the Ramsey-optimal rate structure in order to prevent entry when it is producing in the neighborhood of its current supply configuration. However, even though the firm is a natural monopolist (that is, it has a subadditive cost function), if it does not have a production technology that exhibits both economies of scale and economies of scope, then the monopoly will not be sustainable against competitive entry even though it is the low-cost method of producing the industry's output. In this case government regulation or some other form of protection of the monopolist's markets is necessary to ensure minimal production costs. Subadditivity, economies of scale, and economies of scope are crucial characteristics of the technology of the multiproduct monopolist. These characteristics can be ascertained only from a detailed knowledge of the cost structure.

How this new theoretical literature complicates (and enriches) this analysis is shown by considering, for example, the importance of scale economies. John Haldi argues persuasively that the measurement of economies of scale is irrelevant for the determination of the natural monopoly aspects of the Postal Service: repeal the private express statutes and the natural monopoly position will be tested in the marketplace.[6] The issue is more complicated, however. A cost-effective natural monopolist may *not* win the market test in the sense that it may not be able to prevent entry and the resultant misallocation of resources. But if the natural monopolist exhibits economies of scale and economies of scope as defined by Baumol, Bailey, and Willig, it would be the up-to-

---

[5] It does not correspond to the inverse elasticity rule actually used by the Postal Rate Commission, which allocates residual costs rather than total costs. This issue is discussed in more detail below.

[6] John Haldi, *Postal Monopoly: An Assessment of the Private Express Statutes* (Washington, D.C.: American Enterprise Institute, 1974).

date counterpart of the Haldi proposition. The market test can be expected to force the monopolist wishing to deter entry to reveal its natural monopoly technology by choosing the Ramsey-optimal rate structure in order to deter entry.

The Use of Traditional Cost Allocation Methods to Determine the Cost Structure and to Allocate Costs

The transcripts of the Postal Rate Commission hearings are replete with discussions of how to allocate costs (see, for example, Docket R77–1). A similar characteristic can be found in the transcripts of regulatory commissions such as the Federal Communications Commission (FCC). To an academic economist, traditional cost allocation (sometimes called cost separation) is a futile exercise. Cost separation exists because of regulators' attempts to find average costs upon which to base a rate structure. But a multiproduct technology that exhibits common or joint costs does not yield average costs. Any attempt to distribute costs fully in order to obtain average costs on which prices can be based must be arbitrary since one is attempting to find something that does not exist. The only way to allocate common costs in a nonarbitrary manner is to use noncost criteria such as, for example, the maximization of consumer surplus. Thus, the decision in *National Association of Greeting Card Publishers* v. *United States Postal Service* is misguided since it forces the Postal Service to allocate costs when no cost allocation is logically possible.

The central issue in cost allocation procedures is the identification of cost causality.[7] Perhaps two examples of correct allocation by cost causation will suffice. The first is drawn from the telecommunications industry. The common carriers in the telecommunications industry have argued that the incremental costs of data service are low since it is an adjunct to the extensive monopoly message-switched service that must be provided for voice transmission. If, however, the quality of the entire system must be increased to accommodate an acceptable level of reliability for data transmission, these upgrading costs are "caused" by data users and should be fully charged to them alone as part of the incremental costs of the change in the system. Even though this higher quality of service is provided in common to all users, incremental common costs should be allocated solely to the data users.

The second example is drawn from the *Postal Rate Commission*

---

[7] The practice of the Postal Service from 1929 to 1968 of separating common costs by some measure of relative use does not fall under the category of allocation by cost causation. In general, there is no connection between intensity of use and cost causation.

Opinion and Recommended Decision, Docket R77–1. According to the published service standards of the Postal Service, "preferred" first-class letter mail and parcel mail must be delivered during six delivery days. The service standards for other mail such as third- and fourth-class parcels, third-class circulars, or second-class mail can be met with only three days' delivery service. The cost of providing the additional three days' delivery service is an incremental cost properly allocated to priority services since the additional cost was caused by the service standards related to those services. Hence, the Postal Rate Commission's decision in regard to that matter was, in my view, a correct one in terms of proper cost allocation procedures. However, suppose a large increase in priority mail led to an increase in the number of outside workers used for delivery purposes but no increase in the number of delivery days. Then the increase in costs incurred during the three days needed to maintain priority service is properly allocable to the priority services. But the additional costs in the other three days are not allocable to the priority services. They are common costs that cannot be separated since any attempt to do so would be to use an intensity-of-use criterion. This remark follows from the reasoning that these costs could have been avoided had there been a decrease in nonpriority service at the same time as the increase in priority service. The additional costs were "caused" as much by the fact that the demand for nonpriority service did not decrease as by the fact that the demand for priority service increased.

The latter example illustrates two measures of cost that play a large role in proper cost allocation methodology: marginal cost and incremental cost. Marginal cost is the cost of providing an additional unit of a particular service, given the levels of all other services. The additional delivery costs that would be incurred if there were an increase in the demand for priority services during the three additional days required for priority service are an example of marginal cost. Incremental cost, on the other hand, is the additional cost incurred when a new service is provided, given the levels of all the other services. The cost per unit of providing the additional service is often called the average incremental cost. Again, to use the delivery example, the cost per unit (of the priority services) incurred in providing the additional three days' delivery is the average incremental cost of priority delivery service.

In most cases marginal cost and incremental cost can be properly allocated, but in general this will not solve the cost allocation problem. When economies of scale are present, allocation by marginal costs will not result in the allocation of total costs. Similarly, allocation by means of incremental costs will not fully allocate total costs in the presence of economies of scope. Hence, if the Postal Service's technology yields economies of scale or economies of scope, cost allocation by means of marginal and incremental cost procedures will still leave a residual of common costs to be allocated. On the other hand, if economies of scale and economies of scope are not present, the use of marginal and incremental cost allocation procedures will, in fact, fully allocate costs. In addition, a rate structure based on this cost allocation will yield efficient resource allocation in the sense that it yields a set of subsidy-free Pareto-optimal prices.

The Postal Rate Commission of course realizes the dilemma caused by the existence of nonallocable common costs that essentially belong in their assigned cost category and their residual cost category. The Postal Rate Commission's current procedure is to attribute and assign costs on the basis of assumed cost causality criteria and to allocate the residual costs on the basis of noncost criteria, primarily, it would appear, the inverse elasticity rule. However, the fact that the court has forced the Postal Rate Commission to attribute and assign costs in excess of those that would be attributed under marginal and incremental cost allocation procedures implies that the inverse elasticity rule cannot be applied properly to yield Pareto-optimal resource allocation constrained by the presence of a break-even requirement. In Appendix A to this paper I demonstrate that the application of the inverse elasticity rule to residual marginal costs is not equivalent in terms of its implications for resource allocation to the application of the rule to total marginal costs. Hence, I wish to argue that the appropriate procedure, once one recognizes that noncost criteria are inevitable, is to apply methods such as the inverse elasticity rule to total marginal costs. To do so one needs knowledge of these marginal (and incremental) costs. This knowledge can be obtained from a properly conducted incremental cost study. Alternatively, econometric cost functions can also provide the required information, a fact unfortunately ignored by the Postal Service. It is to these functions that I now turn.

The Use of Econometric Cost Functions to Determine the Cost Structure and to Allocate Costs

In this section, I briefly summarize advances in the econometric literature that have made it possible to represent and to estimate more realistically a multiproduct firm's technology, and I then relate them to my previous discussion of economies of scale and economies of scope. Second, in the light of these recent developments, I analyze two attempts to estimate the cost structure of postal services, those by Leonard Merewitz and R. E. Stevenson.[8] I show that the forms available to these authors at the time their studies were carried out are unduly restrictive with respect to the estimation of the firm's technology and hence with respect to the allocation of costs. Finally, as an example of the recent econometric advances I will give a functional form that overcomes the objections to the forms used by Merewitz and Stevenson.

The Multiproduct Cost Function. A multiproduct production process can be represented by the implicitly defined production function:

$$F(Y_1, \ldots Y_m; X_1 \ldots X_n) = 0 \qquad (1)$$

where $Y_i, i = 1, \ldots m$ are outputs and $X_j, j = 1, \ldots n$ are inputs.[9]

The theory of duality between cost and production[10] assures that for every production function (1) there exists a dual long-run cost function of the form.

$$C = C(Y_1, \ldots Y_m; p_1, \ldots p_n) \qquad (2)$$

where $p_j, j = 1, \ldots n$ are the prices paid by the firm for the inputs X_j, as long as the following assumptions are valid: (1) the production function satisfies the usual regularity conditions (for example, convex isoquants); (2) the firm pursues cost-minimizing behavior;[11] (3) the firm has no control over input prices. Given these assumptions, the cost function is just as basic a description of the technology as the production function and contains all the required information, including information on economies of scale and economies of scope.

Properties of the multiproduct cost function (2) are: C is concave in p_j; C is linear homogeneous in p_j; C is increasing in Y_i and p_j; and $\partial C/\partial p_j = X_j$ (Shephard's Lemma).[12]

---

[8] Leonard Merewitz, *The Production Function in the Public Sector: Production of Postal Services in the U.S. Post Office,* Monograph 14 (Berkeley: University of California, 1971), and "Costs and Returns to Scale in U.S. Post Offices," *Journal of the American Statistical Association,* September 1971, pp. 504–09; Rodney E. Stevenson, "Postal Pricing Problems and Production Functions," (Ph.D. Diss., Michigan State University, 1973).

[9] In the case of a single output, $m = 1$, and equation (1) can be solved explicitly as $Y_1 = f(X_1 \ldots X_n)$, which is the usual form of the production function.

[10] See Diewert, "Application."

[11] This assumption may not be reasonable for the postal services, especially with respect to "regular" workers. If the Postal Service's cost-minimizing choice of inputs is constrained by union agreements regarding the rate at which capital can be substituted for labor, then a restricted cost function should be estimated. For a description of the properties of the restricted cost function, see H. Varian, *Microeconomic Analysis* (New York: W. W. Norton, 1978).

[12] For an introduction to duality theory and the use of Shephard's Lemma, see William J. Baumol, *Economic Theory and Operations Analysis,* 4th ed. (Englewood Cliffs, N. J.: Prentice-Hall, 1977), chap. 14. For a more extensive treatment, see Varian *Microeconomic Analysis,* chap. 1.

Economies of Scale, Economies of Scope, and Subadditivity. If a technology is a multiple output one, then average cost, that is, cost per unit of output, is not defined. This is the fact that makes traditional cost separation of the fully distributed kind an exercise in futility. This fact also makes an analysis of returns to scale somewhat complex since it is no longer possible to measure only the effect of output increases on the average cost of production.

A measure of returns to scale can be obtained by computing either of the following expressions:

$$dC = \sum_{i=1}^{m} \frac{\partial C}{\partial Y_i} dY_i$$

$$d\log C = \sum_{i=1}^{m} \frac{\partial \log C}{\partial \log Y_i} \cdot \frac{dY_i}{Y_i} \tag{3}$$

Equation (3) represents the total change in cost resulting from differential changes in the levels of the m outputs. Unfortunately, unless additional structure is added to equation (3) it is difficult to interpret changes in cost resulting from changes in outputs in terms of returns to scale. The most common procedure analyzes costs along some output ray. An output ray is said to be generated when the firm's expansion path is characterized by equal proportionate growth in all products, that is, $dY_i/Y_i = \lambda$. Then,

$$\frac{d\log C}{\lambda} = \sum_{i=1}^{m} \frac{\partial \log C}{\partial \log Y_i} \tag{4}$$

If $(d\log C)/\lambda > 1$, differential costs along the ray are increasing, hence production is subject to decreasing returns to scale; if $(d\log C)/\lambda < 1$, the technology exhibits increasing returns to scale; if$(d\log C)/\lambda = 1$, constant returns to scale exist. This description of returns to scale may be more problematic in the multiple output case than the single output case, since it requires all outputs to be increasing in strict proportion, which may not correspond to the optimal production plan. Nevertheless, this returns-to-scale measure can be a useful summary statistic and plays an important role, along with the measure of economies of scope, in determining whether a multiproduct firm is a natural monopoly.

To this point in my summary of cost and production functions, I have assumed that the production technology is truly a multiple output one in the sense that it is more efficient to produce the m outputs together than by separate production processes. This efficiency condition is known in the industrial organization literature as economies of scope.[13] The production technology exhibits economies of scope if

$$C(Y_1 \ldots Y_m) < C(Y_1, 0 \ldots 0) + C(0, Y_2, 0 \ldots 0)$$
$$+ C(0, 0, Y_3 \ldots 0) + \ldots + C(0, 0 \ldots 0, Y_m) \qquad (5)$$

That is, it is less expensive to produce the m products using a single firm than to have m firms each producing a single product.

Panzar and Willig have shown that a twice differentiable multi-product cost function exhibits economies of scope if it exhibits cost complementarities,[14] where cost complementarity is defined by

$$\frac{\partial^2 C}{\partial Y_i \partial Y_j} < 0, i \neq j, \quad i, j = 1, \ldots m \qquad (6)$$

Conditions (6) provide a means of testing for the existence of economies of scope once the multiproduct cost function has been estimated.

Expressions (4), (5), and (6) can be used for analyzing the structure of cost of the multiproduct firm. Two other important cost concepts for the purpose of cost allocation, marginal cost and incremental cost, can also be measured once the cost structure has been estimated. The marginal cost for the ith service can be computed as

$$\frac{\partial C}{\partial Y_i}, \quad i = 1, \ldots m \qquad (7)$$

and the corresponding incremental cost from

$$C(Y_1, Y_2, \ldots Y_{i-1}, Y_i, Y_{i+1}, \ldots Y_m)$$
$$- C(Y_1, Y_2, \ldots Y_{i-1}, 0, Y_{i+1}, \ldots Y_m) \qquad (8)$$

In the light of our need to have appropriate expressions for measures of economies of scale, economies of scope, marginal costs, and incremental costs, it is appropriate at this point to review the two previous studies that have estimated the cost structure for the Postal Service. I wish first to emphasize that these papers used "state of the art" procedures at the time they were written. My criticisms are based on the existence of new techniques that were unknown to the authors.

The most extensive and complete study to date that attempts to estimate the cost function for the Postal Service's technology is that by Leonard Merewitz.[15] Merewitz studied the cost-output relationship of

---

[13] See John C. Panzar and Robert D. Willig, "Economies of Scale and Economies of Scope in Multi-Output Production," Bell Laboratories working paper (Holmdel, N.J., 1975), and "Economies of Scope, Product Specific Scale Economies, and the Multiproduct Competitive Firm," mimeographed, 1978.

[14] Panzar and Willig, "Economies of Scope."

[15] Merewitz, Production Function, and "Costs and Returns to Scale."

the 156 largest post offices. For the postal system as a whole, he concluded that "in 1966 there appeared to be economies of scale . . . up to offices of the size of 1400 employees. After that there appeared to be constant returns to scale." There are no discussions of economies of scope and subadditivity, since these concepts were unknown at the time Merewitz produced his research. Underlying Merewitz's conclusions are results based on the estimation of Cobb-Douglas and constant elasticity of substitution (CES) cost functions and input demand functions derived from these cost functions. As shown in Appendix B of this paper, the Cobb-Douglas function has restrictive assumptions built into it which make it unsuitable as a general description of the underlying cost structure. First, the Cobb-Douglas function assumes that the production technology can be separated into two functions: output alone and input alone. This separable description of technology has been demonstrated to be incorrect for railroads and for telecommunications.[16] It is also likely to be incorrect for the Postal Service function.

Second, the Cobb-Douglas function has an inappropriate curvature property. If a profit-maximizing producer were subject to a Cobb-Douglas technology in outputs and faced exogenously determined prices for his outputs, then he would never produce more than one product regardless of the magnitude of these output prices. Merewitz recognized this problem, and that is the reason he also estimated constant elasticity of substitution functions.

Third, and perhaps most important, a Cobb-Douglas function of output can never exhibit economies of scope in the sense that it can never exhibit cost complementarity. The CES transformation function overcomes the problem of incorrect curvature but retains the other restrictive features. In particular, separability is required, and if the production process is subject to constant returns to scale or increasing returns to scale, cost complementarity must occur. Stevenson's study also uses the Cobb-Douglas description of technology for the cost function and derived demand functions. Thus, it is subject to the same criticisms with regard to functional form as the Merewitz study. In addition, Stevenson used an extremely limited data base consisting of only eleven observations on aggregate inputs for the Postal Service for the period 1961 to 1971.[17]

My general conclusion from reviewing these studies is that there is a definite need to update the previous research on Postal Service cost functions using current "state of the art" procedures. This would provide

---

[16] Brown, Caves, and Christensen, "Estimating Marginal Costs; Fuss and Wåverman, "Multi-Product, Multi-Input Cost Functions."

[17] Stevenson, "Postal Pricing Problems."

a more reliable estimated cost structure, which should be used as one of the components of any cost allocation exercise.

An Econometric Cost Function That Provides a General Description of a Multiproduct Technology. A function known as the translog cost function is becoming an increasingly popular specification of the functional form of a cost function.[18] The function is quadratic in logarithms and is one of the family of second-order Taylor series approximations to an arbitrary cost function. Hence, it is only one of a number of possible examples I could have chosen. The multiple-output translog cost function with m outputs and n inputs takes the form:

$$
\begin{aligned}
\log C = \alpha_o &+ \sum_{i=1}^{m} \alpha_i \log Y_i + \sum_{j=1}^{n} \beta_j \log p_j \\
&+ \frac{1}{2} \sum_{i=1}^{m} \sum_{k=1}^{m} \delta_{ik} \log Y_i \log Y_k \\
&+ \frac{1}{2} \sum_{j=1}^{n} \sum_{k=1}^{n} \gamma_{jk} \log p_j \log p_k \\
&+ \sum_{i=1}^{m} \sum_{j=1}^{n} \rho_{ij} \log Y_i \log p_j
\end{aligned}
\tag{9}
$$

where α_o, α_i, β_j, δ_{ik}, γ_{jk}, ρ_{ij} are parameters to be estimated.

Using Shephard's Lemma ($\partial C / \partial p_j = X_j$), the derived demand functions can be obtained in terms of cost shares as

$$
\frac{\partial \log C}{\partial \log p_j} = \frac{P_j X_j}{C} = M_j = \beta_j + \sum_k \gamma_{jk} \log p_k + \sum_i \rho_{ij} \log Y_i
\tag{10}
$$
$$
j = 1, \ldots n
$$

where M_j is the cost share of the jth input.

The system of equations (9), (10) is the cost system to be estimated. However, a number of features of the system reduce the number of parameters to be estimated. Since M_j is a cost share,

$$
\sum_{j=1}^{n} M_j = 1
$$

which implies

$$
\sum_j \beta_j = 1, \ \sum_j \gamma_{jk} = 0, \ \sum_j \rho_{ij} = 0
$$

---

[18] Brown, Caves, and Christensen, "Estimating Marginal Costs"; Fuss and Waverman, "Multi-Product, Multi-Input Cost Functions."

In addition, the linear homogeneity property of cost functions outlined earlier implies the further parameter restrictions

$$\sum_k \gamma_{jk} = 0$$

Finally, the fact that the function is a second-order approximation implies $\delta_{ik} = \delta_{ki}$ and $\gamma_{jk} = \gamma_{kj}$.

The marginal cost elasticity of producing output i is:

$$\frac{\partial \log C}{\partial \log Y_i} = \alpha_i + \sum_k \delta_{ik} \log Y_k + \sum_j \rho_{ij} \log p_j \tag{11}$$

The marginal cost *curve* for output Y_i can be obtained as

$$MCC\ (Y_i) = \frac{C}{Y_i} \left(\alpha_i + \delta_{ii} \log Y_i + \sum_{k \neq i} \delta_{ik} \log \overline{Y}_k + \sum_j \rho_{ij} \log \overline{p}_j \right) \tag{12}$$

where $\overline{Y}_k$, $\overline{p}_j$ are preassigned constant outputs and prices respectively. The returns-to-scale measure can be obtained as

$$\begin{aligned}
\frac{d \log C}{\lambda} &= \sum_i \frac{\partial \log C}{\partial \log Y_i} \\
&= \sum_i \alpha_i + \sum_i \sum_k \delta_{ik} \log Y_k + \sum_i \sum_j \rho_{ij} \log p_j
\end{aligned} \tag{13}$$

Economies of scope in production can be tested in the translog framework using the approximate tests discussed by M. Denny and Melvyn Fuss.[19]

The condition for cost complementarity is that

$$\delta_{ij} + \alpha_i \cdot \alpha_k < 0, \quad i \neq j$$

when the data have been scaled so that all $Y_i = p_j = 1$ at the point of approximation.

In addition, the translog cost function viewed as a second-order approximation to an arbitrary cost function contains the separable cost structure, the CES cost structure, and the Cobb-Douglas cost structure as special cases, demonstrating that it is a more general description of technology than any of the forms that have been applied to Postal Service data.[20]

---

[19] M. Denny and Melvyn Fuss, "The Use of Approximation Analysis to Test for Separability and the Existence of Consistent Aggregates," *American Economic Review,* June 1977, pp. 404–18.

[20] Test statistics for these specialized descriptions of technology can be found in ibid.

Summary and Conclusions

I have argued that the existence of a multiproduct technology for postal services makes the calculation of average cost of any particular service impossible and, hence, any fully distributed cost allocation based on cost criteria alone a futile exercise. Once it is recognized that noncost criteria must be used in any cost allocation exercise that is designed to yield a rate structure, the question remains, how should one proceed? First, more attention should be paid to cost function estimation than has previously been done in the case of Postal Service technology. Given the recent advances in the econometrics literature, it is possible to overcome most of the objections to the earlier attempts at cost function estimation of this technology.

Information on marginal and incremental costs obtained from estimation of the cost structure can be used in conjunction with detailed incremental cost causation allocations such as the delivery example outlined earlier in the paper. The two approaches, econometric estimation and traditional incremental allocation, are complementary activities. Consistency of results can only increase confidence in the usefulness of such results.

Second, once explicit knowledge of the cost structure is obtained, a rate structure and hence a complete cost allocation should be chosen so as to expose the value judgment that went into the choice. Long-run marginal costs and long-run average incremental costs calculated from the cost side alone should serve as lower bounds for the rates charged for existing and new services respectively. It is important that all causally related costs be included and that the "long run" be long enough so that capacity can be adjusted. In the presence of economies of scale or economies of scope, total costs will not be allocated by the above method. However, this is as far as we should go on costing grounds alone. To complete the rate-setting, cost-allocation exercise,[21] we should introduce value judgments explicitly through the use of information on the demand side. An obvious candidate for consideration is the Ramsey-optimal-pricing rule, or perhaps Martin Feldstein's equity criteria.[22]

The explicit rule finally chosen would undoubtedly be heavily influenced by political and social considerations as well as economic considerations. Nevertheless, the methodology I am proposing would avoid the arbitrariness inherent in the current procedure, which requires a

---

[21] The exercise is complete if economies of scale and scope are unimportant. In that case, however, it would be preferable to permit competition and thus allow the marketplace to "allocate" costs.

[22] Martin S. Feldstein, "Distributional Equity and the Optimal Structure of Public Prices," *American Economic Review,* March 1972, pp. 32–36.

particular percentage of the total cost to be allocated in order to satisfy a judicial ruling. In the end, any attempt to base cost allocation on cost principles alone is a will-o'-the-wisp that cannot be attained. Continuation of the current "almost fully allocated" procedures will succeed only in masking the value judgments that must be embodied in any structure of rates charged by the Postal Service.

Appendix A

In this appendix the simple inverse elasticity rule applied to residual costs is shown not to yield the constrained Pareto-optimal cost allocation. Suppose the cost function for m outputs can be written as

$$C(Y_1 \ldots Y_m) = \sum_{i=1}^{m} C_i(Y_i) + RC(Y_1 \ldots Y_m) \qquad \text{(A.1)}$$

where $C_i(Y_i)$ is the allocable cost function specific to output Y_i and $RC(Y_1 \ldots Y_m)$ is the nonallocable or residual cost. Factor prices are ignored for simplicity. For nonzero production of all services, the Pareto-optimal set of prices and quantities satisfies the first-order conditions.[23]

$$p_i^* - \frac{\partial C}{\partial Y_i} = -\lambda \left(MR_i - \frac{\partial C}{\partial Y_i} \right) \qquad i = 1, \ldots m; \ y_i^* > 0 \quad \text{(A.2)}$$

where the * denotes optimal values, λ is a Lagrangian multiplier, and MR_i is the marginal revenue associated with ith service market. The first-order conditions can be manipulated to yield

$$\frac{p_i^* - \dfrac{\partial C}{\partial Y_i}}{p_j^* - \dfrac{\partial C}{\partial Y_j}} = \frac{MR_i - \dfrac{\partial C}{\partial Y_i}}{MR_j - \dfrac{\partial C}{\partial Y_j}} \qquad i, j = 1, \ldots m \qquad \text{(A.3)}$$

If zero cross-price elasticities of demand are assumed, $MR_i = p_i^* (1 + 1/\varepsilon_i)$, where ε_i is the ith own price elasticity of demand. Equation (A.3) becomes

$$\frac{\left(p_i^* - \dfrac{\partial C}{\partial Y_i} \right) \div p_i^*}{\left(p_j^* - \dfrac{\partial C}{\partial Y_j} \right) \div p_j^*} = \frac{\varepsilon_j}{\varepsilon_i} \qquad \text{(A.4)}$$

---

[23] Baumol, Bailey, and Willig, "Invisible Hand."

which yields the inverse elasticity rule applied to total marginal costs. Now, from (A.1),

$$\frac{\partial C}{\partial Y_i} = \frac{\partial C_i}{\partial Y_i} + \frac{\partial RC}{\partial Y_i} \tag{A.5}$$

and (A.4) becomes

$$\frac{\left[\left(p_i^* - \dfrac{\partial C_i}{\partial Y_i}\right) - \dfrac{\partial RC}{\partial Y_i}\right] \div p_i^*}{\left[\left(p_j^* - \dfrac{\partial C}{\partial Y_j}\right) - \dfrac{\partial RC}{\partial Y_j}\right] \div p_j^*} = \frac{\varepsilon_j}{\varepsilon_i} \tag{A.6}$$

We do not have an inverse elasticity proportionate markup rule with respect to the residual price $p_i^* - \partial C_i/\partial Y_i$ since the denominator in the proportion is not $p_i^* - \partial C/\partial Y_i$ but rather p_i^*. The spirit of the inverse elasticity rule is retained, but the simple rule of thumb that the price markup above directly allocable costs is inversely proportional to elasticities is not valid.

Appendix B

In this appendix the Cobb-Douglas and CES cost functions are shown to possess properties that make them less than desirable as descriptions of the Postal Service technology. For the case of two inputs and two outputs, the Cobb-Douglas function can be written as

$$C(p_1, p_2, Y_1, Y_2) = Ap_1^{\alpha_1} p_2^{\alpha_2} y_1^{\beta_1} Y_2^{\beta_2} \tag{B.1}$$

Since $C(p_1, p_2, Y_1, Y_2) = g(p_1, p_2) \cdot h(Y_1, Y_2)$, the theory of duality between cost and production yields the result that the underlying transformation function can be written in the separable form

$$H(Y_1, Y_2) = G(X_1, X_2) \tag{B.2}$$

The marginal rate of transformation (MRT) between the outputs is the ratio of marginal costs. Hence,

$$\text{MRT} = \frac{\partial C}{\partial Y_1} \Big/ \frac{\partial C}{\partial Y_2} = \frac{\beta_1 Y_2}{\beta_2 Y_1} \tag{B.3}$$

Therefore, as Y_2/Y_1 increases, MRT increases, implying a convex curvature. A price-taking, profit-maximizing producer supplies only one of the outputs Y_1, Y_2.

Finally, for cost complementarity we require $\dfrac{\partial^2 C}{\partial Y_1 \partial Y_2} < 0$. It can be shown[24] that

$$\frac{\partial^2 C}{\partial Y_1\, \partial Y_2} = \frac{C}{Y_1\, Y_2}\left[\frac{\partial \log C}{\partial \log Y_1}\cdot\frac{\partial \log C}{\partial \log Y_2} + \frac{\partial^2 \log C}{\partial \log Y_1\, \partial \log Y_2}\right] \tag{B.4}$$

For the Cobb-Douglas function,

$$\frac{\partial^2 C}{\partial Y_1\, \partial Y_2} = \frac{C}{Y_1 Y_2}\cdot \beta_1 \cdot \beta_2 > 0$$

Hence, the Cobb-Douglas function cannot portray cost complementarity.

A typical version of a cost function containing a CES transformation function can be written as

$$C(p_1,\, p_2,\, Y_1,\, Y_2) = A p_1^{\alpha_1}\, p_2^{\alpha_2}\, [\delta Y_1^{-\rho} + (1 - \delta)Y_2^{-\rho}]^{-\mu/\rho} \tag{B.5}$$

It can easily be shown that the function (B.5) implies separability of outputs from inputs and has the correct curvature for $\rho < -1$. The cost complementarity condition stated in the text can be verified by computing

$$\frac{\partial^2 C}{\partial Y_1\, \partial Y_2} = \mu(\mu + \rho)\delta(1 - \delta)Y_1^{-\rho-1}\, Y_2^{-\rho-1}\, [A p_1^{\alpha_1}\, p_2^{\alpha_2}][\delta Y_1^{-\rho} \tag{B.6}$$
$$+ (1 - \delta)Y_2^{-\rho}]^{-\mu/\rho-2} < 0 \text{ if } \mu + \rho < 0$$

Since $\rho < -1$, cost complementarity must occur when the technology is subject to nondecreasing returns to scale ($\mu \leq 1$). This fact eliminates one potentially interesting case of an unnatural monopoly—the case when a limited degree of increasing returns to scale is combined with diseconomies of scope.

---

[24] Fuss and Waverman, "Multi-Product, Multi-Input Cost Functions."

Commentary

Leonard Merewitz

Judge Seymour Wenner, in the administrative law judge's initial decision of August 28, 1975, was concerned that no class of mail, particularly one with an inelastic demand, bear too great a part of the costs. Regulated utilities that operate simultaneously in monopoly and competitive markets are sometimes said to have an incentive to allocate discretionary expenditures to the monopoly service. There exists the temptation to price high in the monopoly market and low in the competitive markets. To the extent that rates are cost based, discretion in price setting is removed from the regulated firm. Judge Wenner was eager to attribute as much cost of service as possible to remove the discretion from the regulatee.

Melvyn Fuss, on the other hand, is concerned with determining the cost structure in an economically defensible manner and with testing interesting hypotheses about the cost structure. If he finds natural monopoly, he is interested in determining a price vector that will be sustainable—that is, it will keep competitors from cream skimming. It is particularly tantalizing that no empirical estimates have been given because the new tools available make the discovery of many interesting facts possible—for example, economies of scale, economies of scope, homotheticity, nonjointness in production. In particular, it would be interesting to know if there are any economies of scale or economies of scope and what the estimates of marginal cost are. In an earlier paper, Melvyn Fuss and Leonard Waverman found that the price of local telephone service in Canada was less than the incremental replacement cost of service whereas the prices for toll and competitive services exceeded their respective incremental costs.[1] This is a surprising finding. The regulated firm has apparently not gone as far as it might have in

---

[1] Melvyn Fuss and Leonard Waverman, "Multi-Product, Multi-Input Cost Functions for a Regulated Utility: The Case of Telecommunications in Canada," Working Paper 7810, University of Toronto, Institute for Policy Analysis, June 1978.

47

charging a high price in the monopoly market. This may cure some cynics.

A time series for a cross-section of post offices would be a good data base from which to estimate marginal costs of several classes of mail. All production processes that can be segregated and do not involve any common costs should be kept separately. Although I think it is unfortunate that to some people U.S.A. means Uniform System of Accounts, I think we should let accounting take us as far as it can and analyze by econometric methods only those accounts that include common costs.

Likelihood of Obtaining Requisite Data

The main data set the Postal Service now has for cost finding is the In-Office Cost System, a probability sample that includes all the largest 150 or so offices; the probability of other offices being in the sample increases with their size. Workers are sampled randomly and asked the activity on which they are working. The system therefore samples labor input and gives only limited information on mail attributes. Perhaps 500,000 observations are taken, but some result in data on mixed mail, such as sacks. There may result 300,000 to 400,000 observations out of the 90 to 96 billion pieces the Postal Service handles each year. Auxiliary cost systems exist for carriers on their routes, transportation, and second-class mail. There is probably insufficient information in these systems to produce data on inputs and outputs at particular offices.

A more promising set of data is the Work Load Reporting System, which improves on the former Work Measurement System. Whereas in the old system measurements had been "linear"—for example, "forty trays of letters"—the new system is based on weight and is therefore less discretionary and more reliable. These data are facility-specific. A data request was filed by the Postal Rate Commission in 1973 for a time series of these data. Only national summary data were made available, and the Postal Service maintains they are not useful for regulation purposes. They are the type of data a study like Fuss's would require.

Some caveats are in order. These data are organized by shape— for example, letters, flats, and small parcels and rolls (SPRs in the postal lexicon)—and there needs to be a careful concordance between shape, data, and products. Data are also not organized by operation performed; sometimes one office will do a primary, secondary, and tertiary sort on mail, and sometimes that same office will do a less thorough sort. The depth of sortation should be investigated.

Researchers need to be on the lookout for multicollinearity. Large offices tend to be large in all aspects of the vector of outputs they produce. Fuss could use some observations of zero outputs to answer some questions he poses. There were some examples of zero output in the Chicago North Suburban and South Suburban facilities in my 1966 sample.[2] I am not too hopeful that we will find post offices that do not produce some of the outputs under consideration. All services are usually available at all offices.

Another pitfall in production function analysis is that, although the amount of labor is readily measurable, capital is usually added in discrete lumps that suffice for several years, and excess capacity usually exists. Therefore, the apparent capital use is higher than the true capital use. Usually output is growing, capital is growing, and costs are growing. Since the apparent costs incurred are larger than the true capital costs, greater costs are attributed to incremental output than are truly attributable.

A mathematical functional form, no matter how well thought out, only approximates the description of a complex production technology. Depending on the data requirements for a precise estimate of the coefficients, I would stratify my group of post offices into at least three groups.

One final caveat: Of most interest is the question of economies of scale to the firm—in this case, the entire Postal Service. The observations are on individual post offices, which are in many cases close to the economic concept of the plant, although frequently a post office includes several facilities or stations. The distinction between economies of scale at the plant level and those at the level of the firm should be kept in mind. In most cases, growth at particular offices simulates what growth of the firm would be like, so this is not necessarily a major problem.

Concepts Worth Underlining

Panzar, Willig, Fuss, and Waverman are asking more fruitful questions than what happens to total cost as all outputs increase in proportion. With these caveats, I think the estimation exercise should be tried. It is important to know the characteristics of postal costs and important to push forward the ability to deal with natural monopoly in a rigorous way. It would be fascinating to see the equation estimates. If the marginal costs end up accounting for only a small share of total cost, I would be troubled by allocating all costs according to the inverse elasticity

---

[2] Leonard Merewitz, *The Production Function in the Public Sector: Production of Postal Services in the U.S. Post Office*, Monograph 14 (Berkeley: University of California, 1971); and "Costs and Returns to Scale in U.S. Post Offices," *Journal of the American Statistical Association*, September 1971.

rule. The inverse elasticity rule or Ramsey rule of pricing serves the economic efficiency objective exclusively. Fuss states correctly that once marginal costs are estimated, any explicit means can be chosen to allocate the remaining costs. The Ramsey rule maximizes economic efficiency. Fuss also suggests a Feldstein rule, which would give great attention to income distribution. I suspect that in the end considerations of efficiency and income distribution will be combined. Perhaps the Postal Service solution was not so bad.

The allocation of all extramarginal costs by the Ramsey rule is a blend of value-of-service and cost-of-service considerations. There is really a great deal of choice in the setting of the final prices—more choice than may seem available at the outset. Any explicitly stated combination of efficiency and income distribution considerations would seem to be acceptable as long as marginal costs are estimated according to econometric regressions of the type Fuss specifies so that they are interpretable as the extra costs of producing units of that service. This is almost certainly better than a constant debate about the proper level of a priori cost attribution where one side wants little attribution and one wants a lot of attribution and the ground rules for attribution are constantly changing. The complete formulation for a decision on prices may involve some constraints, such as subsidization of rural mail service. Whatever the constraints and whatever the blend of economic efficiency and income distribution considerations, a commission of lay persons will be needed to pass on them.

The translog cost function is more general than the Cobb-Douglas or constant elasticity of substitution function. It has the same arguments: outputs and factor prices. It adds cross-product terms between prices, between outputs, and between outputs and prices together. One advantage is theoretical: it allows the possibility of concavity in output-output space. This problem, noted by Yair Mundlak,[3] applies especially in a profit-maximizing behavioral formulation because convex isoquants would lead to a corner solution. These considerations are irrelevant when dealing with a cost-minimization problem where outputs are exogenously determined and multiproduction is assured. It would be curious, however, to have the cost structure differ depending on marketing facts. In the Postal Service, outputs are exogenously determined. That is what makes the estimate of the cost function more advisable than direct estimation of the production function. Nevertheless, the translog cost function allows testing of nonjointness in production, homotheticity, economies of scope, Cobb-Douglas nature, and other technical

[3] Yair Mundlak, "Transcendental Multiproduct Production Functions," *International Economic Review*, September 1964.

features of the technology. According to several empirical studies, a model that allows nonhomotheticity and nonunitary elasticities of substitution is required to represent the structure of production adequately.[4] For example, why should the capital-labor ratio remain fixed as the firm expands? Substitution of one factor for another is usually more than in the Leontief model of production but not so great as in the Cobb-Douglas model.

A repetitive question of public postal policy is: Is it good public policy to allow the Postal Service to become bigger, or should we repeal the private express statutes? Growth of the Postal Service may mean adding to its outputs or absorbing additional services. Is it good public policy to add Mailgram, express mail, or electronic transmission to the current menu of services offered by the Postal Service? Was it wise to drop postal banking?

We have been guilty of fuzzy thinking in the past in looking solely at the inherited concept of economies of scale. We have tended to try to look at the generalized average cost curve as all output increases. Panzar and Willig have sharpened our thinking on these matters and given us the concept of economies of scope.[5] It may be more efficient to produce several outputs together than to use separate production processes (this may also be called production commonality or complementarity in production). Fuss and Waverman treat the concepts of joint production and multiple production together in their empirical work although they make the definitional distinctions.

Although there exists no unambiguous measure of output-specific returns to scale except in the case of nonjoint production, it is fruitful to look at the second partial derivative of cost with respect to first one output and then another. If this is negative, then the extra production of output j reduces $\partial C/\partial Yi$ and there exist economies of scope. For example, if the influence of producing extra units of third-class mail is to reduce the marginal cost of first-class, there is complementarity in production between these two. There may be complementarities between two outputs but not all outputs. Probably banking was not complementary. One wonders whether the production of parcel services is. This expresses the intuitive notion that several outputs might possibly be more efficiently produced together than apart. Therefore, that a private firm can produce third-class mail services for lower marginal costs than the Postal Service is not conclusive. We must look at what

[4] Laurits R. Christensen and W. Greene, "Economies of Scale in U.S. Electric Power Generation," *Journal of Political Economy,* vol. 84, no. 4 (1976); and Fuss and Waverman, "Multi-Product, Multi-Input Cost Functions."

[5] John C. Panzar and Robert D. Willig, "Economies of Scale and Economies of Scope in Multi-Output Production," Bell Laboratories working paper (Holmdel, N.J., 1975).

51

happens to the marginal cost of Y_1 as Y_3 increases. If it goes down, there exist economies of scope, and the synergistic savings *might* justify the combination of production and the giving of monopoly to the Postal Service. The comparison of a single-product firm's average cost of producing Y_3 and the Postal Service's average cost of producing Y_3 is irrelevant, Fuss would claim, because the Postal Service's average cost is inherently arbitrary. Thus, we can begin to answer questions such as: Should the Postal Service drop a service that does not have commonality? We cannot, however, ask a more interesting question from a public policy view: should the Postal Service *add* a monopoly service? This is the implicit question of Part Two of this volume.

4

Has the 1970 Act Been Fair to Mailers?

James C. Miller III and Roger Sherman

It provides that, if the Commission determines, in connection with any request submitted prior to September 30, 1982, that all attributable costs exceed 60 percent of total estimated costs, the attributable costs of each class, subclass or type shall be reduced to an amount that is determined by multiplying the attributable costs of that class, subclass or type by a fraction whose numerator is 60 and denominator is a whole number equal to the percentage of total estimated costs determined to be attributable.

S. 3229

There is little doubt why the Postal Reorganization Act (which S. 3229 would amend) was passed in 1970.[1] First, the Post Office had been accumulating ever increasing annual deficits; by fiscal year (FY) 1967 the deficit had reached $1.17 billion, then almost 20 percent of the total postal budget.[2] At the same time, some mail users were enjoying large subsidies that contributed mightily to the Post Office's deficits.[3] Second, mail service was steadily deteriorating and was the subject of mounting complaints.[4] Service broke down for a short time in Chicago during 1966. The introduction of modern management methods and the adoption of a pricing policy that would ensure that each service covered at least its marginal, or attributable, cost were seen as two essential steps

---

Note: This paper draws in part on research carried out for the Rand Corporation under National Science Foundation grant no. APR 77–15721. The views expressed are those of the authors and do not necessarily reflect those of the institutions with which they are affiliated.

---

[1] 84 Stat. 719 (August 12, 1970), 39 *U.S. Code.*

[2] See *Towards Postal Excellence: The Report of the President's Commission on Postal Organization* (Washington, D.C., 1968), p. 22.

[3] Ibid., pp. 29–31.

[4] Ibid., p. 14.

in restoring postal service viability. Thus, some type of reorganization was seen as the answer.[5]

The Postal Reorganization Act of 1970 made a number of important changes. One was to remove postal service from politics and place it in the hands of a public corporation, the U.S. Postal Service. This new entity was instructed to introduce modern management methods and was given authority to issue bonds up to a limit of $10 billion. Its employees were taken out of the U.S. Civil Service system and given the right to bargain collectively; the expectation was that postal workers would thereby receive wages comparable to those in the private sector. Along with the Postal Service a new regulatory agency, the Postal Rate Commission, was created to oversee the Postal Service's establishment of postal classifications and rates.[6] This approach was viewed as more expert and objective than having Congress set rates on political grounds as it had in the past. Under the rate-setting standards incorporated in the act, each class of mail was to pay all the costs attributable to it,[7] in order to avoid cross-subsidization of one class by another and in hopes of making the Postal Service self-sufficient. Exceptions for some public-service mail categories were planned, and a subsidy of $920 million was authorized to sustain small post offices that would not otherwise be self-supporting.

Performance under the new act has been controversial, to say the least. By most measures, postal reorganization has not lived up to expectations. Although certain new management techniques have been introduced and pricing has arguably been insulated from political forces, problems still abound. For example, the annual deficit has risen from $166 million in FY 1970 to $688 million in FY 1977.[8] The conventional wisdom of the time was that first-class mail was subsidizing other classes and thus rate increases for first-class mail should be limited. Yet the price of a one-ounce first-class letter has risen from six cents in 1970 to fifteen cents today—a 150 percent increase—while the increase in the consumer price index has been less than 60 percent.[9] One reason for this

---

[5] See ibid., chap. 3. Also see Earl M. Collier, Jr., and George H. Bostick, "The Postal Reorganization Act: A Case Study of Regulated Industry Reform," *Virginia Law Review,* September 1972, pp. 1030–98.

[6] The Postal Rate Commission's decisions concerning postal rates and fees are not binding. The commission makes its findings and forwards them to the Board of Governors of the Postal Service, which makes the ultimate decision. The Postal Rate Commission's recommended decision can be set aside only by a unanimous vote of the governors, however, and thus far the board has accepted each of the commission's recommended decisions. See U.S. Postal Rate Commission, *Postal Rate Commission Handbook,* December 1976, pp. 3 and 4.

[7] Section 3622(*b*), which is presented in full in the appendix to this chapter.

[8] Telephone communication with Alfred C. Biggim of the U.S. Postal Service, September 21, 1978.

[9] *Economic Report of the President, 1978* (Washington, D.C., 1978), p. 313.

dramatic rise in postal prices and costs since 1970 is that postal wages have increased much faster than wages for comparable work in the private sector.[10]

In this paper we focus on postal pricing issues and address the question, Has the 1970 act been fair to mailers? We conclude there are serious doubts and explain why. Under the act we find only modest changes in postal pricing, in part because the act allowed for a very gradual transition—an eight-year phasing period that was later extended to sixteen years. But a second and perhaps more important reason is the lack of full enforcement of the aims of the act, apparently because costs have not been identified with enough precision to allow detection of cross-subsidization, which undercuts the goal of making each service self-supporting.

The prefatory quote above from S. 3229 illustrates the costing problem well. In addition to the many other affected parties, members of Congress are here seen wanting to influence postal rates indirectly. For this bill would legislate the maximum proportion of total cost that could be attributed to any class of mail, which in turn would affect rates. Defining what cost can or cannot be is certainly an odd purpose for legislation, as if legislators could revise the laws of economics (and if those, why not the law of gravity?). No wonder the quoted passage appeared in a July 6, 1978, *Washington Star* featured called "Gobbledygook." (Translated, the passage says: "Attributable cost can be no more than 60 percent of total cost.")

Principles of pricing and costing, which were discussed in Chapters 2 and 3, suggest that separating the two tasks is neither easy nor appropriate. Nevertheless, the guiding statutes contain pricing rules that assume costs have already been attributed, insofar as that is possible, to the classes of mail before "pricing" is undertaken. We shall examine the costing and pricing tasks separately because government practice separates them and the record is arranged according to such a division. Next, fairness to mailers will be discussed. Finally, we shall offer some reasons for our finding that appropriate costing and pricing principles are yet to be introduced to postal service.

Postal Service Cost Attribution

The starting point for any discussion of costs (or prices) is economic efficiency. This concept has two principal components. One is mini-

---

[10] See, for example, Douglas K. Adie, *An Evaluation of Postal Service Wage Rates* (Washington, D.C.: American Enterprise Institute, 1977); Sharon P. Smith, "Are Postal Workers Over- or Underpaid?" *Industrial Relations*, vol. 13 (May 1976), pp. 168–76; and "Comments of the Council on Wage and Price Stability Concerning the Private Express Statutes," in U.S. Postal Rate Commission Docket R76–4 (January 16, 1976), pp. 50–57.

mizing the cost of whatever amounts of goods or services are produced, sometimes called technical efficiency. The second is more complex and is called allocative efficiency; it requires that consumers and producers choose the "correct" amount of each good or service, a decision that can be made by relying on prices to convey information. Suppose, for example, that a mail service is priced well below the cost of providing marginal units of it. Then consumers will use the service "too much" because the last units produced will cost society more than consumers actually pay. Unless there is some clear social gain in having some consumers benefit from the low price, the result is obviously inequitable; the consumers do not pay the full cost of their consumption, and the balance of the cost must be borne by others. The result is also inefficient, because the consumers themselves value the additional service only by the amount they pay, which is less than the value the resources used to produce the service would have in some other use.[11] That value in some other use is the cost of the resources, and it must be known so that the product of the resources can have a price that is efficient or equitable.

Thus, a knowledge of cost is essential to determine whether any given price or set of prices is efficient or equitable. Yet the Postal Service's efforts to determine the costs of various services have failed miserably. Without knowledge of costs, the Postal Service cannot meet the strictures against cross-subsidization among various classes of mail, and its compliance with the Postal Reorganization Act has been brought into question. Also, without reasonably accurate cost information, Postal Service management and others cannot evaluate the service's performance in minimizing cost.

That the costs of mail services have not been well identified by the Postal Service is a matter of legal record. In 1972 the Postal Rate Commission issued its first decision (Docket R71–1), based on an extensive review of various cost justifications put forward by the Postal Service. This decision was appealed, and in a concurring opinion to that decision District of Columbia Court of Appeals Chief Judge David Bazelon (joined by Circuit Judge Edward A. Tamm and Senior District Judge Charles E. Wyzanski, Jr.) observed:

> One troubling aspect of the Postal Service's approach in this
> case requires comment. The Act directs that the Postal Rate

---

[11] Decentralized economic systems, such as a competitive market system, tend to reach efficient outcomes because each producer has an incentive to set the price charged at marginal (production and distribution) cost. Unless price covers average cost, the producer will go out of business; if price exceeds average cost, this will attract new entry which, in turn, will force prices back down to average cost. On the other hand, producers that are not competitive—such as those regulated or managed by government—do not face the same set of incentives.

Commission determine rates in accordance with certain guidelines. The most concrete of these, Section 3622(b)(3), estab-
lishes "the *requirement* that each class of mail or type of mail
service bear (1) the direct and indirect postal costs attributable
to that class or type plus (2) that portion of all other costs of
the Postal Service *reasonably assignable* to such class or type."

The Postal Service's response to this requirement was questionable at best. It proposed that the Commission "attribute"
only 49 percent of the ten billion dollars at issue. The remain-
der, it said, should be "reasonably assigned." It presented a
schedule of such assignments that, it said, had been derived
by two of its employees through the use of a formula. The
formula, in turn, was purportedly composed of three factors:
(1) the hypothesized elasticity of demand for each class of mail;
(2) the "value" of each class; and (3) the competitive stance
of the Postal Service in those cases in which it lacked a legal
monopoly. And when application of this vague formula threatened to result in great changes from pre-existing rates, it was
simply suspended and an alternative substituted. The Chief
Examiner aptly concluded: "Distributing billions of dollars on
the basis of thinly supported judgments is not an acceptable
method. And it is an invitation to pressures which Congress
sought to avoid."[12]

The Postal Rate Commission's next major decision came in August 1975
(Docket R74–1), a decision that was again appealed. The court observed
this time:

> We are an appellate court, not an agency possessed of devel-
> oped expertise. We look to the design of the Commission's
> approach not to substitute our judgment for that of the agency,
> but only to determine whether the Commission's adopted
> method falls unconscionably short of the statutory require-
> ments. . . .
>
> The Commission acknowledges that presently incomplete
> data preclude full attribution under its cost variability ap-
> proach. It insists, however, that utmost accuracy in the meas-
> urement of causation must prevail over all else. In our view
> this allegiance to the goal of greatest possible accuracy fatally
> flaws the design of the Commission's adopted method since
> at present the Commission's goal may be obtained only by
> substantially disregarding the Act's express concern for ex-
> tended attribution. . . .
>
> We conclude that in the circumstances of this case the Com-
> mission's almost exclusive reliance on a cost variability ap-

---

[12] *Association of American Publishers, Inc.* v. *Governors, U.S. Postal Service*, 485 F. 2nd
768 (D.C. Cir. 1973), pp. 777–78; footnotes omitted.

proach to attribution contravenes a primary purpose of subsection 3622(*b*)(3) and therefore fails to comply with the Act. . . .

We conclude that the Commission's present method for assigning unattributed costs proceeds from a faulty premise in contravention of the Act and therefore must be rejected.[13]

The procedures followed by the Postal Service, and essentially accepted by the Postal Rate Commission in its early decisions, attributed less than half the total cost of postal operations to the various classes of mail. The Postal Service used old accounting rules. Under them, a fixed cost that was shared by two mail services would be apportioned to all classes of mail, even though the cost was incurred for resources clearly used only by the two services. To be attributed to a class of mail as a variable cost, the cost had to vary directly from year to year with the volume of mail in that class. Even the cost of stamps was excluded from the variable (and thus attributable) category for not varying enough with mail volume to satisfy the Postal Service's strict application of its own extreme rule. To quote from the May 1975 initial decision of the chief administrative law judge in Docket R74–1:

> Thus, "fixed" costs encompass substantially all costs for the purchase and lease of buildings, the purchase and lease of equipment and vehicles, expenses for vehicle drivers, vehicle maintenance, building and equipment maintenance and custodial costs, the cost of a mailman's driving or walking his route to deliver mail, one-third of purchased transportation, most supplies including gasoline and oil, and a considerable portion of clerks' time (including window service)—in summary, substantial parts of many operating costs and many costs that may appear fixed over a short-run time period but are long-term variable or incremental costs (long-term costs).[14]

The Postal Service's approach makes it difficult to separate the excessive costs of inefficient operations from the "true costs" of providing service or even to identify how cost is related to output.[15] For example, if too much capacity is regularly maintained, the evidence will point to increasing returns to scale (that is, decreasing average cost with expanding output), even though excess capacity is the proper explanation. As shown in the next section, the *character* of costs (including whether returns to scale exist) is important to a determination of efficient (and

---

[13] *National Association of Greeting Card Publishers* v. *U.S. Postal Service*, 569 F. 2nd 570 (D.C. Cir., December 28, 1976).

[14] Chief Administrative Law Judge's Initial Decision on Postal Rate and Fee Increases, U.S. Postal Rate Commission Docket R74–1, vol. 1 (May 28, 1975), pp. 8 and 9.

[15] This point is emphasized in Rodney E. Stevenson, "The Pricing of Postal Services," in H. M. Trebing, ed., *New Dimensions in Public Utility Pricing* (East Lansing: Michigan State University Press, 1976).

equitable) postal rates. But traditional estimating procedures assume cost-minimizing behavior by the enterprise examined. As Rodney Stevenson has demonstrated, this condition is usual in competitive markets but may not occur in a monopoly like the U.S. Postal Service, and its absence makes the identification of true cost relationships very difficult, even with the most advanced econometric methods.[16]

Particularly distressing is the lack of empirical evidence for the Postal Service's conclusion that the provision of postal services is characterized by significant economies of scale—a conclusion at variance with available studies of this question.[17] The Postal Service may well *believe* that average costs decline with volume, but though it produces some evidence in support of this conclusion, its analysts use a highly restrictive, short-run definition of marginal cost.[18] Costs have mainly been categorized by accounting rules, not estimated statistically. The portion of costs termed "fixed" by the Postal Service and presumably unrelated to volume appears empirically to rise as much with mail volume as the costs traced explicitly to mail volume. Even in short-run periods, such as from one month to the next, total costs move in almost perfect proportion to mail volume.[19] This result is not surprising, since approximately 80 percent of the Postal Service's expenses are labor costs.

In summary, the careful, objective analyses that would permit a more scientific allocation of postal service costs have not been used by the Postal Service, although eight years have passed since a law requiring such costs as a basis for rates went into effect. Recent cases have seen modest changes in Postal Service costing, brought about by gentle nudging from the Postal Rate Commission and more formidable shoving by the courts. In the 1976 postal rates and fees case the Postal Rate Commission succeeded in getting the Postal Service to attribute about 60

---

[16] Ibid., pp. 437–40.

[17] Even the Post Office Department's own empirical study found no economies of scale. See Bureau of Finance and Administration, U.S. Post Office Department, *Summary Report of Cost System Task Force on Incremental Costs* (Washington, D.C., May 1970). See also the review of studies in U.S. Postal Rate Commission, "Economies of Scale in Postal Service" by Leonard Merewitz (August 30, 1973, processed); and the review contained in the Initial Decision, Docket R74–1, pp. 78–90. No general economies of scale were found in Rodney E. Stevenson, "Postal Pricing Problems and Production Functions" (Ph.D. diss., Michigan State University, 1973). However, a finding of some modest economies of scope is contained in George M. Wattles, "The Rates and Costs of the United States Postal Service," *Journal of Law and Economics*, April 1963.

[18] That postal service is characterized by increasing returns to scale is thus an *assumption* built into the Postal Service's costing methodology; the conclusion is not a product of any analysis.

[19] Initial Decision, Docket R74–1, pp. 80–81.

percent of its total cost to mail classes,[20] and in the 1977 case the attributed cost component reached nearly 65 percent.[21] In addition, in the most recent case some 7 percent of total cost was deemed reasonably assignable to mail classes, so that more than 70 percent of total cost was in effect assigned to classes of mail. But the underlying basis for these cost imputations remains contentious and negotiated rather than professional and scientific. It is therefore not certain that costs are better estimated in these recent decisions, although most evidence in early cases indicated the fraction of costs allocated to the classes of mail then was too low.

Postal Service Pricing

In contrast to its rather rudimentary approach to costing, the Postal Service has endorsed, and even relied upon, sophisticated principles for pricing. Most attention has centered on the Ramsey or inverse elasticity rule, which says that if demands are independent the profit margin for each service should be inversely proportional to that service's price elasticity of demand.[22] But the application of this principle has been marred in two respects. First, to use the rule we must know the marginal or incremental costs, and as we have seen, this information is woefully

---

[20] Opinion and Recommended Decision, U.S. Postal Rate Commission Docket R76-1 (June 30, 1976).

[21] Opinion and Recommended Decision, U.S. Postal Rate Commission Docket R77-1 (May 12, 1978).

[22] The principle is often called the Ramsey rule after Frank P. Ramsey, "A Contribution to the Theory of Taxation," *Economic Journal*, vol. 37 (March 1927), pp. 47–61. A modern derivation of the rule is contained in William J. Baumol and David F. Bradford, "Optimal Departures from Marginal Cost Pricing," *American Economic Review*, June 1970, pp. 265–83. In precise terms, the rule says that $(P_i - MC_i)/P_i = K/E_i$, where P_i = price of the ith service; MC_i = marginal cost of the ith service; E_i = price elasticity of the ith service; and K is a "proportionality constant" chosen so the enterprise will just satisfy its budget constraint. (E_i is defined simply as the percentage change in the ith service divided by the percentage change in P_i.) This simple form of the inverse elasticity rule assumes that cross-elasticities of demand are zero (that is, changing the price of one service has no effect on sales of any other service), and that it is infeasible to adopt more efficient pricing schemes such as second-degree price discrimination. Strictly speaking, the Postal Service's use of the rule was not precise inasmuch as the cross-elasticities are not zero; see explanation by one of the Postal Service's own expert witnesses, William Vickery (U.S. Postal Rate Commission Docket R74-1, *Transcript*, vol. 2, p. 423); this point was discussed at great length in Docket R76-1 (see Recommended Decision, Docket R76-1, pp. 133–38). Pricing rules to deal with nonzero cross-elasticities, including those with private-sector services, are derived in Roger Sherman and Anthony George, "Second-Best Pricing Rules for the U.S. Postal Service," *Southern Economic Journal*, vol. 45, no. 3 (January 1979), pp. 685–95. In addition, the Postal Service did not explore the possibility of employing forms of second-degree price discrimination (such as a yearly charge for having a mailbox), as was suggested by witnesses in rate cases.

inadequate. Second, the Postal Service's elasticity estimates have been highly subjective and judgmental. In Docket R74–1, estimates of different Postal Service witnesses were inconsistent;[23] other methods were used in Docket R76–1, and results then were quite different from those offered in Docket R74–1.

˙If only a small fraction of the cost were not attributable (and therefore the amount to be "marked up" over marginal cost were small), this lack of reliable elasticity estimates might be tolerable. But in the early cases the Postal Service appeared to understate marginal costs and left more than half of all its costs in the "fixed" category, not allocated to any class of mail and therefore to be recovered in rates through application of the inverse elasticity rule. In Docket R74–1, for example, the enormous sum of $6 billion was to be recovered on the basis of the Postal Service's subjective views about demand elasticity and rather incomplete knowledge about the true marginal or incremental costs of providing services. Even though a smaller fraction of total cost was left unassigned in the most recent decision (in Docket R77–1), between $4 billion and $5 billion still remained "fixed" and not allocated on a cost basis among the various classes of mail.

As Melvyn Fuss has pointed out, the inverse elasticity rule can be used to allocate costs, for it is difficult to separate costing from pricing.[24] Indeed, the Postal Service and the Postal Rate Commission have applied second-best pricing rules to the task of allocating costs.[25] If the elasticity of demand is used to assign costs to classes of mail, however, cross-subsidization as considered in the act will never be detected. Cost essentially will then follow whatever price is set and can never be above price. That is, if the Postal Service can make apparently reasonable assignments of cost by the inverse elasticity rule, it can always satisfy subsection 3622(b)(3) of the act: "the requirement that each class of mail or type of mail service bear the direct and indirect postal costs attributable to that class or type plus that portion of all other costs of the Postal Service reasonably assignable to such class or type." This subsection surely did not anticipate the use of demand factors in the *assignment of cost,* because by using them the Postal Service could always satisfy it and the subsection would have no meaning. The consideration of demand elasticity is invited for setting rates in subsection 3622(b)(4) (see the appendix to this chapter), which calls attention to

---

[23] See Initial Decision, Docket R74–1, vol. 1, pp. 90–105, esp. p. 104.
[24] See Melvyn A. Fuss, Chapter 3 herein.
[25] The following quotation, for example, comes from Recommended Decision, Docket R76–1, p. 12: "As we have done in the past, we use market demand forces and relative price sensitivities as a guide to judgment in assigning institutional costs to classes and services."

the effects of rate increases on the general public and business mail users, and also on private enterprises that deliver mail other than letters (such as the United Parcel Service and the Independent Postal System of America). In addition, subsection 3622(b)(2) invited attention to the value of mail service actually provided by class or type to both sender and recipient. Thus, in the law, whether or not it is technically advisable, costing and pricing are separate tasks. Costs are first to be traced to classes of mail that cause them, and every price is to be set so it will bear at least that cost, in order to meet 3622(b)(3). In terms of the act, marking up that cost is regarded as pricing.

In advancing the inverse elasticity approach, the Postal Service has argued that its circumstances fit those necessary to have the rule apply. The rule is appropriate for a public enterprise that realizes economies of scale and economies of scope. If the price of each service were equal to its marginal or incremental cost, such an enterprise would lose money. And if the enterprise is constrained not to lose as much money as it would under marginal cost pricing, it must set prices above marginal costs. The inverse elasticity rule guides the enterprise in setting prices above marginal costs while interfering as little as possible with an efficient allocation of resources. Resulting prices are often called second-best. That is, while they are not ideal, they contribute as much as possible to efficiency while departing from it only enough to meet the budget constraint.

Although the inverse elasticity rule might be appropriate, its application has been impeded by inadequacies in the Postal Service's tracing of costs to the mail classes that cause them. To quote again from the administrative law judge's decision in Docket R74–1,

> For example, the new $1 billion bulk mail system will handle bulk third and fourth-class mail and some second-class mail. Because Postal Service classifies buildings and equipment as "fixed" costs, 58 percent of the cost of this system will be charged to first-class mail on the basis of its relative inelasticity of demand, even though it will not use any of these facilities. [26]

We do not mean to imply that attributing cost to classes of mail is a simple task for, as Fuss indicates, the problem is a difficult one. [27] But if costs are traced only partially to mail classes and the inverse elasticity rule is applied, resulting prices may exploit the classes of mail where monopoly power is greatest. Prices will be high, not necessarily because costs of providing services are great but because monopoly power is high as indicated by less elastic demand. And where demand is more

---

[26] Initial Decision, Docket R74–1, vol. 1, p. 10.

[27] Fuss, Chapter 3 herein.

elastic, perhaps because competing services exist, prices may be set low, even below true marginal costs. Thus, by inadequate attribution of costs to classes of mail, the Postal Service may fail to comply with the terms of the Postal Reorganization Act. That has been the major concern of administrative law judges and appeals courts in postal rate cases throughout the 1970s.

Fairness to Mailers

Fairness may be defined in many ways. One notion of fairness takes the status quo as legitimate and sees changes from it as undesirable. In this view, those receiving favored treatment have a right to its continuation. Another view holds that none should be favored and none benefited. Each party pays the cost of service it consumes, not less, and does not bear the cost of others' consumption. A third idea of fairness involves value judgments about which persons or which services are to be benefited or encouraged as compared with others; prices would be adjusted relative to costs in order to achieve those aims. The Postal Reorganization Act sought primarily the second view of fairness in that no party is to be subsidized by another. The first view was acknowledged, inasmuch as provision was made to move gradually, in phases, to rates that would comply with the act's pricing guidelines. Little scope was given to the third idea of fairness, because no group was to enjoy a price lower than marginal or incremental cost.

If fairness is defined as an absence of change, postal pricing since 1970 appears to have been fair. Table 4.1 shows indexes of prices for four important mail classes to indicate changes since 1970 (when all indexes equal 100). All postal rates have increased by comparable

TABLE 4.1
PRICE INDEXES FOR MAIL CLASSES AND OTHER CONSUMER GOODS
(1970 = 100)

	1971	1973	1975	1977
First-class letters (first ounce)	133	167	217	250
Second-class regular	150	167	212	273
Third-class bulk	120	158	193	210
Parcel post	100	116	128	172
Consumer prices	104	114	139	156

SOURCES: U.S. Postal Rate Commission Recommended Decisions, Dockets R71–1, R74–1, R76–1, and R77–1; and *Economic Report of the President, 1978*, p. 313.

amounts, much more than the consumer price index, since 1970. Only second-class mail (the regular rate for nonadvertising material) has increased more than first-class mail, and parcel post has increased the least. Because second-class mail was thought to be heavily subsidized in 1970, whereas first-class mail was seen carrying too great a burden then, this result is not surprising. The very small difference in their price increases is surprising, however, as is the relatively small increase in parcel post rates, because parcel post was also thought to be subsidized in 1970. For many years before 1970, special interests lobbied long and hard to win favorable treatment from Congress for their postal rates. Not only magazines and newspapers but churches, book clubs, record clubs, nonprofit organizations of all kinds, libraries, mail-order houses, direct-mail advertisers, and many other users were favored with low rates. Since 1970, the Postal Service's reluctance to attribute costs to mail classes, together with its extremely subjective assumptions in applying the inverse elasticity rule, apparently has allowed essentially the same pricing structure to persist through most of the 1970s. The relative prices in Table 4.1 are full rates, not counting the effects of phasing appropriations that softened the impact of change, and they show no radical change in the structure of postal rates.

The lack of change in Postal Service rates would not be fair to mailers, according to the second notion of fairness which bans cross-subsidization. This notion of fairness is embodied in the terms of the Postal Reorganization Act of 1970. Indeed, on this point the Postal Rate Commission's administrative law judge concluded in Docket R74–1:

> The Postal Service has become a tax-collecting agency, collecting money from first-class mailers to distribute to other favored classes. Every time a person pays 10 cents to mail a first-class letter he is paying his appropriate attributable cost plus his proportionate share of residual cost, and in addition, he is contributing almost 2 cents to pay the costs of other services. [28]

Using his own estimates of costs drawn from evidence in the case, the chief administrative law judge concluded that certain groups of mailers were recipients of this subsidy: second class (periodicals, including newspapers), single-piece third class (printed matter and merchandise weighing less than one pound), and fourth class (printed matter and merchandise over one pound), especially parcel post users. [29] In Table 4.2 are the net contributions found for the four mail classes for which

---

[28] See Initial Decision, Docket R74–1, vol. 1., p. 13.
[29] Ibid., pp. 110–15.

TABLE 4.2

CROSS-SUBSIDY FOUND BY POSTAL RATE COMMISSION ADMINISTRATIVE
LAW JUDGE IN DOCKET R74–1

	Postal Service Revenues Less Judge's Estimates of Attributable Costs (millions of dollars)	Difference per Piece of Mail (in cents)
First-class letters	2,143.4	4.25
Second-class regular	−200.5	−4.05
Third-class bulk	260.8	1.61
Parcel post	−335.6	−78.59

SOURCE: Initial Decision, Docket R74–1, vol. 1, pp. 113, 114, and appendix C.

price indexes were reported in Table 4.1. To be sure, the cost data with which to analyze cross-subsidization well are not at hand. But a reasonable case was presented in Docket R74–1, and since it is the Postal Service that must gather data to settle this charge, its failure to answer makes such criticism more convincing. In the latest case (Docket R77–1), the Postal Service's estimates of cost have come more nearly to reflect those of the administrative law judge's in Docket R74–1.

It might not be unfair for some users of postal services to subsidize others if the explicit form of the cross-subsidy were deemed fair and desirable, thus meeting the third idea of fairness. Such a cross-subsidy would have to be mandated in postal or other legislation, however. The Postal Reorganization Act explicitly sought an end to favoritism that was not explicitly mandated. Its continuation therefore cannot be regarded as fair, no matter how long it may have existed before the act was passed.

The Postal Service will continue to have great discretion to favor one mail class over another as long as it is not forced to trace costs with accuracy. Although a requirement that rates be tied to accurate costs would reduce its discretionary power, the Postal Service would, almost paradoxically, improve its financial position by using cost-based rates. Their use would probably cause the Postal Service to lose some mail volume in classes such as parcel post, but much of this business has already gone to private competitors, and the rest is probably retained only because rates for this class are so low that losses on it are significant. The contributions from mail classes that now have very high rates may be increased under cost-based rates, at least in the long run.

Another benefit of cost-based rates could actually be the survival of mail classes that may now have rates well above marginal costs. In the long run, placing an extra burden on, say, first-class mail users may be self-defeating because very high rates will invite the substitution of other services. Since some 80 percent of first-class mail users are businesses, it is reasonable to expect that some of them will try cost-cutting alternatives, drawing from the range of new technologies that have been developed for transmitting messages. [30] By exploiting its monopoly now, the Postal Service may speed the day when it no longer exists.

Reasons for the Failure of the Postal Reorganization Act

As we have seen, Postal Service costing and pricing techniques do not appear adequate to meet the requirements of the Postal Reorganization Act. Apart from any faults in its rate-setting goals, those charged with implementing them have not begun to achieve them. Although the agency has a new name, bargains collectively with its employees, and handles its own financial matters, and although the Postal Rate Commission is in place and processes rate requests through ponderous proceedings, postal rates have nevertheless been rising, service complaints continue, and charges of cross-subsidization are commonplace. Because these postal problems continue, Congress is on the verge of another reorganization of the service. What accounts for this failure?

One clear feature of the postal problem is inadequate cost identification. If costs are not identified, they are not easily controlled. And without cost knowledge, pricing may be misguided. The lack of progress may be partially explained by the fact that the Postal Service has enjoyed a monopoly on first-class mail ever since the Postal Act of 1845 outlawed private express service. [31] Without extremely skillful oversight the Postal Service will retain great discretion in setting rates as long as it has this monopoly. And of course its own life will be more comfortable as long as it has power to juggle rates as it chooses. This would lead one to suspect that the Postal Service would prefer not to have its costs well identified as a basis for rates—a suspicion that seems confirmed by all available evidence. Also, one would expect the agency to oppose the

---

[30] Donald R. Ewing and Roger K. Salaman, "The Postal Crisis: The Postal Function as a Communications Service," U.S. Department of Commerce, OT Special Publication 77–13 (January 1977). See also Charles L. Jackson, Chapter 7 herein.

[31] 5 Stat. 732 (March 3, 1845). Not known to many people is the fact that the pony express—a frequent symbol of U.S. mail service—was not an invention of the U.S. Post Office but was introduced by private postal companies that were, in turn, put out of business by the private express statutes.

repeal of the private express statutes; it does so with extraordinary vigor.[32]

Another problem is that the Postal Service insists on allocating costs to the conventional categories of mail such as first class and parcel post, rather than analyzing costs in terms of principal components—speed of delivery, distance, size, weight, handling, and so on. A functional cost analysis in terms of speed, size, weight, and so forth could probably reveal more appropriate mail categories. It might also indicate the extent of cross-subsidy currently embodied in such policies as uniform first-class and book rates across the entire country.

Unfortunately, turning Postal Service pricing around is not a simple matter, partly because the public has come to view it as analogous to the weather: Everyone talks about it, but no one does (or perhaps can do) anything about it. Apparently over the years the organization has come to *believe* that its costs are largely fixed, that they cannot be attributed to mail classes, and that no scientific costing methodologies will show otherwise. Without experience in competitive circumstances, no challenge to these beliefs has been made for generations. Decent people can remain confident in beliefs that are wrong[33] even when they are the basis of unfair and inefficient pricing of postal services.

Strong forces that thrive on these ancient beliefs about costs are embodied in the special interest groups that helped to foster them. As an example, when Congress created the Commission on Postal Service in September 1976, there were to be seven appointed members, plus the postmaster general and the chairman of the Postal Rate Commission as members ex officio. Of the seven appointed members, two were to be Postal Service employees. As it turned out, two more were affiliated with magazines, important beneficiaries under the old practices. It is not surprising that the *Report of the Commission,* issued on April 1977, found the Postal Service providing "comprehensive and generally acceptable levels of services at reasonable rates."[34] The commission even went so far as to suggest limiting to 60 percent the fraction of total cost

---

[32] The Postal Service opposes moves to repeal the private express statutes and urges prosecution of private firms that crop up from time to time to provide mail services. Recently the Postal Service proposed a limited suspension of the private express statutes *in the event of a strike.* Obviously, one motive here was to make a strike less likely; another was to diminish criticism of the Postal Service should a strike occur.

[33] One is reminded of Proust's observation about the persistence of beliefs: "they can aim at them continual blows of contradiction and disproof without weakening them; and an avalanche of miseries and maladies coming, one after another, without interruption into the bosom of a family, will not make it lose faith in either the clemency of its God or the capacity of its physician."

[34] See U.S. Congress, Commission on Postal Service, *Report of the Commission on Postal Service* (April 1977), vol. 1, p. 5.

that could be attributed to individual classes of mail. [35] What is surprising is that legislation to limit the percentage of costs in this way was introduced seriously in Congress. Such a proposal reflects either a blind faith in patterns of cost that available facts show to be wrong or a deliberate effort to influence for private gain the billions of dollars at stake in Postal Service rates.

The evidence indicates that if the Postal Service were to make appropriate cost attributions and set postal rates at marginal costs, the deficit would be reasonably small; this deficit could then be narrowed (even to zero) if postal rates were set slightly above marginal costs. But we do not know what these marginal costs are. Since the Postal Service seems unwilling to make the needed estimations, one would expect the task to be accomplished by the Postal Rate Commission. So far, however, the commission has been reasonably sympathetic to the Postal Service's defense of current practices and has not performed cost analyses of its own. Although the trend may be in the right direction (as more costs are very gradually being attributed to mail classes), we cannot yet be sure; the process is interminably slow and imperfect.

What is to be done? If, as many have alleged, the market could coordinate private postal services, probably the most effective action would be to repeal the private express statutes. This would force the Postal Service to reform its rate structure and improve its operations or else go out of business. [36] But numerous attempts to repeal the private express statutes have been mounted, and all have failed. Perhaps the only recourse is to demand that the Postal Rate Commission do its job.

Appendix: Pricing Guidelines

The Pricing Guidelines of the Postal Reorganization Act, Subsection 3622(b) follow:

> Upon receiving a request, the Commission shall make a recommended decision on the request for changes in rates or fees in each class of mail or type of service in accordance with the policies of this title and the following factors:
>
> 1. the establishment and maintenance of a fair and equitable schedule;
>
> 2. the value of the mail service actually provided each class or type of mail service to both the sender and the recipient, including but not limited to the collection, mode of transportation, and priority of delivery;

---

[35] Ibid., p. 64.

[36] For an analysis of this alternative, see U.S. Department of Justice, *Changing the Private Express Laws: Competitive Alternatives and the U.S. Postal Service* (January 1977).

3. the requirement that each class of mail or type of mail service bear the direct and indirect postal costs attributable to that class or type plus that portion of all other costs of the Postal Service reasonably assignable to such class or type;

4. the effect of rate increases upon the general public, business mail users, and enterprises in the private sector of the economy engaged in the delivery of mail matter other than letters;

5. the available alternative means of sending and receiving letters and other mail matter at reasonable costs;

6. the degree of preparation of mail for delivery into the postal system performed by the mailer and its effect upon reducing costs to the Postal Service;

7. simplicity of structure for the entire schedule and simple, identifiable relationships between the rates or fees charged the various classes of mail for postal services;

8. the educational, cultural, scientific, and informational value to the recipient of mail matter; and

9. such other factors as the Commission deems appropriate.

Commentary

Michael A. Crew

I should like to commend James C. Miller III and Roger Sherman for their very lucid exposition and application of some relevant economic theory to problems of the U.S. Postal Service. I find myself in almost complete agreement with their analysis. My one reservation concerns their concluding remark. They mention briefly the potential benefits of placing the Postal Service under competitive pressures by repeal of the private express statutes but reject the idea on the pragmatic grounds that numerous previous attempts at repeal have failed. They then rightly point out that in the absence of repeal all that seems to be left is "to demand that the Postal Rate Commission do its job." If their pragmatism in this regard is well placed, the prospects for improvement in the performance of the Postal Service do not seem very good, as my subsequent remarks will indicate. My approach in reviewing some of the proposals made by Miller and Sherman and discussing their potential for improving the performance of the Postal Service will be to examine some relevant experience of the Post Office in the United Kingdom.

Miller and Sherman have indicated very clearly the arbitrary nature of the Postal Service's cost analysis and its overzealous or even misguided use of the inverse elasticity rule. I think they have covered the issues very clearly. They show that the existing system of costing has some major flaws and that the system of Ramsey pricing, as employed by the Postal Service, causes many inefficiencies. In addition, they examine some ways in which the system might be considered unfair to mailers. With these important parts of their analysis I am in almost complete agreement, and so I will confine my comments to discussion of their proposals for improvements in pricing and costing procedures.

One proposal concerns the need to get the Postal Service to stop allocating costs on the basis of the conventional categories of mail, such as first class, second class, and parcel post, and to move toward an analysis based upon the principal components of cost, for example, speed of delivery, size, weight, and distance. This is an interesting proposal, particularly because the British Post Office has had experience with this approach for several years. In 1968 the Post Office introduced a two-tier pricing system that is rooted in the kind of cost analysis proposed by Miller and Sherman. The system allowed the customer to choose whether he wanted fast or slow service, paying a higher fee for the prospect of earlier delivery. The rates (converted into U.S. currency) in 1968 were five cents for first class (the faster service) and four cents for second class, for up to four ounces in each case. Both rates were raised frequently and the initial weight allowance reduced, until now the rates (at current exchange rates) are twenty-one cents and sixteen and one-half cents, respectively.

The importance of the two-tier system was not that it miraculously kept prices down, which it clearly did not, but that it introduced some principles of efficiency into postal pricing. Pricing was now, to some extent, related to cost. Instead of being based on some arbitrary distinction between printed paper and sealed letters, it was based on two of the main determinants of cost. One consequence of the change was greater efficiency. For example, the two-tier system was a means of reducing the evening peak that occurred in sorting the mail, since more mail was put to one side for sorting during the slacker period the next day. The effect was that of a peak-load pricing mechanism. The resources that had gone into sorting a large volume of mail in the evening were reduced. With less demand at this time, a better service could be offered to the higher-priced first-class mail.

Commenting on the proposal to move to the two-tier system, the National Board for Prices and Incomes made some remarks that might be particularly relevant in the U.S. context. The board saw it mainly as a means of ending the printed-paper service "which was conceived in the last century in circumstances when to subsidize the book trade was regarded as a proper aim of Post Office policy." The board also emphasized the complexity of the printed-paper regulations, which had "come to include within their compass various forms of printed matter the development of which was not foreseen by the original architects of the service."[1] These comments would apparently apply even more strongly in the United States, where, as Sherman and Miller argue, low rates for second-class mail force the individual to subsidize it by paying

---

[1] U.K., National Board for Prices and Incomes, *Post Office Charges,* Rept. 58, H.M.S.O., Cmnd. 3574 (March 1968), p. 30.

higher rates for other classes.[2] He may further cross-subsidize other services by accepting inferior service on his first-class mail.

If the Postal Service were to adopt the reforms suggested by Miller and Sherman it could offer a better first-class mail service and improve consumer choice. At the moment, I usually have no choice but first-class mail, for example, to pay my bills. If there were a two-tier system, I could pay most bills by the slower service with a resultant saving. Similarly, companies could send out most bills by the slower service. The slower service would cost significantly more than the printed-paper and other low bulk rates currently in force, however, and would discourage the use of the Postal Service for mail that is not priced high enough to cover costs.

Together with such a reform, the Postal Service might offer to deliver completely unaddressed circulars at rates dependent on the capacity utilization of the individual post offices and parts of the system involved. For example, a supermarket chain might wish a flyer delivered to every address in the area served by the local post office. The Postal Service could develop a rate structure for such unaddressed items, which presumably would have reduced handling costs, since nobody would actually have to read an address. Such a service, offered only at offices and parts of the country where capacity was available, together with a simple two-tier system based on speed of delivery and weight, would be consistent with the general proposals of Miller and Sherman and might play a part in solving some of the major problems of the Postal Service.

Even with rate reform along the above lines, the prospects for the Postal Service are not good. The two-tier rate structure in Britain did not leave the Post Office without problems. In 1969 it ceased to be a government department and became a public corporation. Like the U.S. Postal Service, it has consistently found the tide running against it, with a declining volume of traffic without a corresponding decline in addresses, and continually rising costs. As a result, the prices of *both* first-class and second-class letters have risen, from a base in 1968 of 100, to 450. Over a similar period (1968–1977) consumer prices have risen from 100 to 287. Correcting for the increase in the general price level means

---

[2] Leonard Waverman (Chapter 2, herein) citing J. K. Horsefield, "British and American Postal Services," in R. Turvey, ed., *Public Enterprise* (Baltimore: Penguin Books, 1968), indicates something of the extent of the problem in the United States, where apparently 67 percent of all magazines are delivered through the post. In addition, James C. Miller and Roger Sherman (Chapter 4 herein) give some idea of the magnitude of the subsidy involved (about four cents per piece of second-class mail). In comparison, in 1966–1967 the British Post Office's income from newspapers was £3.6 million out of a total income from postal services of £340.6 million. The loss attributed to this service was £1.5 million.

that letter rates have increased by 60 percent in real terms over the period. If we use Miller and Sherman figures for 1970–1978, the corresponding figure for first-class mail for the United States is also about 60 percent. Over this period, however, the losses by the British Post Office on mail have been very small compared with the losses by the U.S. Postal Service.

To conclude then, in the absence of major changes such as repeal of the private express statutes, the proposals of Miller and Sherman, while providing some long-overdue reforms, would still leave the U.S. Postal Service in the position of many other mail services throughout the world. It would still be a challenge to run the service efficiently. Miller and Sherman have provided a good discussion of one of the first steps toward efficiency for the Postal Service.

5

How Have Postal Workers Fared Since the 1970 Act?

Douglas K. Adie

What was the effect of the 1970 Postal Reorganization Act on postal workers? The act changed the name of the Post Office to the Postal Service and changed the organizational structure and some of the higher administrative communication channels. The act removed postal workers from the Civil Service system and replaced the patronage system for selecting postal management with a career system. The intent of these changes was to decentralize authority within the Postal Service, provide a meaningful work situation for postal employees, and allow management to introduce more efficient production methods. Unfortunately, the day-to-day operations, incentive systems, and modus operandi of the service have remained almost intact. Before the act, incentives for employees to assume increased responsibilities, take initiative, improve their skill, or work diligently were weak, but they have been further eroded since the act.

The Postal Service is an enormous employer with a work force of nearly 700,000. Its operating budget of $17 billion approaches 1 percent of GNP, 85 percent of which is for labor—up from 82 percent in 1970. Its workers inhabit 132 million square feet in 29,000 locations across the country. In such a geographically and occupationally diverse enterprise, the question in the title of this paper needs to specify which workers, where, and how. I would like to break down the title's question into three parts. First, since passage of the act, are all postal workers taken together better off than workers in the private sector with respect to wages, benefits, and working conditions? The answer is yes. Second, has the act changed the work environment of all postal workers to one where the work is satisfying and challenging and where initiative and effort are rewarded? The answer is no. Third, how does the change in welfare affect different groups of postal employees within the Postal

Service: namely, distribution or scheme operators and highly skilled employees as compared with employees in the unskilled and more numerous crafts; temporary and substitute employees as compared with regulars; and workers in large cities as compared with those in small towns and rural areas. In each of these cases, inequities have increased since the act as the former groups have lost to the latter. It is my hope that answering these questions of how postal workers have fared will shed some light on the overall fairness of the act.

Wages and Benefits

Are postal workers better off since the act with respect to wages, benefits, and working conditions? A comparison of the percentage increases in average hourly earnings for postal workers and for manufacturing workers suggests that there has been a tendency for the Post Office/Postal Service to grant its employees greater-than-average increases. Before the act, wages paid postal employees were on average excessive.[1]

Before the reorganization and its accompanying sizable wage increases, the salaries of nonsupervisory postal employees were considered to be more than competitive with those paid to similar employees by private companies in most areas. (The postal employee annual quit rate in 1969 was only 13.4 percent whereas that of manufacturing employees was 32.4 percent.)

The wages of postal workers increased by 51 percent between fiscal years 1960 and 1969 compared with an increase of only 33.2 percent for manufacturing employees. Since the act, postal workers have gained even more on workers in the private economy (see Table 5.1). Between 1969 and 1977, postal workers' hourly wages increased by 95 percent while the wages of workers in private nonfarm economy or all manufacturing have increased only 73 and 76 percent respectively. The contract just negotiated, granting postal workers a 21.5 percent increase in wages over the next three years, could result in postal workers earning in excess of 40 percent higher wages than the average American and enjoying far greater job security, pensions, and fringe benefits.

Consider how support for the act was assembled. At first, all postal

---

[1] This conclusion has been arrived at independently by different researchers using different techniques with a remarkable correspondence of results. See Douglas K. Adie, *An Evaluation of Postal Service Wage Rates* (Washington, D.C.: American Enterprise Institute, 1977), pp. 89–101. My own conservative estimate of excess wages in 1972 is 32.8 percent, established on the basis of efficiency criterion without reference to any particular group of employees, and calculated using actual wages as the base for the excess. If the optimal wage were used as the base, the excess would have been 48.2 percent.

TABLE 5.1

AVERAGE HOURLY EARNINGS FOR POSTAL WORKERS AND FOR
NONSUPERVISORY WORKERS IN THE PRIVATE SECTOR

	Hourly Earnings[a]			Percentage Change		
	1969	1975	1977	1969–75	1975–77	1969–77
Postal workers	3.65	6.23	7.12	71	14	95
Private nonfarm economy	3.03	4.53	5.24	50	16	73
All manufacturing	3.19	4.18	5.63	31	35	76

[a] Average hourly pay for postal workers does not include overtime, while average hourly earnings data for the private nonfarm economy and all manufacturing do. A review of the Postal Services' National Payroll Hours Summary Report for Accounting Period 1, FY 1976, indicates that 4 percent of clerks' pay was at overtime rates. Hence, including overtime would increase Postal Service hourly earnings slightly. Figures given are for July of each year.
SOURCE: U.S. Bureau of Labor Statistics, *Employment and Earnings*, table C–2.

union leaders opposed the reorganization because they preferred the existing situation to collective bargaining. Although philosophically committed to collective bargaining, they did not want authority over postal matters to shift from Congress, where they could exercise their political influence, and so resisted a new set of rules. It took a substantial increase in postal wages for them to change their minds, and in the end it was the rank-and-file union members who persuaded their leaders to support reorganization because of the proposed wage increase.

The administration gave postal employees pay raises totaling more than 14 percent and gave the AFL-CIO an opportunity to strengthen itself immensely in the federal sector in return for their support of the reorganization. National postal unions received increased recognition and a greater opportunity to unionize all federal employees.

As a result of the deal, the wage increases for postal workers for fiscal years 1969–1970 and 1970–1971 were almost twice as large as those received by manufacturing workers. On November 19, 1970, approximately three months after the Postal Reorganization Act was signed into law, labor and management announced their agreement to compress the time required for employees to reach the top of the pay scale from twenty-one years to eight years, in effect providing a second increase in pay. This move, along with the 14 percent wage increase, greatly increased the attractiveness of postal jobs, as indicated by a decline of more than 50 percent in the already low quit rate between 1969 and 1971 (see Table 5.2).

TABLE 5.2

WAGE RATES AND QUIT RATES IN THE POST OFFICE/POSTAL SERVICE

Year	Annual Quit Rate (percent)	Hourly Wage Rate (dollars)
1958	5.35	2.39
1959	6.89	2.40
1960	6.67	2.41
1961	6.09	2.63
1962	6.20	2.62
1963	5.03	2.85
1964	4.75	2.92
1965	—	3.08
1966	—	3.19
1967	12.39	3.26
1968	12.56	3.44
1969	13.42	3.64
1970	10.80	4.03
1971	6.21	4.51
1972	6.70	4.79
1973	7.43	5.07
1974	5.64	5.65
1975	4.70	6.23
1976	4.40	6.77
1977	4.00	7.12

NOTE: Dashes indicate data not available.

SOURCE: Douglas K. Adie, *An Evaluation of Postal Service Wage Rates* (Washington, D.C.: American Enterprise Institute, 1977), pp. 91, 109, 128, 140. Average hourly wages for nonsupervisory or bargaining employees can be calculated by dividing the salary from the PFS schedule, level five, step six, by 2,080, the number of hours per year (Forest Benkenney, U.S. Postal Service). Another estimate can be calculated by dividing the average salary of postal employees in the *Budget* of the United States government by 2,080. The average hourly wages calculated by either way are quite similar.

After slipping back a little in the years 1971–1973, postal wages then moved ahead with increases of 11.4 percent in 1973–1974 and 10.3 percent in 1974–1975 (see Table 5.3). In 1973 the Postal Service and the unions signed a new national agreement covering the period from July 21, 1973, to July 20, 1975. As of July 30, 1973, the basic wage increase of postal workers for 1973 was exceeded only by that of workers in the electrical equipment industry, who received a 7.5 percent raise. The postal agreement provided for a $700-a-year increase effective July 21, 1973, and another $400 a year effective July 21, 1974. The 90,000 nonunion supervisory workers received a similar increase on November

TABLE 5.3

CHANGE IN AVERAGE HOURLY WAGES, 1960–1977

(percentage)

	Postal Workers	Manufacturing Workers
1960–69	51.0	33.2
1969–70	10.7	5.5
1970–71	11.9	6.4
1971–72	6.2	6.8
1972–73	5.8	6.5
1973–74	11.4	7.9
1974–75	10.3	7.8
1975–76	8.7	7.3
1976–77	5.2	8.2

SOURCE: The percentage change for manufacturing workers is calculated from average hourly earnings, private nonfarm economy, in Bureau of Labor Statistics, *Employment and Earnings,* tables C-15 and C-17.

12, 1973. According to the Cost of Living Council, increases for union members worked out to 6.8 percent in the first year and 3.9 percent in the second. (There was an additional 0.9 percent qualified-benefits increase in the first year and 1.2 percent in the second that the council excluded from its computations in determining whether the settlement was consistent with government pay standards—generally holding increases to 3.5 percent a year.) Included in the agreement was an increase in the Postal Service's share of the premium payment for basic life insurance. In the second year of the contract, the Postal Service paid the entire premium for basic life insurance. The agreement also provided for four cost-of-living adjustments during the two-year period. By November 9, 1974, cost-of-living pay adjustments added another $998. From 1970 to 1975, average hourly earnings of postal workers rose by 51 percent while those of private nonfarm workers increased by 40 percent, both exclusive of changes in fringe benefits.

The contract signed in September 1975 covering three years added an average 4.2 percent a year increase in wages and benefits, plus semiannual cost-of-living adjustments. During fiscal years 1974, 1975, and 1976, when the consumer price index increased a total of 29 percent over fiscal year 1973, cost-of-living allowances produced compensation increases of $2.9 billion. This description suggests that postal workers in general have fared well under the act with respect to wages and benefits as compared with workers in the private sector.

The repeated pay increases have not been justified by economic necessity. The long queue of would-be job applicants together with the almost imperceptible voluntary quit rate, especially for regulars, suggests very strongly that privilege has been created for the relatively few fortunate citizens who have regular employment in the Postal Service. This means that large numbers of people who would like to have jobs with the Postal Service are systematically excluded.[2] This strategy of excluding large numbers of qualified persons from economic opportunity within their own government enterprise because of the gross privilege given to the relative few is antithetical to the foundation of this great democratic republic. The continued success of postal unions in creating privilege for their members can only bring about the eventual collapse of privilege when the public reacts.[3]

Physical Working Conditions

Before the act, Post Office physical working conditions were somewhat inferior to those of many other industries. Many post offices were built in the 1930s or before, when mail volume was less than half what it is today. Twelve percent of departing employees, before the act, said that poor physical working conditions either caused or contributed to their decision to quit. They complained about crowded and noisy work areas, inadequate locker space and rest rooms, poor lighting, poor heating and cooling systems, excessive noise, excessive heat from mail-processing equipment, and insufficient janitorial service. At some facilities

---

[2] The rate of new applicants for beginning Postal Service jobs is very revealing. Some 679,000 Americans applied to take a test for Postal Service employment after an announcement that 10,200 jobs would open up in fifty-nine cities. This amounts to sixty-seven applicants per job (*Wall Street Journal,* March 14, 1978). In the Civil Service there are eleven job applicants on the rolls for every person expected to be hired, and inquiries numbered 12 million last year (*U.S. News and World Report,* April 3, 1978, p. 12).

[3] The working situation in the Canadian Post Office is not unlike its U.S. counterpart. A Canadian postal worker who did not wish to be identified said the Post Office situation is "ridiculous." Workers, including himself, were grossly overpaid. He said he has seen workers playing football and hockey with parcels in the station, and workers spend more time on coffee breaks than at their posts. He said workers get paid for eight hours and work four or five, earning more than the average steelworker does for his extremely hard work. "It's just a honeymoon in there," he said. "You have people who can't read or write making $20,000 a year, and they're still not satisfied. If any private company ran a business the way that union runs it, it would be broke by now" (*Hamilton Spectator,* October 21, 1979).

A public reaction has recently surfaced in Canada with regard to the Post Office. In response to a 1978 strike, the Canadian Parliament passed a back-to-work law and jailed union leaders for not publicly supporting the law. Private action was taken when a Hamilton letter carrier was assaulted by two strangers in apparent retaliation against the post office and the current inside workers' strike (Mary K. Nolan, *Hamilton Spectator,* October 21, 1978).

the parking lots were so small employees were forced to walk long distances through unsafe areas with risk of assault. The problem was even more acute when women employed as clerks or mail handlers were assigned night-shift duty at facilities located in or near poorly lighted areas. In Chicago's South Suburban facility, perhaps the most outmoded post office in the country, the turnover rate was much higher than in Detroit's modern post office, with its enclosed docks, excellent lighting, adequate parking, and many other features that enhance the working environment.

Since reorganization, the Postal Service has been correcting such conditions through its Working Conditions Improvement Program. In fiscal 1973, for instance, $27 million was committed to improve plant heating, ventilation, lighting, and other conditions affecting the work atmosphere. By 1976, 99 percent of postal employees were working in what were or would soon be satisfactory facilities. Thus, physical working conditions have been improved since the act.

Other Working Conditions

Before reorganization, the Civil Service Commission exercised control over personnel regulations for examinations, hiring, employment, supervision, and discipline of employees. Through these regulations, not necessarily designed for postal employees, the Civil Service Commission preempted much of the personnel administration of the Post Office. The act was intended to place personnel practices within the Postal Service where authority could be decentralized, the work situation humanized, and efficiency increased.

Reorganization abolished the practice of political appointments in the Postal Service but left most other hiring and personnel procedures untouched. The creation of the Postal Service as a government corporation has not provided the incentive to reform such procedures. The act has reduced the all too few incentives that previously existed for employees to assume more responsibilities, take initiative, or improve their skills. The vested interests of regular workers are still enhanced by the cumbersome hiring procedures and seniority rules, at the expense of other workers and overall efficiency.

What is the nature of the working situation within the Postal Service? It is important for personal well-being, interpersonal equity, and efficiency of postal operations for workers to have satisfying, challenging work where personal initiative, effort, and honesty are recognized and rewarded.[4] To what extent, if at all, has the act achieved these goals? Postal workers collect cards, envelopes, newspapers, magazines, catalogs, and parcels. They separate the mail into airmail, mail suitable for machine processing, and items of unusual size or shape that must be handled manually. Machinable mail is fed through a complicated device that faces it, so stamps are in a position to be canceled, and then cancels the stamps. Postal workers place mail in trays for sorting at manual cases or at letter-sorting machines. Local mail is sorted by carrier routes for delivery the next day. Mail leaving the city is sorted into canvas sacks, transported by truck, plane, train, or boat to its destination post office, and then sorted for delivery. Deliveries are made to almost every office and residence in America six days a week by rural and city carriers who travel over 3 million miles each day.

Not all mail passes through each stage of this process. Second-class publishers' mail is often hauled privately to the city where it is to be distributed, and mail addressed to boxholders is not delivered. Window clerks collect revenue for stamps, parcel post, and special services. Collections for permit mail are also made at post offices or at mailers' premises. There are a host of support functions such as industrial management, research and development, accounting and finance controls, and general management that do not ordinarily involve the handling of mail but are concerned with the control of the whole process. This brief description of postal operations is sufficient to indicate the nature of the work process. The most startling aspect of this routine process is that most of the functions are performed by hand labor.

Because the Postal Service is labor intensive, it depends primarily on employee performance in individual and group tasks rather than on machine performance. Hiring, training, supervising, promoting, and directing a large, dispersed body of postal employees is an extensive and complex undertaking not unlike that of the army, where functions and procedures are stated, rules apply, and authority is delegated.

The Postal Service organization is designed to be directed from the top rather than to be responsive to changes from below. One has only to memorize the postal manual to be a satisfactory Postal Service employee. This manual defines relationships, procedures, and attitudes

---

[4] Adam Smith describes graphically the personality disintegration that can take place gradually over time because of an adverse work environment. "The man whose whole life is spent in performing a few simple operations, of which the effects too are, perhaps, always the same, or very nearly the same, has no occasion to exert his understanding, or to exercise his invention in finding out expedients for removing difficulties which never occur. He naturally loses, therefore, the habit of such exertion, and generally becomes as stupid and ignorant as it is possible for a human creature to become. The torpor of his mind renders him, not only incapable of relishing or bearing a part in any rational con-

and confers authority to organizational units to perform the duties and responsibilities assigned to them. It is intended to be a self-contained guide covering all foreseeable contingencies for all decisions to be made regarding the administration of postal affairs. With few changes from the Post Office days, it has remained the handbook for postal employees since reorganization. In a word, the Postal Service goes by the book just as the Post Office did.

Higher officials receive documents from their superiors that expand on their job descriptions and become the basis for further subdivisions of responsibilities to permit the assignment of tasks to subordinates. It is the responsibility of each person to relate any particular situation to the existing regulatory framework—the general rule being that nothing can be done unless there is specific authority for doing it. Tasks are so greatly subdivided that no one carries out what could be called a complete unit of work.

Any deviation from the manual ordered verbally must be confirmed by a written memorandum or order, and postal inspectors are directed to charge as "irregularities" any deviations not properly authorized. Except in emergencies such as fires or floods, one goes by the rules or risks punishment.

The postal manual states: "Any communication on matters requiring discretion or policy determinations shall proceed through each successive level of authority upward and downward without bypassing any." This practice is followed to give an officer who is accountable for any activity the opportunity to pass judgment on matters under his jurisdiction. Because irregularities uncovered by the postal inspectors can have serious consequences for the local supervisor, employees' initiatives are fraught with risk. Irregularities are easy enough to uncover because it is beyond the capability of any single individual to know all the rules. Many in the organization can recall instances when such irregularities were used to fire postmasters or to block promotions. The lesson is: "Don't stick your neck out; don't rock the boat; don't make waves." The safest course is to stick to the book or pass responsibility up the line. By following this comprehensive book of rules, individual managers and supervisors can avoid personal responsibility for their

---

versation but of conceiving any generous, noble or tender sentiment, and consequently of forming any just judgment concerning many even of the ordinary duties of private life . . . . the uniformity of his stationary life naturally corrupts the courage of his mind. . . . It corrupts even the activity of his body, and renders him incapable of exerting his strength with vigour and perseverance, in any other employment than that to which he has been bred. His dexterity at his own particular trade seems, in this manner, to be acquired at the expense of his intellectual, social and martial virtues." Adam Smith, *The Wealth of Nations,* Modern Library (New York: Random House, 1937), pp. 734–35.

actions. When routine employees occupy standardized positions governed by general instructions recorded in the postal manual,[5] it is clear that the act has failed to encourage initiative and reward effort.

In a work environment of impersonal hierarchical control and boring repetitive tasks, postal workers can be dehumanized. Also, the repetitive performance of minute functions under seemingly arbitrary circumstances with vague goals can lead to frustration and a decrease in productivity. Centralized organizations can create low morale, diminish incentives, and cause worker attitudes that are not conducive to productivity advances. Is there a solution to this problem in the Postal Service? The implementation of modern technology and decentralization of managerial control can rehumanize the work process. Instead of turning skilled artisans into cogs in a machine, new techniques can substitute machines for workers in the performance of repetitive tasks. For instance, it can be more interesting for a postal worker to diagnose a defect in a letter-sorting machine when it breaks down, and fix it, than to sort letters all day. Since these techniques require skilled engineers to manage and repair machines, they put more decision-making responsibility into the hands of workers and increase workers' directing roles.

What success has the Postal Service had since the act in bringing about increased mechanization? Before reorganization Congress was reluctant to approve major mechanization and modernization of postal operations that would affect the number and activity of employees. While the unions did not publicly oppose increased mechanization within the department, it is thought that they influenced Congress in this direction. Since the Postal Reorganization Act became effective in July 1971, postal unions at the national level have to be informed, according to their contract, not less than ninety days in advance when major new technology or equipment is to be purchased and installed. A committee composed of equal numbers of management and union representatives is notified of each innovation, and it attempts to resolve any questions about the impact of the proposed change upon affected employees. If these questions are not resolved within a reasonable time, they are given priority in arbitration under the grievance procedures. Needless to say, these cumbersome procedures have helped to keep innovations from reaching the discussion stage, let alone being implemented. The Postal Service further agreed, however, that no employee

---

[5] "Each installation head makes the Postal Service Manual available to all employees. When there is no personnel office the availability and location of a reference copy of the Postal Manual is posted on employee bulletin boards. Supervisors and personnel officers counsel and advise employees on the meaning of the various sections of the manual." See "General Transmittal Letter," in U.S. Postal Service, *Postal Service Manual,* chap. 6.

in the regular work force would be laid off involuntarily because of mechanization if that employee applied for a new position at his or her former wage level. In commenting on his attempts to improve efficiency, former Postmaster General Bailer said that "opposition to our cost-cutting efforts has in most cases far outweighed any support we have received."[6]

Until recently, the Postal Service has not been able to reduce significantly the number of its employees by mechanization.[7] Advanced equipment such as multiposition letter sorters, parcel sorters, sack sorters, and cullers are limited to large post offices. Where used, they have resulted in more than a proportionate increase in errors, with the result that more and more manpower is needed to handle mail volume. Since there is no reward for producing "surpluses," there is no incentive to decrease the number of jobs and labor costs.

The second solution to the problem of dehumanization of workers and low productivity lies in decentralizing managerial control by increasing the responsibility and importance of jobs. In private industry these changes have been made with considerable success.[8]

What success has the Postal Service had in bringing about these changes? Carl C. Ulsaker, the senior assistant postmaster general for manpower and cost control, attempted to change the work environment and instill some incentives for superior performance and the use of cost-saving techniques by decentralizing budgets. In several cases this backfired when regional managers falsified mail volume figures to appear more efficient.

---

[6] U.S. Congress, House, Committee on the Post Office and Civil Service, *Proceedings*, March 15, 1977, p. 12.

[7] Since 1975 the Postal Service has been moderately successful in reducing its employees by nearly 50,000. In 1977, 63 percent of all letters were sorted mechanically compared with 25 percent in 1971. This has resulted in increased productivity. It took 683,590 man-years to deliver 89.8 billion pieces of mail in 1976 as compared with 723,581 man-years to deliver 87 billion pieces in 1971—an increase in productivity of 1.8 percent per year. While not as great an increase as that in the private sector, it represents an improvement over past postal experience.

[8] "Detroit Edison reduced office costs by making clerical jobs more complicated, less repetitive, and more interesting. At Lincoln Electric increasing opportunities for initiative through decentralization had the effect of raising productivity. Corporations such as General Electric, Allis-Chalmers, and Sylvania have replaced giant plants employing tens of thousands of workers with scattered plants employing a few hundred workers. General Motors and Sears, Roebuck and Company have given more decision-making power to division managers. Suggestion systems and incentive pay plans can increase productivity, since they give workers an opportunity and a reward for exercising initiative. Initiative, morale, and output may be increased by choosing techniques for administration and production that rely on decentralized decision-making." Douglas K. Adie, "Are Corporations Indifferent to Worker Job Alienation?" in M. Bruce Johnson, ed., *The Attack on Corporate America: The Corporate Issues Sourcebook* (New York: McGraw-Hill, 1978), pp. 45–46.

What negative incentives exist to exact performance from recalcitrant and irresponsible postal workers and deal with insubordination? Adverse action procedures were imposed on departments and agencies for the disciplining of employees on January 17, 1962, by Executive Order 10988. If an employee against whom an action is brought does not agree with the proposed action, he may make a reply to the responsible official in the Postal Service hierarchy. If the employee is unable to receive satisfaction, he may pursue the action within the Postal Service to the regional level and the appropriate regional executive (before reorganization, he could appeal to the Civil Service Commission).

After a decision at the regional level, the employee still has three options: he can go to the Postal Service's Board of Appeals and Review (or to the Civil Service Commission before reorganization), or with the concurrence of his union he can request advisory arbitration. The Civil Service Commission, when used before reorganization, would only reverse a decision on procedural violations and, reportedly, did not usually accept claims of mitigating circumstances. Employees felt that the Civil Service Commission gave the local postmaster the benefit of the doubt as far as substantive issues were concerned and heard appeals only for procedural violations. Almost all employees involved in adverse actions before reorganization took the departmental route. Postal employees apparently felt confident of a fair hearing on the merits of the case within the department or, since 1971, the Postal Service. For this reason, losing the right to appeal to the Civil Service in reorganization imposed no great hardship on postal workers.

Officials in local installations complain about the length of time it takes to get rid of "incompetents" or "troublemakers." The process of preparing documents and appearing at conferences, meetings, and hearings discourages adverse actions by managers. An employee against whom a removal action is pending can stay on the active roll until the appeal is decided at the regional level, a process that takes sixty to ninety days. During this time the employee, if he or she expects to be dismissed, may disrupt the morale and discipline of the office. Fellow workers generally are unaware of the adverse action because the supervisor cannot disclose it. When employees witness an apparently helpless supervisor repeatedly being challenged, discipline breaks down and may not be restored for a long time. Because of the difficulty in applying disciplinary actions, supervisors have only informal power over their subordinates. They are helped by the sense of commitment to "moving the mails" that prevails throughout the organization, but when this commitment is insufficient they must coax or bluff employees to get the job done. Disciplinary action is rarely used because the procedure is too intricate, time-consuming, and cumbersome. Thus, negative incentives to work performance, such as discipline, are not very useful.

One might think that procedures that give employees so much protection from the arbitrary discipline of their employer would work to benefit the employees, but this is not so. The general breakdown of morale and morality that these procedures can foster is destructive to the work environment and makes jobs in the Postal Service less satisfying to most employees. For instance, in a local post office with which I am familiar, there is a serious problem of morale. Postal workers, particularly clerks and mail handlers, are not doing their jobs during regular working hours, necessitating overtime work and overtime pay. Overtime work has shot up with little or no change in productivity. (This is a regular occurrence after a contract has been negotiated that does not meet the workers' expectations.) What is the effect of this on postal workers? There is an incentive for postal workers to put off doing their work during regular hours and receive overtime pay. Some workers are making much more by engaging in this practice; others, whose sense of personal honesty is more deeply ingrained, refuse to take advantage of this situation and are forgoing the extra earnings and incurring the displeasure of their fellow workers for not condoning these practices. Some workers who know the practice is wrong but are morally weak are succumbing to the social pressure or the financial gains. In this way dissension is bred among employees, morality is weakened, and morale lowered.

Before reorganization, lack of opportunities for advancement because of the political patronage system and local residence requirements demoralized employees aspiring to be postmasters, and postmasters of small post offices aspiring to larger responsibilities. The emphasis given to seniority and political acceptability in determining promotions created an environment in which employees were more concerned with job tenure and convenience than with performance. Because they could not earn promotions based on merit, they had little incentive to do more or better work. Those without the right political connection could not even aspire to leadership of their own post offices. Even with the right connections, a first-line supervisor typically waited from twelve to twenty years for his promotion to postmaster. A ruling by the Civil Service Commission made it practically impossible to transfer postmasters from small post offices to larger ones, and this also dampened morale. The patronage system limited advancement opportunities of career employees with management potential and inevitably harmed morale.

Under Postal Service regulations since reorganization, patronage appointments have been eliminated, and promotions are supposed to be made on the basis of merit. From the time of reorganization until early 1977, selection boards chose 15,500 new postmasters under the merit selection program. A new rule, however, requires a postal employee to serve four or five years before becoming eligible for the supervisory examination. This prevents college graduates from moving directly into middle-management positions in the Postal Service and substantially reduces the prospects of upgrading the quality and training of supervisors. While the merit system makes more opportunities available to current postal employees, it effectively closes all would-be employees out of postmaster jobs, whereas the patronage system closed out only members of the "wrong" political party.

The wage scale can provide an important incentive to workers within a large enterprise, encouraging them to work harder and learn new jobs in the hope of promotion when an opening arises, as long as more difficult jobs are differentiated by higher pay. In the Postal Service schedule are eleven pay levels that are supposed to be related to the degree of skill and responsibility required for the jobs at each level. Within each pay level are from ten to twelve steps, which represent pay increases achieved solely through seniority. Two changes in the salary schedule after reorganization have implications for motivating workers: First, the differentials between levels associated with jobs of differing difficulty have been compressed, and second, the time required to receive pay increases though seniority has been shortened.

Before reorganization, a new employee would begin a job at step one of that job's level. Except for professional, scientific, or managerial personnel, who accept employment with the Postal Service in regional, district, or headquarters positions, new employees are always appointed to step one of the salary level. Step increases were given annually for six years in the lower grades and every three years thereafter until the top was reached in twenty-one years. In level eight before reorganization, the top was reached in eighteen years; in levels nine–nineteen in fifteen years; in level twenty in nine years; and in level twenty-one in four years. These increases were based entirely on tenure and were in addition to all bargained increases. On November 19, 1970, as a result of negotiation after passage of the Postal Reorganization Act but before it took effect, the time required to reach the top step in each level was shortened to eight years.

On October 7, 1967, all jobs were upgraded one level in the wage schedule. This phenomenon (which consists of raising the pay level of a particular job without upgrading the responsibilities), is common in the federal Civil Service and is called "grade creep." On October 7, 1967, the wage differential between grades three and ten was 68 percent, whereas after November 4, 1977, the wage differential between grades four and ten was 30 percent. The comparison has been made between grades three and four on the lower end of the schedule because the most populous crafts were just above these levels at the respective times. In 1978 the percentage increases in salary between consecutive pay levels were between 4.2 and 5.4 percent, while within a level pay differentials because of longevity range between 20 and 23 percent. In a relatively short time, because of the step increases postal workers can be earning more than the beginning salary of a job two or three levels higher.

There is little or no wage distinction or possibility of promotion within a craft to differentiate more difficult assignments or higher degrees of skill because all the jobs within a craft are salaried at the same level. Neither is there any practical financial incentive to improve efficiency on the job as long as one remains a clerk or a carrier. Only seniority yields better working conditions, preferable tours of duty, and step increases. This arrangement discourages capable employees from volunteering for more responsible positions. In fact, within a job at a particular level employees often "bid off" successive assignments until they reach the easiest assignment for which they are eligible.

The compression of differentials between grades, the speeding up of step increases since reorganization, and grade creep have reduced the incentives for postal workers to aspire to more difficult jobs at higher pay levels. The pay differentials between levels give employees little or no incentive to apply for a promotion to a more responsible job.

Distributive Justice: Inequities between Classes of Postal Employees

The main postal crafts are window clerks, mail handlers, city and rural carriers, maintenance employees, motor vehicle employees, special delivery messengers, and distribution or scheme clerks, the last of which have some of the most difficult assignments. Window clerks perform a variety of services at public windows of post offices, branches, or stations. As representatives of the Postal Service, clerks must be familiar with postal laws, regulations, and procedures and maintain pleasant and effective public relations with patrons. Mail handlers load, unload, and move bulk mail; perform sorting duties not requiring scheme knowledge; and operate certain mail-processing machines. City and rural letter carriers sort mail for their own delivery. They receive less supervision than clerks because most of their work is performed individually outdoors. Rural carriers, in addition to delivering mail, provide such services as selling stamps and receiving parcels. Their compensation is based on route length, patrons served, and mail volume. Their workday ends when they complete their deliveries and a few clerical duties. Independent contractors called star-route carriers deliver mail in remote areas where other service cannot be provided easily. Maintenance employees operate elevators; repair vehicles, air-conditioning and mail-processing equipment; and serve as janitors. Motor vehicle employees pick up and transport mail by truck on regularly scheduled routes. Special delivery messengers deliver all classes of special delivery mail, usually by vehicle.

Each occupation is strictly regulated by a job description supplemented by manuals and letters of instruction that detail the nature of the work and the manner of performing it. The employee is responsible for performing a minutely described, routine job. The technology is basically simple, notwithstanding the use of machines in some phases of the operation. Except for a relatively small number of jobs, mainly maintenance positions requiring mechanical or technical skills and some scheme jobs, the occupational requirements in postal crafts are not exacting.

The distribution or scheme clerks have some of the most difficult assignments. They must possess scheme knowledge (that is, a large number of destination and distribution points must be committed to memory), and they must separate incoming or outgoing mail by machine or by hand. These clerks are required to take a state scheme examination covering every post office, station, and branch listed in the scheme. A city scheme examination requires knowledge of a local scheme. A grade of 95 percent must be obtained to pass. Though clerks must qualify and requalify every two years to hold their positions, they are not paid for the time spent in mastering schemes or compensated according to the extent and complexity of their scheme knowledge.

The highest training costs are for scheme distributors and particularly for incoming rather than outgoing distributors. Incoming distributors in large cities are required to learn two incoming primary schemes (recently reduced from four) as well as one or two incoming secondary schemes. It takes approximately one full year for a clerk to learn his or her incoming schemes. On outgoing schemes, distribution practice is usually not given until the clerk qualifies on all sections of the scheme exam. It is generally thought to take up to one year for a clerk to become proficient on outgoing schemes. A relatively large percentage of clerks are separated for scheme failure (21 percent based on the turnover study), and a large percentage probably separate before receiving an adverse action for scheme failure.

Departing scheme operators have said that a main reason for leaving was that they were required to study, on their own time, schemes that were seldom used. Although new employees were told about the need for home study during their preinduction interview, they were frequently surprised by the complexity of the schemes and the amount of home study required and regarded this requirement as a breach of their agreement. Although training of up to thirty hours of official work time is authorized by the regional manual for scheme employees, some large offices do not provide any and others limit the training because of manpower budget requirements.

The complexity of the schemes most clerks have to know has no relation to their salary. Experienced clerks bid off assignments for which they have been trained and give more difficult schemes to new employees. Increasing compensation for more difficult scheme knowledge would probably decrease the turnover associated with scheme clerks and reduce errors and some inequities.

The loss of trained scheme distributors contributes to excessive overtime at post offices where there is difficulty in replacing separated scheme employees. The cost of underproduction of new employees, other than in scheme work, is thought to be nominal because new employees can become reasonably efficient in a few days, but distribution clerks do not reach peak efficiency until two years after they start learning schemes. In addition to increased costs because of slowed distribution, the use of partially trained clerks increases the quantity of misdirected mail. The Bureau of Operations has stated that offices with a shortage of scheme distributors will often have a very high distribution error rate—25 percent being not uncommon. This involves double handling of mail and increased costs.

Distribution clerks with complicated schemes have difficult jobs and are not compensated adequately, whereas most unskilled jobs are more than adequately compensated. The internal organization system within the Postal Service does not permit the placing of people in the jobs for which they are best suited. Seniority governs the selection of tasks, and uniformity of pay makes those with seniority choose the easiest jobs. This system reduces incentives for efficiency and is inequitable.

In addition to the craft distinction there are four principal categories of employees. In descending pecking order, they are career regulars, hourly-rate regulars, career substitutes, and temporary substitutes. Career regulars include postmasters, supervisors, and rural carriers as well as most clerks, carriers, and mail handlers. These permanent full-time employees make up about 70 percent of postal employees. Since they are salaried, their earnings are unaffected by the number of hours worked (unless overtime is involved); and since they cannot be discharged except "for cause," they enjoy almost continuous tenure. Once assigned to a post office, career regulars may not be transferred against their will. Hourly-rate regulars are permanent part-time employees with fixed work schedules usually not exceeding twenty hours a week. Career substitutes have no fixed schedule and are used to augment the regular work force during peak periods. Substitutes must be available for call but have no assurance of any fixed amount of employment. The hourly-rate regulars and the career substitutes make up about 15 percent of postal employees. Temporary employees, who in some offices serve an apprenticeship of from three to six months and then are routinely re-placed, account for another 15 percent of the work force.

The initial job with the Postal Service is usually as a substitute or temporary employee. Because of the seniority system, newly hired em-ployees are assigned to the least desirable positions under the least desirable conditions. Substitute employees often have unpredictable and erratic work hours, variable and sometimes insufficient take-home pay, and weekend work. For instance, rookie mail handlers are assigned to the graveyard shift in the terminal, and rookie scheme clerks get the most difficult schemes. Substitutes, who are not guaranteed a forty-hour work week, often have insufficient work and low pay. To approach forty hours of work a week they often have to work six days a week with ten- or twelve-hour shifts on some days and two- or three-hour shifts on others, and they have to work weekends and holidays with no premium pay. If called to work, the temporary or substitute is guaranteed only two hours of employment that day.

New employees are first hired as substitutes and temporaries and require time and training to achieve full productivity. According to Postal Service sources, six months to a year is necessary for most new employees to reach a satisfactory level of performance. They must learn procedures for handling mail, postal organization, the details of their own and others' jobs, civil defense and safety procedures, and many other subjects. Much of this knowledge must be acquired on their own time. In some post offices temporary employees serve an apprenticeship of from three to six months and then are routinely replaced. In smaller post offices where substitutes are allowed to stay on, it may be many years before they succeed to a regular or full-time position. This ar-rangement is almost like an initiation ordeal. For these reasons, turnover among temporary and substitute workers is much higher than among regulars. The regular postal workers with seniority benefit from turnover because it enhances the value of their jobs. Turnover among substitutes and temporaries also increases the amount of overtime pay of regulars.

Regular permanent employees, on the other hand, make their jobs pleasant and secure through the use of seniority privileges. They have been successful in influencing the rules and conditions of employment to enhance the nonpecuniary and pecuniary aspects of their jobs at the expense of newer substitute and temporary employees.[9] Their demands were acceded to by Congress, which did not understand the consequences, by inadequately trained managers, and by top executives who had no reason to resist. Elimination of the present classification of temporary, substitute, and regular employees and improvement of working schedules would reduce the inequities among these classes of employees.

Finally, under the postal pay system of no regional differentiation, the same pay schedule is used for postal employees in all parts of the country. Those in high-cost-of-living areas in big cities where market conditions suggest higher wages receive the same compensation as those in small towns and other rural low-cost-of-living areas where market conditions suggest lower wages. Because of this the postal officer in a small town can be the wealthiest and most influential man in his area while his counterpart in a large city, with increased responsibilities and work load, may be struggling to survive financially. In small towns and rural areas the pay schedule can be so far removed from the local market conditions that it is disruptive to community standards.

A letter I received from a former Postal Service employee, dated December 5, 1977, graphically describes this condition:

> I saw a comment on your study of postal pay in Joseph Young's newsletter and your conclusion coincides with my views on the matter. I used to work in a post office and if education and ability matter, the pay is close to twice what it should be. What you have is 600,000 file clerks and messengers [clerks and carriers], and after 12 automatic increases in 8 years, they make close to $15,000 per year.
>
> I now work for social security as a GS–10 claims authorizer at $20,496 and in all honesty, that's too much.
>
> Our module (50 people) handles all of the Social Security numbers issued in South Dakota (503–504) and semi-skilled labor there seems to be like 7 or 8 thousand [dollars] per year, with no lush fringe benefits. In those small towns up there the guys handling the mail are among the most affluent people in town, paid more than bank officers. Most begalling! It is a real rip-off and I hope your study helps to put things right. . . .
>
> Someone who went to work at the post office in July 1970 has had about 25 pay raises since then and howling for more! They are paid more than GS–7's and to be a GS–7 around here

---

[9] While the annual voluntary quit rate for all postal employees has varied between 4.0 and 13.42 percent per year between 1969 and 1977, the quit rate for career regulars who comprise approximately 70 percent of the postal work force has been quite stable at about 1.8 percent—perhaps varying at most one percentage point in either direction (J. G. Tiedemann, Personnel Research Division, U.S. Postal Service).

you have to have something on the ball. You just don't put pieces of paper in order and deliver them.

Recommendations

On the first issue—wages, salaries, and benefits—the postal employees in general are overpaid in relation to the wages necessary to attract and maintain a competent work force, and in relation to workers in the private sector of similar educational background and ability. This differential is almost at the point of triggering a public reaction that could jeopardize all the gains postal workers have made. Union leaders would be wise to reduce their demands in subsequent collective bargaining sessions; postal management would be wise to resist any further widening in the excess wage differential.

On the second issue—providing a meaningful work situation—much remains to be done. Mechanization and innovation should go forward at full speed. Authority should be decentralized, and cumbersome disciplinary procedures streamlined so that irresponsible employees can be easily removed. To provide incentives for achievement, step increases based on seniority should be eliminated and differentials between levels should be increased. Jobs within a craft might also be evaluated and differentiated according to difficulty by salary level.

The requirement of seniority should be abolished for candidates for supervisory positions, thus opening up employment opportunities to interested persons of all political parties, within and without the Postal Service. Equity could be restored among groups of postal workers if the salaries of scheme operators and others with particularly difficult assignments reflected the requirements of their jobs; if the distinction between regulars, temporaries, and substitutes were eliminated; if most seniority privileges were allocated on the basis of merit; and if lifetime tenure of regulars were abolished. Regional differentials in pay scales should be introduced so that postal workers in rural and urban areas receive only what is necessary for their local post offices to attract and maintain an adequate labor force.

Since it is highly unlikely that a quasipolitical institution such as the Postal Service can muster the resolve to implement these recommendations (it has already had the opportunity and been unsuccessful), I recommend denationalization of the Postal Service, coupled with repeal of the private express statutes that grant the Postal Service a monopoly on first-class mail. A private business operating under the incentives of profit and loss and the threat of potential competition could not afford to wait around for another presidential commission study before implementing some of these measures.

Commentary

Sharon P. Smith

The United States Postal Service, with a work force of nearly 700,000, is the second largest agency of the federal government. (The largest is, of course, the Department of Defense.) It is, as Douglas Adie notes, a highly labor-intensive operation, with 85 percent of its budget going to labor. Indeed, the old Post Office Department was reorganized into the Postal Service in the hope of replacing the old patronage system of choosing postal managers with a career system containing some elements of professionalism that would greatly improve the efficiency of postal operations. Thus, in evaluating the 1970 act, a key consideration is the impact of the reorganization on postal workers.

The perspective Adie takes in making this evaluation is to question whether the act has been "fair" to the workers. An evaluation along such lines is certainly of primary interest to the postal workers themselves, especially since the 1970 act was passed after a nationwide postal strike raised the issue of whether the old Post Office Department had been fair to workers. Adie appears to take a somewhat unusual view of what constitutes "fairness," however. He suggests that this question can be answered by considering three subsidiary questions: Are postal workers better off with respect to wages, benefits, and working conditions since the 1970 act? Has the 1970 act led to more challenging working conditions in the Postal Service than in the Post Office? And has the 1970 act resulted in a change in the comparative welfare of different groups of workers in the Postal Service?

Although answers to these subsidiary questions do provide important information about the impact of the 1970 act on postal workers, they are insufficient to indicate whether the act has been "fair" to postal workers. To reach a conclusion about fairness, it is necessary first to spell out what is meant by the term. The dictionary defines "fair" as

---

Note: These comments represent the opinions of the author and not necessarily those of the Federal Reserve Bank of New York or the Federal Reserve System.

meaning "free from favor toward either or any side . . . implies an elimination of personal feelings, interests, or prejudices so as to achieve a proper balance of conflicting needs, rights or demands."[1] In asking whether the act has been "fair" to workers, we are asking whether these workers have been free from favoritism of any kind, either for or against them. Since treatment is "fair" only in relation to the treatment given other workers, however, we must compare the treatment postal workers have received since the 1970 act with that received by nonpostal workers.

Accordingly, Adie's first subsidiary question—Are postal workers better off with respect to wages, benefits, and working conditions?—is misdirected. To conclude that an improvement in these conditions for postal workers suggests fair treatment under the act implies that postal workers were at a relative disadvantage before passage of the 1970 act. The evidence Adie presents with respect to working conditions is consistent with this. Thus, the improvement Adie observes in postal working conditions suggests that the 1970 act has helped correct an unfair situation.

However, the evidence Adie presents here and in his earlier work indicates that postal workers enjoyed a wage advantage over nonpostal workers prior to the 1970 act and that this advantage has grown since then.[2] If postal workers receive higher wages than nonpostal workers of comparable qualifications and the 1970 act has either maintained this differential or helped increase it, then the act has been unfair to nonpostal workers, because it supports favoritism (in the sense of a net wage advantage) to postal workers. Research I have done in this area confirms the point that postal workers have enjoyed a substantial wage advantage over comparable private-sector workers both before and after the 1970 act (see Table 5.4 for estimates for 1973 and 1975). These estimates, and similar estimates for 1970, strongly suggest that an improvement in average wages and benefits for postal workers relative to nonpostal was unnecessary for "fair" treatment under the 1970 act. Instead, postal workers enjoy a favored wage position that for males is approximately the same as that of private-sector union members and for females is significantly greater than private-sector union members.

Adie's second subsidiary question—Has the 1970 act led to more challenging working conditions in the Postal Service than in the Post Office?—should also be placed in a relational framework. Certainly one of the goals of the act was to provide greater incentives to employee efficiency. Adie concludes that because working conditions have not

---

[1] *Webster's New Collegiate Dictionary* (Springfield, Mass.: G. C. Merriam, 1976), p. 411.
[2] See Douglas K. Adie, *An Evaluation of Postal Service Wage Rates* (Washington, D.C.: American Enterprise Institute, 1977).

TABLE 5.4

WAGES OF UNIONIZED AND NONUNIONIZED POSTAL WORKERS AND
UNIONIZED WORKERS IN THE PRIVATE SECTOR, BY SEX, 1973 AND 1975

	Males		Females	
	Wage effect	Differ-ence[a]	Wage effect	Differ-ence[a]
1973				
Unionized private workers	0.25		0.22	
	(33.25)		(18.71)	
Nonunionized Postal	0.25	0.01	0.49	0.27
Service workers	(5.81)	(0.00)	(7.14)	(3.89)
Unionized Postal Service	0.26	0.01	0.58	0.36
workers	(8.69)	(0.33)	(8.21)	(5.04)
1975				
Unionized private workers	0.22		0.21	
	(31.39)		(21.38)	
Nonunionized Postal	0.25	0.03	0.46	0.25
Service workers	(5.42)	(0.65)	(6.49)	(3.49)
Unionized Postal Service	0.24	0.02	0.53	0.32
workers	(8.52)	(0.68)	(10.50)	(6.13)

NOTE: t-values in parentheses.
[a] Postal Service wage effect minus wage effect for unionized private sector.
SOURCE: Sharon P. Smith, *Equal Pay in the Public Sector: Fact or Fantasy?* Research Report Series no. 122, Industrial Relations Section (Princeton University, 1977), p. 127.

become more challenging the 1970 act has been unfair to postal workers, implying that working conditions were more challenging for *comparable* nonpostal workers prior to the act and have continued to be so. If, other things being equal, workers prefer more challenging working conditions, then the extent of challenge may be expected to influence the kind of worker an industry attracts and retains. The relatively low quit rates in the Postal Service cited by Adie would therefore imply that working conditions elsewhere for comparable workers are not more challenging. However, the existence of a positive net wage differential for postal workers means that all other things are not equal. This net wage differential may, in fact, compensate workers for less challenging working conditions. Alternatively, if working conditions were made more challenging, the Postal Service might attract a different kind of worker than it does at present.

Adie's third subsidiary question—Has the 1970 act changed the comparative welfare of different groups of workers in the Postal Service?—is indeed an important part of determining whether the 1970

TABLE 5.5

POSTAL WAGE DIFFERENTIALS BY SIZE OF STANDARD METROPOLITAN
STATISTICAL AREA (SMSA), 1973 AND 1975

| | Non-SMSA | SMSA Size[a] | | | | |
		Less than 250	250–500	500–1M	1M–3M	More than 3M
1973						
Males	0.22	0.12	0.04	0.09	0.04	(0.02)
	(4.39)	(1.29)	(0.40)	(1.24)	(0.80)	(0.37)
Females	0.58	0.54	0.53	0.37	0.18	0.40
	(6.83)	(1.79)	(3.16)	(2.48)	(1.63)	(3.91)
1975						
Males	0.13	0.08	0.05	0.09	0.12	0.04
	(2.50)	(0.94)	(0.67)	(1.22)	(2.44)	(0.72)
Females	0.53	0.69	0.46	0.42	0.42	0.21
	(4.78)	(2.34)	(3.39)	(3.13)	(5.92)	(2.71)

NOTE: *t*-values in parentheses.
[a]SMSA sizes below 1 million in thousands.
SOURCE: Smith, *Equal Pay,* p. 100.

act has been fair to postal workers. Fair treatment of postal workers does require comparisons both between similar postal and nonpostal workers and among different kinds of postal employees. The growing inequities among different classes of postal workers that Adie notes do suggest that the 1970 act has been unfair to workers from this internal perspective. Research I have done confirms the inequities among postal workers according to where they reside (see Table 5.5). Although there is no indication that postal workers in large cities are paid less than comparable workers in the private sector, whether they enjoy a net wage advantage and, if they do, its size depend very much on where the worker lives. In general, the largest net wage differentials occur for postal workers outside of Standard Metropolitan Statistical Areas (SMSAs) and in very small SMSAs. This is a clear indication that if the 1970 act had been fair to postal workers, it would have set up area pay scales so that salaries would reflect differences across labor markets in costs of living and in pecuniary and nonpecuniary opportunities. Instead, the national postal salary schedule results in higher wages in certain regions than are necessary to attract qualified manpower.

In answering the basic question—Has the 1970 act been fair to workers?—Adie implies that the "net" answer is no since, although the act has improved wages, benefits, and working conditions of postal

97

workers, it has not made postal working conditions more challenging and has increased the inequities among different groups of postal workers. Recalling that "fair" means "free from favor toward either or any side," I would argue that the answer to this question is an even stronger no. The average postal worker enjoys a substantial wage advantage over a comparable private-sector worker, while working conditions for postal workers have also improved—facts that suggest the 1970 act has been unfair to nonpostal workers. Although Adie's question of the amount of challenge in postal working conditions concerns an interesting and important effect of the 1970 act, it is not relevant to a consideration of fair treatment of postal workers. Finally, it is clear that the 1970 act has increased the existing inequities among different groups of postal workers. In conclusion, the 1970 act appears to have increased both existing favoritism for postal workers, on average, relative to nonpostal workers and the inequities among particular classes of postal workers.

A point not considered by Adie is that, although postal workers appear to have received favored treatment since 1970, the act itself may have been neutral in this. Perhaps what occurred is attributable to the postal unions and would have happened even if the Post Office Department had never been reorganized into the Postal Service.

Discussion

CHAPIN CARPENTER, Magazine Publishers Association: Professor Waverman, I am curious about your definition of a subsidy as it pertains to second-class mail. Are you saying, on the basis of your own preferred economic theories of cost allocation, that second-class mail receives a cross-subsidy from first class? Are you critical of the so-called subsidy you referred to? Are you talking about a federal money subsidy for second class?

DR. WAVERMAN: I was talking about the direct subsidy. I am not sure there is a cross-subsidy from first-class mail, given the evidence.

MR. CARPENTER: I would like to point out that the so-called continuing appropriation, which second class and certain mailers in third class receive, is only for nonprofit mailers, as required by statute. The *Wall Street Journal,* under the Postal Rate Commission's interpretation of the statute, is not receiving any subsidy, or at least will not be after next July when the so-called phasing appropriations end.

DR. WAVERMAN: Very well, then, let me rephrase what I said. When we attribute a certain percentage of cost to second-class mail and then say that the total price is 102 percent of the attributable costs, I think there is a subsidy to second-class mail.

MR. CARPENTER: Then in your judgment the subsidy comes from other classes of mail?

DR. WAVERMAN: Yes.

DR. INGO VOGELSANG, Massachusetts Institute of Technology: I have a question for Professor Fuss. Knowledge is always potentially dangerous, and I think the knowledge about sustainability is very dangerous. How does one establish sustainability, in an econometric way, if a franchised monopoly already exists? That is, how can we know the pro-

99

duction function of potential competitors of the natural monopoly, or of the monopoly firm? I would think that one of the advantages of competition is that it reveals information about production processes. If there were no franchised monopoly, this information would come from the fact that there are competitors. But when a franchised monopoly already exists, how then can we econometrically test for sustainability?

DR. FUSS: If I entirely understand the general thrust of your question, I believe I would agree in part and disagree in part. It is true that one could not test for potential sustainability, in the sense that we do not really know what the future will bring with regard to technologies. Given the current range of technologies, however, even with a franchised monopolist it should presumably be possible to test these issues, particularly if one broadens the scope a little to include current competitors in certain areas, such as the United Parcel Service. But if we are talking about the potential for the future, I would agree that these issues really cannot be answered entirely by looking at past historical data.

The suggestion was made that we ought to open up postal services to market forces, in order to determine the sustainability. I would not necessarily disagree with that. As I stated in my paper, if there are no natural monopoly aspects, or if the natural monopoly aspects are in the form of both economies of scale and economies of scope, such cases are potentially amenable to being opened up to competition, so that the market can test the proposition.

The theoretical literature indicates a somewhat troubling possibility of a natural monopoly that does not have some of these characteristics and, therefore, could lose the market test. I am not quite sure what one does about that. In such a case, an enfranchised monopolist seems to make sense for purposes of allocating costs or determining the minimal cost of production. Again, future technologies may change what perhaps should be an enfranchised monopoly to one that should not be, but historical data do not provide any evidence on that issue. As Dr. Merewitz stated earlier, these techniques cannot really tell us when to introduce a new service, since by *new,* we mean essentially something in which there has been no historical experience.

BERNARD SOBIN, Civil Aeronautics Board: Dr. Merewitz said that he would be doubtful about using a Ramsey rule where the marginal costs are unusually low in relation to the total costs of the agency. I wonder whether he had any critical point, and if there is such a critical point, what would he substitute?

100

DR. MEREWITZ: Professor Fuss makes the point in his paper that one should use an inverse elasticity rule, based on total marginal costs, rather than marginal costs as they have been attributed. The inverse elasticity rule serves the objective of economic efficiency, which is certainly not the sole objective in postal pricing. But the utility of Fuss's method is that we are forced to be explicit about what criterion we are using, once we have established those marginal costs econometrically.

Fortunately, these things are delegated to expert commissions, and I am not a commissioner. I think it should be the responsibility of lay people to make social decisions, after listening to economists, engineers, and accountants. And I would not give the final word to economists.

ARTHUR EDEN, National Economic Research Associates: My question can probably be answered by either Professor Waverman or Professor Fuss. Both, I believe, have indicated that the Postal Service is not a natural monopoly. On that assumption, I believe both gentlemen would agree that the Postal Service should be open to private competition. Were that the case, would the private entrant be required to assume the public service responsibilities that are now fulfilled by the Postal Service?

DR. WAVERMAN: Actually, I do not argue in my paper that the Postal Service is not a natural monopoly—if I may state it that way. Whether it is a natural monopoly is at this moment open to question. I think it was a natural monopoly in 1775. It clearly will not be in twenty years. Eighty percent of first-class mail is business related, and I am not sure how invoices bind the nation together. But when the Postal Service loses that portion of the mail—and as we get into alternative ways of transmitting messages I am sure that will happen—then the public-service aspects probably diminish, unless it is argued that the postal monopoly should be extended somehow to electronic media.

There are public-service aspects to communications lines. We do want people to be able to yell "Fire" into a telephone, and to be connected to the center. I am not sure, however, that in twenty years the post office will be a very important ingredient of that kind of public service.

DR. FUSS: I, too, do not really state in my paper that I think the Postal Service is not a natural monopoly. The main point I make is that we do not know; we do not have the evidence at hand. When one says that the Postal Service is not a natural monopoly, however, it is assumed that one cannot find a pricing scheme that enables public services to be provided; or else one finds a pricing scheme that is deemed not in the public interest in some way.

My first inclination is to say that providing those services is essentially a political decision, and some explicit subsidization ought to go along with that political decision.

DR. WAVERMAN: We could take the experiment at the Civil Aeronautics Board as an example of what happens when we do move to a more efficient pricing scheme. We buy off certain groups by subsidizing those who would be hurt, which is what the CAB is doing with the small carriers. We could do that also. Simply allowing competition does not necessarily mean that there will be no post office delivery to Mississippi. It can be subsidized directly. An underlying notion of efficiency does not imply that the world is terribly efficient in everything it does or that the market is best for everything. Services have to be provided, which we think the market will provide at an incorrect price, although I disagree with Professor Visscher that having postal service makes people move out of the city. That is a very small subsidy, in effect.

EDWARD DAY, attorney for Associated Third Class Mailers and former postmaster general: I want to ask Professor Waverman about his statement that television transmission is not subsidized. Does he know how much Channel 4 pays for the incredibly valuable monopoly of using one of the six available VHF channels in Washington? Would he accept, subject to check, that it is not one thin dime?

DR. WAVERMAN: I know that it is not one thin dime. I agree that we give away television channels. That, to me, is different from subsidizing the recipient of that message. I do not think we subsidize the purchase of television sets by people in small, rural communities for the same purposes that we subsidize the mail.

MICHAEL CAVANAGH, Post Office and Civil Service Committee staff member: First, I have a question for Dr. Smith or Professor Adie. I wonder if the use of the fact that the number of people applying for the postal jobs far exceeds the quit rate is entirely fair at a time when we have moderately high unemployment in this country. When the Postal Service makes a standard public announcement that there will be additions to the rolls, it would seem that a number of applicants for these jobs are perhaps unemployed or seriously underemployed. I do not think Dr. Smith or Professor Adie would want to suggest that postal employees' salaries should be set on the basis of what unemployed individuals would be willing to accept above their unemployment checks.

Second, when Dr. Smith talks about comparable employees, what employees are meant? Are we talking about nonfarm workers, or is it a little more specific than that?

Finally, in regard to fairness, in view of the postal workers' contract settlement, could we say that the recent railroad settlement was unfair to postal workers, or could we say that the mine workers' settlement was unfair to postal workers, and so on?

PROFESSOR ADIE: First, I disagree on a factual point—5.9 or 6.0 percent unemployment is low, not high. People may differ on that, but I think we are going to see much higher unemployment in the next year or two.

And yes, I am suggesting that a statistic such as the quit rate be used as a guide to setting wages. The questioner's point is a valid one— such statistics will fluctuate over the business cycle, and for that reason they need to be examined. However, the absolute level of the quit rate in the Postal Service is so low compared with that of private industries, whether we are in an expansion or in a recession, that it suggests the absolute level of wages has quite a large cushion in it at present.

I suggested elsewhere that an average annual quit rate of 12 percent be used as a guide, not as an absolute, to indicate a particular wage differential. That quit rate is slightly lower than the highest quit rates the Postal Service has had over the last ten years.

MR. CAVANAGH: Some of the very high statistics that are used involve 300,000 applicants for postal jobs and were specifically in areas where the unemployment rate was far above the national average.

DR. SMITH: But there were also queues of people for postal jobs in Houston, where the unemployment rate is far below the national average.

It was asked what I meant by "comparable." I have done a regression analysis in which I make a comparison between postal workers and other workers in the federal government who are not in the Postal Service, and workers in the private sector—people employed in private industry other than farms and private households. I look at such characteristics as education, experience, race, sex, occupational status, union status, whether one is a part-time worker, whether one is a dual jobholder—all the things that enter into determining a person's wage rate.

I take a representative individual who can get a job in any one of these sectors and ask, What are the comparative pay levels? The data

103

that I used were from the 1960 and the 1970 censuses and the 1973 and 1975 Current Population Surveys. Plenty of people are involved, and there is a separate analysis for each of those years.

MR. CAVANAGH: Did you look separately at, for instance, the United Parcel Service or one of the other delivery companies?

DR. SMITH: No, because they could not be identified. As for the question, Are these other settlements unfair?, before we could answer that we would have to compare the composition of the work force in each industry with that of the Postal Service, compare their past pattern of wages, and so on. We cannot simply say that because a given percentage is higher for one industry settlement than for the postal settlement, the postal workers' settlement is unfair.

COLEMAN HOYT, *Reader's Digest:* I am concerned that we have been discussing the comparability of postal pay with private-sector pay. I am under the impression that postal workers' pay, as set by Congress prior to the Postal Reorganization Act of 1970, was roughly comparable to that of government workers at the GS–5 level. I wonder why our attention has not been directed to the comparison between the growth in postal wages since 1970 and the growth in government wages since 1970.

DR. SMITH: First of all, the linkage, prior to the Postal Service, was made at unequal levels. The GS level was a college entry grade, and it was linked to a postal field schedule grade that was basically for a postal clerk.

It was recognized that the levels were unequal, but the linkage was justified on the grounds that most postal workers would spend most of their careers at that grade. Congress wanted, as shown in the testimony, to be fair to these people, who would have family obligations, and to make sure they had a living wage.

The linkage started off at unequal levels, and Postal Service wages have gone up faster than federal wages. At the same time, as I have shown, on average most federal workers are paid significantly more than comparable private-sector workers. Everybody is doing better, but postal workers are doing best.

JACK RABINOW, National Bureau of Standards: Is it not true that the compression of jobs between the top and bottom hurt the Civil Service as well? For a while, for example, the director of the Bureau of Standards was getting $36,000 for running a $100 million business; my salary was $36,000 for supervising two people. With all due respect, I think this is silly.

The point, however, is this: Whenever we compare wages in government against those in industry, we must remember that union wages have always been higher than nonunion wages for similar work. Whether it is fair or not, we have to admit that union wages did raise all salaries, ultimately. Unions argue that if unions are unfair to the rest of the world—and I do not mean to say that the postal union is more unfair than others—the fact is that they do raise the total salary level in general. To use as the criterion the number of people who want the job or do not want the job or quit is a very dangerous thing. It implies that if unions were abolished things would be perfectly fair, which is obviously nonsense. The fact is that unions have raised the standard of living of the worker in general.

My question is: Is it not true that the unions in the long run make things fairer but that in the short run they make things look bad?

PROFESSOR ADIE: Although unions claim to have raised the overall level of wages, the studies I am familiar with seem to suggest a different impact of unionism—not that they raise overall wages but that they raise the wages of union members vis-à-vis nonunion members. The differential is affected, not the overall level of wages.

DR. SMITH: I would agree with Professor Adie. The company that raises the wages of its union members in response to union pressure will, in the long run, reduce its work force, because it is a profit-making enterprise and it has to consider what impact the increase in cost has on its profits. That is one of the major differences between pay determination in the private sector and pay determination in the government. Government is not a profit-making enterprise, and it does not have to consider whether it is going to go out of business. So it does not have to be as conscious of how much it is paying its workers.

There is also a political consideration in any of its pay decisions, because the people who ultimately decide pay levels are people who are elected, and they have to care about what effect their pay decision is going to have on their vote-getting ability in the next election.

ROY NIERENBERG, Council on Wage and Price Stability: Among the four negotiated settlements recently completed, the last two were seen to slow down the increase of postal wages. Are there any economic or other factors that can explain the slowdown?

DR. SMITH: The slowdown might reflect an increased awareness of economic factors, so that there is more pressure from voters who are taxpayers, and not postal workers, for wage restraint than from the postal workers for a wage increase. There is more willingness to take a little harder line on that.

The existence of queues has not been formally acknowledged in the structure, but there is some awareness of how many people want to come into the Postal Service, which might also create a greater tendency toward wage restraint.

MR. EDEN: Professor Sherman, in regard to the concept of attributable cost used by the Postal Service in the *NAGCP* 1 case, was it your understanding that when the Postal Service found costs to be shared by two services those costs were not attributed?

PROFESSOR SHERMAN: Yes.

MR. EDEN: I would like to correct that. Most of the costs attributed by the Postal Service are, indeed, shared costs. What the Postal Service did not attribute were those *fixed* costs that were shared by two or more services. I wonder whether that would affect your judgment concerning the reputed restrictive character of these attributions.

PROFESSOR SHERMAN: No. I was thinking of what are defined as fixed costs that seem to me potentially assignable to, say, two classes of mail. The most prominent case, which is no longer treated this way, is that of the bulk mail centers. The centers were to serve mainly third- and fourth-class mail, and I would like to have seen the fixed elements of those costs divided between those two classes in some way. Instead, they were lumped into institutional costs and essentially borne by all classes of mail, which, in the end, turned out to be mainly by first-class mail. That is a couple of rate cases back, but it is the sort of problem I had in mind.

DR. MEREWITZ: I wonder if any evidence can be deduced from the other social sciences about job satisfaction. My understanding is that the Postal Service, since reorganization, has cut down the work force, which is, in itself, an achievement. And the workhorse of the Postal Service, the letter-sorting machine, has now been introduced in many post offices. Under the old system, the Post Office Department was starved for capital. The Postal Service has the ability to spend on capital now.

My impression is that Postal Service employees have been upgraded and that they in fact are more than encouraged—they are forced—to work overtime. That is one of the things there have been grievances about. Are there any studies that make comments on the level of job satisfaction in Postal Service workers?

DR. SMITH: I have not seen anything on the level of job satisfaction, but I would like to comment on the points Dr. Merewitz brought up, because I think they are significant. First of all, a decrease in the number of postal employees has taken place, but it has only been over the last year or so. The 1977 annual report shows a decrease of about 50,000.

DR. MEREWITZ: But the labor force was up around 720,000 when I wrote my thesis in 1966, and it was coming down into the 600,000s in the annual reports of 1971 and 1972, as I recollect.

DR. SMITH: I think that from 1966 to about 1975 or 1976 there may have been a decrease of about 20,000, which does not amount to very much per year. But in the last year and a half, there was a decrease in excess of 50,000, which is dramatic.

The second point has to do with the letter-sorting machines. They have been around for quite some time, but they have not been fully utilized. My understanding is that they are now being used in many more applications, and used much more efficiently than they have been. I think this is another noteworthy event.

DR. WAVERMAN: I have a question for Michael Crew. To the best of your knowledge, has the sending of newspapers or magazines been subsidized in the British postal service?

PROFESSOR CREW: Yes, it was subsidized for a while. I am not sure, but I think the element of subsidy has now been removed.

DR. WAVERMAN: If periodicals were subsidized in the United States, would you think, therefore, that the British society is less literate than American society?

PROFESSOR CREW: I do not know what the comparative scores are on literacy tests in British and American universities, do you? I have been here less than two years as a permanent resident, so I think I am going to duck that question.

Part Two

The Present: Postal Rate Oversight

6

The Postal Rate Commission

Clyde S. DuPont

The Postal Rate Commission's most challenging functions are its rate-making responsibilities and its regulatory relationship with the Postal Service. The relationship is unique in national regulatory experience and unique in worldwide postal rate setting. Government regulation of private industry is commonplace in our society, but there are few examples of one federal agency regulating another. In fact, the Postal Service is in many ways very different from other utility and transportation enterprises. In implementing postal reorganization, we have faced a wide array of novel problems.

We can divide the substantive problems of postal regulation into three categories: (1) achieving a sound conceptual framework for postal rate setting; (2) making sure that the regulatory program is carried out efficiently, expeditiously, and fairly; and (3) ensuring the proper application of both the regulatory theory and the efficient procedures through the acquisition of detailed, reliable, and relevant data.

When postal reorganization got underway in 1970, both the commission and the Postal Service were at the starting gate in all three areas. Since then, I believe our progress has been notable—but it has not been uniform in all three categories of problems. We have achieved a regulatory theory that is both advanced and workable. We have also refined our procedures to the point where we can claim with pride, and good conscience, to have met the statute's demand for the "utmost expedition consistent with procedural fairness." Because of the vast spectrum of rates and services offered by the service, however, there is still much to be done in the area of data collection and organization.

The Conceptual Framework for Postal Rate Setting

Since 1971 the commission has conducted four major rate proceedings in which postal costing and pricing have steadily developed into fields

111

of sophisticated technical analysis. In each succeeding case, we were able to attribute more of the costs to classes of mail, on the basis of demonstrated causation. When the Postal Service submitted its first rate filing, it proposed to attribute about 49 percent of the total costs. By the end of the fourth case, we had raised the attribution level to 65 percent, without departing from our basic theory that volume variability should be the major basis for attributing costs. However, total costs directly related to the classes and subclasses of mail are 75 percent of those costs; residual costs are 25 percent.

This refining process has by no means been all smooth sailing. A landmark court decision in December 1976 caused us to search diligently for other ways to relate costs to mail classes. The resultant changes in our basic incremental cost theory are seen in our most recent rate decision. In my view, some of the changes necessitated by the court's interpretation of our statute are highly questionable, and I share the view of Judge MacKinnon who sat on the panel in the *NAGCP* 1 case. He protested, in a separate opinion, against what he saw as the tendency of the majority opinion to ignore the noncost rate-making factors contained in our statute.

Nevertheless, the decision in the *NAGCP* 1 case must be regarded as controlling, at least until Congress—or the Supreme Court, should a parallel issue come before it—declares otherwise.

Of course, the development of sound regulatory theory involves more than costing and pricing, although these are perhaps the key elements. For example, in the third rate case, the Postal Service for the first time asked us to include in its revenue requirement an element for recovery of past years' losses. Many people, as might be expected, objected. They were able to produce an impressive number of cases from other fields of regulation disallowing such cost-of-service elements. As we analyzed the situation, however, we observed that the rationale generally expressed by courts and commissions was that the utility's shareholders were compensated, through the allowed return, for the risk of such losses. The Postal Service, of course, has no allowed rate of return; it is confined, by statute, to breaking even. Our ultimate conclusion was that the generally applicable principle forbidding the recovery from present rate payers of past losses was not appropriate, in all its customary rigor, to the situation of the Postal Service. This is but one example of the necessity we have faced of adapting well-tried regulatory theory to the unique context of postal regulation. In general—and subject, of course, to the final resolution of the issues raised by the *NAGCP* 1 case—I believe we have made excellent progress in this field.

Procedural Problems

There is a general tendency today to inquire closely into the costs of regulation and to question whether they are in proper proportion to the benefits. We at the commission have tried, and I think with significant success, to minimize the costs and—what is frequently the same thing— to minimize the time consumed by our proceedings. In 1975 the Congress was contemplating legislation that would place a time limitation on rate cases before the commission. We decided—in advance of any legislation—to see if this could be done. Our first case had consumed sixteen months, and the second (which, because the parties had had more time to develop their competing theories, was in fact more complex than the first) had taken twenty-three months. The third case—from the time of filing to the issuance of the decision—was finished in less than ten months. The most recent rate case—the first to be tried under a *statutory* time limit—was also successfully concluded within the deadline. This is perhaps more remarkable, since in the fourth case we had the *NAGCP* 1 decision as an added complication, and new theoretical work was required to accommodate it.

We accomplished this by using a number of procedural innovations. A stranger to our proceedings might find it unusual that the commissioners hear a case directly, unlike the federal agencies which generally employ administrative law judges and the initial decision procedure. The hearing itself is conducted in accordance with procedures designed to minimize hearing time while assuring a full and representative record as required by sections 556 and 557 of the Administrative Procedure Act. Judge Seymour Wenner was largely instrumental in developing the highly efficient written cross-examination procedure that we have employed ever since. We have also developed methods of uncovering issues that seem likely to be material but that the parties have not addressed clearly in the early stages. The commission addresses notices of inquiry to the parties, designed to ventilate questions that seem important and to elicit comments, argument, and the submission of record evidence. Matters of clarification—especially in the filings made by the Postal Service—are often dealt with at an early stage through information requests issued by the commissioner acting as presiding officer. In this way, we attempt—I think successfully—to develop the issues early, to ensure that the record deals with them, and to produce an ample record without interminable oral proceedings.

As a result, I believe the commission can claim to have largely fulfilled Congress's expectation that its proceedings would be expeditiously completed. I do not know of any other regulatory field in which an $18 billion rate proceeding, involving over forty main classes of service and a number of subsidiary special services, is filed, tried, and heard on a 12,500-page evidentiary record and decided in so short a time as ten months.

The Problem of Data

When we turn from the theory and its implementation to the needed improvements in cost data and analysis we find we have the most left to do. Progress has been made in the context of cases actually heard, but it is the area of postal rate making in which we have advanced the least. More needs to be done outside the hearing room, and it needs to be done faster. We now have—and are monitoring through monthly technical conferences—a program of advanced studies conducted in Docket MC76–5.

Our desire for more refined data, I must emphasize, does not stem from dissatisfaction with the results obtained in past cases. I am satisfied that our evidentiary records were more than adequate, and were properly used, to arrive at fair and equitable decisions. I do believe that we should strive to reduce the need for cost estimation and the use of proxy analyses—now necessary where the data are insufficiently refined. Because the Postal Service has required four rate increases in seven and a half years, in order to break even as the statute requires, we have not been able to afford the luxury of withholding action until highly refined Postal Service data are available. On the other hand, our success in reaching sound decisions on first- or second-generation data must not obscure the real need for third- and even fourth-generation data and analysis.

The Kappel commission outlined, in 1968, the need for an extensive overhaul in Postal Service data systems. The Congress and the Kappel commission leveled harsh criticisms at the Post Office Department's forty-year-old cost ascertainment system. The Kappel report also called for functional analysis of postal costs, identification of peak load costs, and data on value of service. After four rate cases, we can endorse those recommendations; and although we are not so lacking in information as the Kappel commission was ten years ago, the job is not yet complete.

Part of the data problem is perhaps inherent in the nature of the postal system. The Postal Service renders a great many different services—far more than the typical utility—and has a high percentage of its costs common to several services. These facts make analytical data collection difficult and complicate the costing out of hundreds of functions and subfunctions to over forty mail classes and numerous special services.

Part of the problem too, is the lack of any *explicit* statutory authority for the commission to prescribe or require the Postal Service to collect particular types of data. Although our discovery powers are generally sufficient to permit us to test and clarify evidence presented in our proceedings, the service has treated the actual collection of data as its exclusive domain. It reserves the design of its statistical systems and the data to be released as a matter of unilateral discretion. We recognize that the collection of data on postal costs or value of service is expensive and in some areas quite possibly infeasible. No intervenor in commission proceedings has as yet undertaken this collection and analysis. For the commission to attempt it would require a substantial increase in our budget; and it is perhaps questionable, given our past experience, whether the funds would be forthcoming under current budgetary arrangements. Thus, the commission and the parties to our proceedings have been tied to the data the Postal Service is willing and able to make available.

I do not wish to be unfair to postal management, however, and I willingly acknowledge not only that not every desirable data project can be fitted into its budget but also that there has, over time, been significant improvement in the data and, more important, the related analyses made available. But areas singled out for special attention in our rates and classification decisions, including costs by certain significant functions and subfunctions, peak load costs, and carrier street time, have not been comprehensively addressed. The officer of the commission and some parties attempt to fill the gaps, but their efforts, while helpful, serve mostly to demonstrate the service's effective monopoly on relevant information.

Perhaps more important than the steady, if not entirely satisfactory, improvement in the data supplied in the successive rate cases are the service's comprehensive, long-range studies of mail classification. These studies, when completed, should provide extensive information on functional costs, peak load costs, value of service, mail flow, and a wide range of other essential subjects. Some studies, such as the household mailstream study, have been completed already. The service has been willing, from the outset, to accept input from us and from outside parties as to the planning of studies and the collection of data. To this end, the service has participated in numerous technical conferences. We are profoundly pleased with this cooperation, and we have tried to assist by holding monthly hearings for discussion of the progress being made by the conferees and particularly the service.

There are, however, still some large deficiencies, which we have temporarily overcome with interim and, we believe, essentially fair solutions. Nonetheless, these deficiencies cause the commission concern. For example, carrier street time is an area we consider of critical importance. Our second and third postal rate decisions called for more work in data collection for carrier street time. Two billion dollars of cost are distributed to the classes of mail on the basis of this factor alone. Again, the Postal Service has not yet responded usefully to these requests. At one time it undertook to include an effort along these lines in the long-range study program, but the service appears to have recently withdrawn this commitment.

In Dockets R74–1 and R76–1 we stressed the potential importance of peak load costs and instructed the service to undertake an analysis of them. At that stage, we did not know what these costs were, what categories of mail caused them, or even whether they were a material part of the total cost picture. The service, after all, is not a capital-intensive enterprise. It may be that peak load costs should not be treated in the same way as they would in regulating an electric utility or gas pipeline. Obviously, though, we eventually must have data to answer these questions authoritatively. We are encouraged that there is a peak load study in the long-range classification study program, but we are disappointed that it is only in the initial stages. Years may elapse before it produces data that can be usefully analyzed.

A slightly different problem arises from the Postal Service's long-standing policy of releasing only final study reports. This is an understandable decision. When experts are satisfied that their final effort is the best that can be offered, it is natural to believe that inquiries as to why it differs from earlier attempts may be less concerned with understanding the data than with fishing for potential weaknesses to exploit in litigation. Nonetheless, the supplying of preliminary data—on the understanding that they might be corrected later—would be most helpful to the commission and to the parties.

The commission has had to redefine regulatory concepts and adapt principles of long standing in other regulated industries to the peculiar circumstances of postal regulation. Under these circumstances, it is not surprising that progress has at times been less rapid than we could wish. I am confident, however, that progress will continue to be made and that the result will be a fairer, more efficient postal rate system and mail classification schedule from which we will all benefit.

Part Three

The Future: Technology and the Mail

7

What Will New Technology Bring?

Charles L. Jackson

What will new technology bring? Disruption, disequilibrium, disturbances, but not disaster. New technology will bring lower costs through more effective electronic communications. Such developments will greatly change the role of the Postal Service, and network externalities will cause the change to be rapid. This paper briefly describes current and expected competitive technologies and examines how such technology will affect the markets currently served by the Postal Service.

The future is uncertain. Costs of electronic alternatives to the Postal Service are dropping dramatically. An approximately true catch phrase is that price/performance ratios in electronics and computers improve by a factor of two every two years. Such an improvement rate will move the costs of an electronic competitor to the Postal Service from an order of magnitude higher than postal service costs to an order of magnitude lower in less than fourteen years. Such a dramatic rate of change overwhelms the imagination and the consumer. The controlling factor will not be the cost of the new technology; rather, it will be the inertia of the people who build and use the systems. Before the new technology can substitute for the mails, consumers must learn new skills and accept new ways of communicating. Once a "critical mass" of consumers has accepted the technology, however, substitution will proceed extremely rapidly.[1]

Technological Options

Two technologies form the key footings upon which all new telecommunications systems will be built. One such footing is electronics, in particular large-scale integration (LSI), which will continue to allow

These remarks are those of the author and do not necessarily reflect the position of the House Subcommittee on Communications or any of its members.

[1] For further information, see Hollis L. Caswell and others, "Basic Technology," *IEEE Computer Magazine*, vol. 11, no. 9 (September 1978), pp. 10–19.

enormous reductions in the costs of processing and storing messages.[2] The other footing is transmission system technology for moving electronic messages around, including fiber optics and communications satellites.

Cheap Electronics. The social and economic effects of large-scale integration can be understood, at least in part, by imagining that electronic hardware will become physically small and that manufacturing costs for the electronic portion of the equipment will almost vanish. It will then be possible, for example, to build a computer into the base of a "Selectric"-style typewriter without significantly changing the cost or size of the typewriter. A computer-typewriter could provide many useful services, including such conventional ones as storage of mailing lists and such unconventional ones as detecting misspelled words.

Before 1948 the two fundamental electronic components were the relay and the tube. Both allow a small current to control a larger current; that is, they provide "amplification" of electrical signals. Tubes and relays were the building blocks of all pre-1950 electronics. They were large (even "miniature" tubes were over an inch long) and expensive, costing a few dollars for each amplifying element. In 1948 the invention of the transistor made possible a substantial reduction in the size of electronic equipment. Within five years transistor costs came down so far that the cost of entire electronic systems was reduced.

But evolution did not stop. Around 1959 or 1960 the integrated circuit was developed. It allows several transistors and supporting circuit elements to be combined on a single small chip of semiconductor material. With the development of integrated circuits, a dollar could purchase several amplifying elements. Later, in the mid-1960s, the research goal became the development of large-scale integration—a goal reached about 1970. Current research and development efforts focus on the development of very-large-scale integrated circuits (VLSI), which allow a single chip to contain hundreds of thousands of amplifying elements.

In September 1978 Texas Instruments announced a new product, a semiconductor device capable of storing 65,536 bits of information. This device, which is about the size of a 1940s miniature tube and costs ten times as much, contains approximately 70,000 amplifying elements. From the point of view of the designer accustomed to working with 1947 devices and prices, the cost of amplifying elements has gone to zero. If one were to try to build a 65,536-bit memory using tubes, the solder needed to connect wires to the tube sockets would cost more than does one of the new generation of 65,536-bit memories.

---

[2] Robert Noyce, "Large-Scale Integration: What Is Yet to Come?" *Science*, vol. 195, no. 4283 (March 18, 1977), pp. 1102–6.

It is not 1948; it is 1978. But the vast preponderance of published studies, both projections of current trends and examinations of fundamental limits, indicates that improvements of the cost/performance of electronic hardware will continue at the pace of the last ten years until at least the early 1990s.

Cheap Transmission. At the same time as the transistor and LSI were changing the nature of electronics, a revolution took place in information transmission systems. Its roots are in the nineteenth century, with Morse and Marconi, but the revolution has speeded up substantially since World War II. Five fundamentally different systems play important roles in improving the transmission functions: satellite systems, fiber optics, enhanced copper pairs, enhanced cable TV cables, and radio systems.

Satellite communication systems are simple in concept. A package consisting of a radio transmitter and receiver along with necessary power supplies, antennas, and so on is orbited around the earth. It can then serve as a relay station, connecting any two points on earth it can "see." Advantages of satellites include flexibility, rapid movement of capacity from route to route, low average cost if fully used, high capacity, and economic distribution of signals to multiple destinations. Disadvantages include large fixed costs, ease of eavesdropping, transmission delay of a quarter of a second, and susceptibility to jamming.

Reasonable projections for satellite systems indicate increasing capacity and decreasing costs over time. A major trouble spot in satellite systems is allocation of the orbital-frequency resource. Which nations should benefit from access to a limited world resource? What trade-offs should be made between such alternative uses of satellite systems as direct broadcast satellites and large-capacity point-to-point satellites?

Fiber optics, also called fiber optic wave guide or dielectric wave guide, is a development of the seventies, although it is based upon earlier work. Optical fibers are thin, threadlike fibers of glass that can carry light waves miles with only minimal attenuation. Fiber optics appears to be the most promising technology for guided signal transmission in the future. It is compact, lightweight, and should become reasonably inexpensive. Current optical fiber systems have many problems, but these seem to be related more to the relative newness of the technology than to fundamental limits.

Electronic technology can improve the usefulness of older transmission technologies such as copper wire pairs, cable television's coaxial cables, or radio systems. Electronic systems can extend the productivity of plants already in place or increase their capacity. Two examples might make this point more concrete. During the last few years many vendors have developed data communications equipment (known as modems) that allows ordinary voice circuits to be used for high-speed data communications. Recently, the 3M Corporation announced a new line of products that allow a two-way cable television system to carry telephone calls as well.

Radio systems offer another route to low-cost transmission. Microwave radio has already become the primary technology for carrying intercity telephone calls. The explosion in citizens band (CB) radio use and the drop in the costs of high-quality CB radios illustrate how modern electronics and mass production can reduce the costs of radio systems.

Subsystems

The building blocks for new communications services are such subsystems as terminals, software packages, communications networks, and computers. This section discusses some of the key subsystems required for any electronic alternative to the Postal Service and attempts to show that most of the necessary subsystems will be economically justified on their own and will be put in place without anyone having to consider their utility for carrying message traffic.

Computer Terminals. A computer terminal is an input/output device usually consisting of a keyboard for input and a display or printer for computer output. Terminal costs range from a low of about $800 to a high of around $5,000. Computer terminals are being installed widely in government and business for use with computer data bases, management information systems, computer models, and time-sharing services.

Smart Typewriters. "Smart typewriter" is a misleading but commonly used phrase. It refers to the use of electronics to enhance the office typewriter, thereby creating an advanced, semiautomated word processing (text management and production) system. Functions of improved typewriters include document storage, the ability to cut and paste documents without retyping, document updating requiring the typing of only the changes, and the ability to merge letter text and mailing lists to create mass mailings. The essential components of smart typewriters include a keyboard, document storage media, display, hardcopy preparation facilities, and minimal computation facilities. University and industrial research facilities now routinely use comprehensive document preparation systems that include such features as spelling correctors and automatic preparation of document tables of contents and indexes.

Smart PBXs. "Smart PBX" (private branch exchange) is another improper, overly anthropomorphic use of the word "smart." PBXs switch telephone calls within offices or hotels and serve as the gateway connecting such sites to the public switched telephone network. Computer control systems allow modern PBXs to take on functions that were previously impractical. As one example, computerized PBXs allow a busy-party callback feature. When a call is made to a busy extension, the PBX notes the calling extension and the called extension; it then waits until both are free and rings them. This and similar features are useful and time-saving in many circumstances.

Facsimile Terminals. Electrical transmission of facsimile images of documents was invented in the nineteenth century. Modern technology allows facsimile terminals to be built at relatively low cost. Several firms, including Xerox, 3M, and Exxon, offer facsimile terminals that can transmit a copy of a typewritten page over the telephone network in a few minutes.

Home Computers. Several firms offer computers for home and small-business use. These computers consist of a keyboard, a display unit, a storage unit, and a simple central processing unit. Frequently, the display unit of the home computer is nothing more than the home television set. Home hobby computers fill no well-defined market need today. Nevertheless, large firms appear to be interested in this market. It seems reasonable to believe that the home computer, augmented with high-quality software for education, for game playing, and for use as a smart typewriter, might be attractive to many consumers.

The home computer, the smart typewriter, and the advanced computer terminal possess very similar architecture. System block diagrams of the three are almost interchangeable. The differences lie in the specific software governing the operation of the components and in the realization of the component parts. For example, the CRT display of the Vydec smart typewriter is of substantially higher quality (and therefore more costly) than the display on the Radio Shack TRS–80 computer.

Communications Facilities. The communications backbone needed by any electronic alternative to the Postal Service is being put into place today. Best known of the networks in place is the telephone system. The telephone network reaches essentially all homes and businesses in this country. Telephone circuits can carry data communications at rates of up to about a thousand characters per second. Top-of-the-line facsimile machines can transmit a page over a telephone line in about thirty seconds. But the telephone network was designed and optimized for voice communications. Most of the data and image communications systems that use it were designed to take advantage of the ubiquitous telephone network and are not complete systems optimized for data communications. Systems designed for efficient data communications are being developed, however. Telenet, a value-added communications common carrier, provides a data communications service using packet-switching technology. This technology can provide substantial economies over traditional telephone circuits when dealing with some kinds of terminal-to-computer communications.

American Telephone and Telegraph (AT&T) has requested FCC approval of its potential new offering, Advanced Communications System (ACS). ACS would offer a variety of flexible data communications options, including packet switching similar to that offered by Telenet, and store-and-forward message service. ACS would provide the nation with a digital communications backbone capable of carrying all transaction mail and typewritten (character by character) correspondence at low cost.

Applications

To what uses will these subsystems be put? In particular, how will these subsystems affect the traffic carried by the Postal Service today? This section looks at some typical applications and tries to impart a qualitative feel for the impact of these new subsystems.

Telephone Bill Paying. Some banks provide bill-paying and funds-transfer services using Touch-Tone telephones as simple computer terminals. In order to pay a bill, a consumer calls a special number, and a recording answers requesting the customer to key in his or her identification number. The customer, helped by further voice promptings, enters the rest of the information required for the transaction. Clearly, paying monthly bills this way would be no more troublesome to most people than writing checks, but many customers will be uncomfortable with a change to telephone bill paying. Banks are faced with a difficult marketing problem, because not all households have Touch-Tone telephone service. Thus, they must either offer the enhanced service to only some of their customers or they must find another, perhaps much more expensive way of serving customers who do not have Touch-Tone telephone service. Telephone bill paying illustrates well how technologies developed for other purposes may have a major impact on Postal Service traffic.

Prestel and CeeFax. The British Post Office (BPO) has developed a new communications service called Prestel, formerly known as Viewdata, a computer-based information utility. Business and residential subscribers will be able to access large data bases using slightly modified television sets as computer terminals. Data expected to interest residential subscribers include weather forecasts, sports results, restaurant menus, consumer information, and so on. Business subscribers are expected to be interested in more specialized services, such as stock market quotations, commodity quotations, international news, and crop reports. The BPO designed Prestel to be a common carrier service. The Post Office provides the communications links and the computers, but the data banks are open to all suppliers. Any information vendor can put data in the Post Office's computers and can attach a price to those data. The price is automatically charged to anyone who accesses the data. The BPO is currently market-testing Prestel service, and it is not yet clear how Prestel will evolve.

It is clear that the problems of Prestel and similar services are fundamentally organizational and social, not problems created by hardware costs. The terminals are inexpensive; the computers are inexpensive. The problems lie in putting the package together.

The most elementary Prestel terminal, a CRT display with only a numeric keyboard for input would be an excellent terminal for a consumer to use in dealing with a bank's computer and in paying bills. The more advanced Prestel terminals feature full alphanumeric keyboards and can be used for terminal-to-terminal electronic correspondence as well.

Closely related to Prestel are the teletext broadcast systems, CeeFax and Oracle. Teletext broadcasting takes an unused portion of the television signal and fills it with written information that can be displayed on modified television sets. Such an enhancement to the television signal can be used to carry captions for the deaf, headlines, or a specialized news magazine. Careful selection of standards at an early stage in the development of CeeFax and Prestel resulted in extensive commonality between a CeeFax compatible television set and a Prestel terminal. This means that product experience can be shared and production of both products will follow the same learning curve. In addition, a combined Prestel/CeeFax terminal will cost little more than a standalone Prestel terminal.

Office of the Future. Many experts see automation increasing in the office, raising worker productivity, and eliminating some repetitive tasks. Putting office automation systems into place will also put into place the terminals needed for electronic message services.

Computer Message Sytems. The combination of computers with communications networks has created a new kind of communications, the computer message system. A user of a computer message system types a message into the computer, using a terminal. The user indicates to the computer the subject or topic of the message, the address, any other individuals who are to receive copies, and the text of the message. The computer then files the message until the addressee asks to have it printed out at his or her terminal. Such a bald description makes computer message systems seem as simple as they are. It hardly describes the great advantages these systems provide for some kind of communications, nor does it explain why people become enthusiastic about them. They are more convenient than a telephone or a letter for many kinds of correspondence. Computer-mediated messages are rapid; yet, because they are held for delivery until called for, they do not interrupt the recipient. Other major advantages of computer message systems include speed comparable to that of a telephone call, the ability to send a message even if the recipient is unavailable, economical transmission of messages to many addressees, and computerized management of files of received messages. Such file management techniques can provide remarkable flexibility, far surpassing that of traditional manual filing systems. One can request the computer to find all messages from Robert Brown during July or August concerning the Postal Service. Or one can request the system to find the most recent message with the word "history" in it.

Computer message systems are still expensive, with costs in the neighborhood of fifty cents to a dollar per message. Nevertheless, they have been used successfully in the academic world, in business, and in government.[3]

Voice Forwarding Systems. One possible enhancement of a PBX or of the telephone network would be the addition of a capability for forwarding stored voice messages. If, for example, one were making an intraoffice call and the number called were busy, one could dictate a short message to the PBX. The PBX would record the message and hold it until the called party became free. Then it would ring the telephone and, when the telephone was answered, play back the recorded message. The recent growth in telephone-answering machines is another example of stored-voice-message technology.

[3] Konrad K. Kalba and others, "Electronic Message Systems: The Technological Market and Regulatory Prospects," report prepared for the Federal Communications Commission by Kalba-Bowen Associates and the Center for Policy Alternatives, Massachusetts Institute of Technology (April 1978).

Markets

Electronic communications and computer systems substitute most effectively for transaction mail and business correspondence. Bills, statements of account, payments, and other transaction-related mail make up 40 percent of the mails (36 billion of the 89 billion pieces of mail in 1974) and an even larger fraction of first-class mail. Correspondence, a far smaller market, totaled only 20 billion pieces of mail in 1974, and only 4.5 billion pieces out of this total flowed between business addresses. Thus, a substantial fraction of the Postal Service's current market, somewhere around 10 to 30 percent of all mail, is exposed to competition from electronic alternatives.

The George Washington University report by Fred B. Wood and others contains an extensive and detailed discussion of the potential diversion of current mail traffic to electronic systems. Anyone desiring more detail on the exposure of the mailstream to electronic competitors should look at this report.[4]

Network Externalities

Each additional subscriber or user of a communications service creates an important external effect that is almost always positive because most people value the ability to communicate with others. This external effect can substantially influence the growth of communications services. Rohlfs discusses such effects with particular attention to the implications for the pricing of newly introduced communications services.[5]

The general thesis is that each additional subscriber to a communications service enhances the value of that service to other users. A telephone system that allows one to call department stores as well as emergency services is more valuable than a system that only allows one to call emergency services. A telephone system that allows one to call almost all homes and businesses is more valuable still. Similarly, a bank credit card that can be used in 80 percent of retail establishments is much more convenient than a credit card that can be used in only 20 percent of establishments.

The implications of such externalities for the growth of services can be striking. If all consumers are homogeneous and the value they place on a communications service is directly proportional to the number of

---

[4] Fred B. Wood and others, "USPS and the Communications Revolution: Impacts, Options, and Issues," report prepared by the Program of Policy Studies in Science and Technology (Washington, D.C.: George Washington University, March 5, 1977).

[5] J. Rohlfs, "A Theory of Interdependent Demand for Communications Service," *Bell Journal of Economics and Management Science,* vol. 5, no. 1 (Spring 1974).

other subscribers, then for any given cost per subscriber, there is a minimum number of subscribers needed for economic viability. Call this number the critical mass. If the number of subscribers is below the critical mass, then the value offered to subscribers is less than the cost of the service and subscribers will tend to quit subscribing. Similarly, if the number of subscribers exceeds the critical mass, then additional subscribers will be attracted to the service, the service will become more valuable to all, and still more subscribers will be attracted.

This phenomenon is not limited to common carrier communications nets of the kind considered by Rohlfs. I believe that it was a major factor in the growth of CB radio in 1974 and 1975, although the publicity given CB by the truckers' strike undoubtedly helped as well. (Note that the probability that a call for assistance or information on a CB channel will be received grows much faster than does the fraction of CB-equipped cars.)

If the critical mass theory applies even approximately to the electronic alternatives to the Postal Service, then we should expect to see a relatively slow growth of these alternative systems until the critical mass is reached. After the critical mass is reached, growth should be rapid.

Consider what this theory says about the use of home computers as terminals to connect with a bank's bill-paying computer. Until a significant fraction of consumers has terminals, there is no reason for banks to develop the necessary computer interfaces and software. But once a large enough fraction of consumers has some form of home terminal, it seems reasonable to expect that banks will rapidly develop the required facilities.

Predictions

The subsystems necessary for electronic alternatives to the Postal Service will spread. They are justified on their own as stand-alone systems or in conjunction with computer systems.

Terminals will move rapidly into the office as part of the growth of office automation. These terminals will reduce secretarial costs, improve work quality and turnaround time, and improve management effectiveness. Office automation systems will include substantial intraoffice and intrafirm computer message system facilities. Use of these technologies in the workplace will educate people to the potential that similar technologies have for the home.

The communications backbone needed for an electronic alternative to the Postal Service is already in place. The telephone network will be enhanced, and competitive alternatives will expand. Current needs of the business world will ensure that an effective communications network will be available for any electronic add-on to the Postal Service or for any electronic alternative to the Postal Service.

Terminals will spread more slowly into the home than into the office. The economic justification for the computer or terminal in the home is less clear than in the office. The home terminal will probably come into being as a game or learning toy with the capability to act as a minimal terminal.

The costs of electronics are dropping dramatically. As already noted, improvements by a factor of two every two years in price/performance ratios are frequently encountered. Price reductions will follow suit. At the same time, the critical mass characteristic of the growth of communications also pushes in the direction of rapid change. Because both factors favor rapid growth of electronic alternatives to the Postal Service, we should prepare ourselves for this transition and should not be surprised when it occurs.

Commentary

Bridger M. Mitchell

The Postal Service and Developing Technologies

In nearly every regulated industry, developing technologies have exerted pressures for pricing changes and new services. While outside competitors have tried to skim the cream of the market, regulated oligopoly and monopoly suppliers have used the regulatory process to protect their traditional markets from competition. In this environment of widespread ferment in the regulated sector, the Postal Service poses a particularly interesting case.

Charles Jackson reminds us that the technology of electronic communication is evolving with extraordinary rapidity; he predicts that the costs of electronic alternatives to much of today's postal service will drop to the point where costs will soon be an insignificant factor.

Do such changes mean that there are no important *economic* issues raised by the new technology? With a somewhat different emphasis from Jackson's, I suggest that for the Postal Service and for public policy the following consequences will result from the impact of technology:

- The Postal Service will lose large portions of the message and financial transactions markets to electronic services.
- The Postal Service must consider different pricing structures if it wishes to compete with suppliers of these services— or even undertake to supply some electronic transmission and delivery services itself.
- Regulation for entry into and competition within the market must be seriously considered, since the Postal Service presently lacks the protection of a regulatory commission.

Natural Monopoly and Competition

Renewed interest in the performance of economic regulation has led economists to reexamine the venerable subject of natural monopoly.

These remarks were prepared under the auspices of National Science Foundation Grant APR77–16286 to the Rand Corporation.

Simply stated, a monopoly is "natural" if it is less expensive for a single firm to meet the market demand for its goods and services than it would be for several firms to produce the identical output.[1] Provided that regulation does not itself impose significant additional costs, in these circumstances society makes the most efficient use of its resources by permitting (private or public) monopoly production and using a regulatory mechanism to limit the monopolist's power to set prices and earn above-normal profits.

Theoretical attention to the problem of natural monopoly focuses on the potential role for competition. Recent studies explicitly recognize that all important monopolies are multiproduct firms that frequently produce a wide variety of services. The cost advantage of the natural monopoly derives not only from long-recognized economies of scale but possibly also from economies of scope that result from joint production of several services.

In this context the economic issue of competition is almost invariably whether production of a particular service by more than one firm will increase the total costs of producing the full set of monopoly services. The issue can be cast in terms of the following questions:

1. Is production of one or more of the monopoly services fully separable from the production of other services? If so, the service is incidental to the monopoly business and can be supplied by competitors without loss of efficiency. Express mail and vertical telephone equipment (such as private switchboards and call-answering machines) are likely examples of separable services.

2. Is there a market-clearing price for each of the monopolist's services sufficient to earn the firm a normal rate of return but yet so low that no competitor can profitably enter any market? This is a question about both the technology of production and the market demands. If such prices exist, the monopoly is termed "sustainable" against competition. In such circumstances, if competitive entry does occur it is a signal that the existing prices involve elements of cross-subsidy between services. Entry (or the threat of entry) will lead the monopoly to align prices more closely with costs.

3. What if there are *no* prices at which the monopoly is sustainable in its (nonseparable) services? In this case, competitive entry will be profitable but will result in less efficient production and consequently higher overall costs to society. In these instances, if the social benefits of monopoly are to be preserved the regulator must act positively to prevent entry or levy taxes on competitive firms.

[1] In the economist's parlance, the cost function of the firm is subadditive.

Whether competitive efforts to enter a regulated market are evidence of a separable service, indicative of cross-subsidies, or an actual threat to the lowest-cost method of organizing production is an empirical issue requiring data on technologies, costs, and market demands. We know, however, that prices that are at variance with costs lead to "cream skimming"—that is, selective entry by competitive suppliers into the high-margin markets.

If entry is allowed, cream skimming by competitors will prevent a regulated monopoly from maintaining its prevailing prices.[2] For example, in the telecommunications industry new microwave firms are supplying private line circuits on traffic-intensive routes, and this competition is forcing AT&T to seek rate changes. The Postal Service faces similar competitive pressures on its high-density, low-cost routes. Although direct federal subsidies give the Postal Service an advantage not enjoyed by most other monopolies, it may nevertheless be forced to depart from its long-standing practice of rate-averaging on first-class and parcel services.

Changing Technology and the Postal Service

The Postal Service confronts many of the market structure issues that face regulated monopolies in other industries today. But in the postal industry changing technology raises another set of vexing issues. Nearly all the new technology is developing outside the boundaries of the Postal Service's long-standing monopoly market. The question for the Postal Service, unlike AT&T and the independent telephone companies, is not primarily whether traditional markets must be insulated from entry by competitors. Rather, a key issue is whether the Postal Service itself should enter the new electronic communications markets.

The appropriate scope of the regulated firm in an environment of changing technology has not yet been subject to systematic economic analysis. In particular cases, it may be that production efficiency will be increased by expanding the scope of the natural monopoly to encompass new techniques and markets. If so, when is it desirable to enlarge the span of economic regulation to levy taxes or erect entry barriers in these new markets? What constitutes an efficient market structure if the Postal Service's competitor is itself a natural monopoly in some other industry?

For Postal Service customers, the impact of the new electronic technology will be felt in first-class mail rates. Until now, first-class mail service has enjoyed some economies of scope with delivery of second-

---

[2] Cream-skimming opportunities are frequently the result of rate-averaging—the practice of combining high- and low-cost markets into an average value for pricing purposes.

and third-class mail and perhaps some economies of scale as well. Moreover, in the preelectronic era one first-class envelope had the same cost implications as another, so that from the supply side of the market first-class mail could be regarded as a homogeneous service. Revenues from all services were potentially available to support the common costs of the home delivery network. Now, electronic communications systems are on the verge of offering lower-cost alternatives for large segments of first-class mail, especially those consisting of financial transactions. This development means that what has been a homogeneous service for the postal system will be split into a host of similar serivces, each tailored to the particular characteristics of the message conveyed.

Two outcomes are conceivable. Most probably, the Postal Service will lose very sizable portions of the financial transaction (and other business message) market to new electronic services offered by competitors; declining first-class mail volume will increase unit costs and require still higher rates for the residual monopoly services. Alternatively, the Postal Service could differentiate its first-class services: raise rates for letters but cut rates on messages subject to electronic competition and perhaps also undertake to supply some electronic transmission and delivery services.

In short, technology has not smiled on the letter writer. Instead, cost-reducing innovation is dramatically favoring one segment of the market, making financial transactions much cheaper to conduct than personal correspondence. The impact that changing technology has had on the telephone system is closely analogous. Marked gains in long-distance telephone technology have far outdistanced the improvements achieved in local-exchange plant and equipment and resulted in sizable reductions in long-distance telephone rates. During this period, costs of local telephone service have risen, and substantially higher local rates have been avoided only by using accounting procedures that transfer local-exchange costs to rates for interstate calls.

The outlook for the Postal Service is a rapidly changing market structure in which cream skimming will occur on a grand scale. The Postal Service lacks the protection of a regulatory commission that can prevent entry into its vulnerable markets. Its one alternative is to become a major supplier of electronic communications, yet it is unlikely to possess the cost advantages needed to succeed in competition with other suppliers. Most probably, the Postal Service can anticipate losing not merely the cream but virtually the entire dairy business to the new electronic competitors.

Commentary

Jacob Rabinow

The paper by Charles Jackson is devoted to the wonders of modern electronics, the greater wonders yet to come, and the way these wonders of communication, computer storage, high-speed image reproduction, and so on, are bound to affect the postal system. I am an electrical engineer who loves electronic machinery as much as anyone else, certainly more than most. I was privileged to become involved with the computer art very early when the Bureau of Standards helped to buy the first UNIVAC for the Census Bureau and when it developed its own computers, and my involvement has continued over the years. I have no quarrel with the technical aspects of Charles Jackson's paper, although I do have some minor reservations about a point or two.

I have very serious objections to his general theme on what effect new technology can have on Postal Service operations. One should not compare apples and oranges. When Jackson speaks of large-scale integration, he does not compare these devices with Marconi's coherer, and he should not compare large-scale integration with the present technology of the U.S. Postal Service.

The magnificent electronic industry of the United States spends a very large part of its income, somewhere between 3 and 10 percent of its gross sales, on research and development. Moreover, this R&D is done by really outstanding people. It is no accident that Bell Laboratories has produced a large number of Nobel Prize winners. When one compares this kind of R&D effort and its results with the present operation of the Postal Service, one is doing a disservice to science and to this country. If the Postal Service spent a similar percentage of its gross receipts on R&D, if the people were of the same caliber as those

---

Note: Time did not allow full discussion of this subject at the conference. Mr. Rabinow, who probably has contributed more to the development of mail-handling technology than anyone else, made this discussion available after the conference, and the editor is glad to be able to include it here. These comments are the personal opinions of the author and do not reflect those of his part-time employer at the National Bureau of Standards.

who work in the industry that Jackson and I so obviously admire, and if this were done for several decades, one could then argue and worry about whether modern electronics really could replace the delivery of letter mail or, for that matter, the delivery of packages.

This short communication is not the place to say what a post office of the future could be. But when one thinks of the control of the documents, of the formats, of the fonts, and of the signals as exercised in the communications industry and then compares it with the lack of control and the absolute chaos of the letter-handling business, one begins to see some of the difficulties. There is a plane leaving Washington, D.C. for New York approximately every fifteen minutes. There are some 300 flights daily between San Francisco and Los Angeles. There are literally dozens of flights between Washington and every major city in the country. Why should it take a day or two to deliver a letter when the average flight time between cities is about one hour? When one is flying west, one flies almost as fast as the sun.

I have heard various arguments attempting to explain slow mail delivery, with the main theme being that the Postal Service is a government operation and the electronic industry is private and driven by a profit motive. This is a gross oversimplification and really has nothing to do with what technology could bring. The Census Bureau, which is also a government agency, has been a pioneer in information technology. We should remember that the punch card was invented by the Census Bureau in 1890 and that the first civilian computer was built for and used by the Census Bureau when Presper Eckert and John Mauchly could not get financial support from any commercial institution because it was thought the computer was a white elephant.

I do not wish to dwell upon the unfortunate political history of the old Post Office and its sorry inheritance with which the Postal Service is still plagued, but, as engineers who talk about the future and what it could do, we should be careful about several things. One is the inherent advantage of sending original data where not only the information content but the physical aspect of the message is important. The physical content may include diagrams and photographs in color. Emphasis can be achieved by arrangement, style of print, type of paper, and color of parts of the message. In general, the information content (the resolution) can be infinitely greater than one could afford with the best present day message-transmitting techniques. I am fully aware that high resolution color photographs can be sent by wire today, but this is slow, very expensive, and justified only for special requirements. We should not assume that information channels are free. We should know that if everyone uses the telephone nearly continuously the switching and line problems are not reduced in proportion to use but get much

TECHNOLOGY AND THE MAIL

worse. We should be careful when we compare information stored in computers with information stored on paper or, even better, on photographic microcopies. We should ask people who write letters, like me, why it is that they dictate letters when they have available the use of facsimile transmission, teletype, telegraph, and unlimited telephone services. When we hear a union leader say that the Postal Service is some 85 percent labor-intensive, we, as good engineers, should ask why much of that is really necessary.

If the mail were properly addressed for machine use and if the proper machinery were used, it could be delivered not only to the block but also to the building and, finally, to the correct person with very little human intervention. What would be the relative cost? One should always remember that the actual transmission of a letter by air is so inexpensive that it has no real part in the Postal Service unit costs.

After many years of designing equipment for the Post Office Department and arguing, sometimes rather bitterly, with some of its technical staff, I believe that Postal Service technology has not yet entered the twentieth century. While we should consider very seriously the impact that electronic communication will have on its future, the Postal Service should not become terrified by the miracles of which Jackson speaks but should be more concerned with the miracles that it, itself, can achieve.

8

What Can Markets Control?

Robert D. Willig

The writings in this volume describe a wide array of postal problems and issues that leave me, as a citizen-mailer, perturbed and perplexed. Further, this volume contains portrayals of tomorrow that, although presented calmly and enticingly, nonetheless threaten my equanimity with future shock. Moreover, the contributors clarify how the complexity of current postal issues concatenates with the prospect of rapid technological advance to make policy analysis formidably difficult.

Consequently, I feel fortunate to be charged with the analysis of a relatively simple policy approach to postal issues, namely, free markets. This topic permits me to protect my equanimity by relabeling future shock and social issues as scientific problems and by proceeding to analyze them as best I can. Toward this end, a necessary first step is to group them into categories that are, perhaps, amenable to analysis. Replacing my citizen's perplexity with economic focus, I proceed to list (nonexhaustively and with some overlapping) potential postal problem areas in generic terms:

1. Cost inefficiency in the provision of services
   a. Inefficient choice of inputs
   b. Inefficient utilization of inputs chosen
   c. Inappropriate prices paid for inputs
   d. Inefficient industry structure
2. Cross-subsidization of services
3. Overall deficit
   a. Shield for cost inefficiency
   b. Protection from competition
4. Instability of enterprise as supplier of traditional set of products and services because of competition from private purveyors who utilize traditional technology

5. Arbitrary and socially inefficient rates
6. Instability of enterprise as supplier of traditional set of products because of the introduction of new products based on new technology; impediments to socially desirable product innovations
7. Endangerment of social aims presently served by enterprise, such as:
   a. Rural communication
   b. Public-service mail categories.

This paper addresses the questions of how well economic markets can control these problem areas. My answers are provisional and largely conditional on matters of fact of which I, and perhaps we, are ignorant. Thus, I place myself in a traditional economist's role—"answering" questions by asking other questions. Yet, I feel that this can be a worthwhile contribution if the new questions are narrower and more easily answered than the original ones.

Essentially, I will argue that problems 1–5 could probably be well controlled by economic markets that permit postal services to be priced with great flexibility and that subject the U.S. Postal Service to vigorous potential competition. Yet, such markets would generally exercise less socially reliable control of problem 6. Although problem 7 cannot be reliably controlled by the market, there may be practical mechanisms capable of handling this area that do not impede the operations of the market.

The analysis will support neither complete deregulation of postal services nor the status quo. Instead, it will attempt to identify basic forces that themselves each argue one way or another. I cannot assess the balance at this time. Even if the balance were toward regulation, however, the analysis may provide guidance as to how market forces could be permitted to temper the potential problems therefrom.

First, drawing heavily on the theory of sustainability, I describe how idealized, frictionless free entry could control the performance of an incumbent firm so as to minimize problems 1–5. Second, I discuss the applicability of these results to a dynamic environment with technological change. Conditions are identified under which markets deal poorly with problem 6, and suggestions are offered for the improvement of such performance. Third, I analyze the relationships between the operation of economic markets and the fulfillment of special social aims of pricing. Fourth, I discuss some of the features of reality that would weaken the control of markets over performance. Finally, I recapitulate the questions that the analysis suggests are critical for assessing the desirability of relying on market control of postal services.

ROBERT D. WILLIG

Sustainability Theory

The theory of sustainability shows that in principle and in favorable circumstances idealized economic markets can control performance so as to eliminate problems 1–5.[1] In this section, I will detail the mechanisms of such control and the nature of the performance that results.

Idealized Economic Markets. Idealized economic markets are open to entry by entrepreneurs who face no disadvantages vis-à-vis incumbent firms. Incumbents receive no subsidies that are not also freely available to newly entering firms. The potential entrants have available the same best-practice production technology, the same input markets, and the same input prices as those utilized by the incumbent firms. There are no legal restrictions on market entry, and there are no special costs that must be borne by an entrant that do not fall on incumbents as well. Consumers have no preferences among firms except those arising directly from price or product-quality differences in firms' offerings.

Entrepreneurs are profit seekers who are assumed to respond with production to profitable opportunities for entry. Potential entrants assess the profitability of their marketing plans by making use of the current prices of incumbent firms. Thus, for example, an entrepreneur will enter a market if he anticipates positive profit from undercutting the incumbent's price and serving the entire market demand at the new lower price. Potential entrants are assumed to be undeterred by prospects of retaliatory price cuts by incumbents and, instead, to be deterred only when the existing market prices leave them no room for profitable entry.

It is important to distinguish this concept of an idealized market from the textbook notion of a perfectly competitive market. A perfectly competitive firm, like an enterprise operating in an idealized economic market, does indeed face frictionless free entry. But, in addition, perfectly competitive markets must contain so many incumbent firms competing among themselves that each perceives that its production decisions have no effect on market prices. In contrast, both incumbents and potential entrants in an idealized market recognize their power over prices and realize that they cannot sell more than consumers demand at given prices, without bidding market prices down. Consequently, an

---

[1] This theory originated in John C. Panzar and Robert D. Willig, "Free Entry and the Sustainability of Natural Monopoly," *Bell Journal of Economics,* vol. 8 (Spring 1977), pp. 1–22; and in William J. Baumol, Elizabeth E. Bailey, and Robert D. Willig, "Weak Invisible Hand Theorems on the Sustainability of Prices in a Multiproduct Natural Monopoly," *American Economic Review,* vol. 67 (June 1977), pp. 352–65.

139

idealized market need not be populated with a great many firms, although, if it is so populated, it is perfectly competitive. Yet, an idealized market may contain only a single monopoly enterprise that faces frictionless free entry.

Sustainable Industry Configurations. Let us define a "feasible industry configuration" to be a set of products or services, their associated market prices, and a set of firms, each at least breaking even, which together produce the quantities of the goods demanded by the market. A feasible industry configuration is said to be sustainable if it yields no incentives for entry in an idealized market setting.[2] As such, sustainability is a prerequisite for industry equilibrium when there is frictionless free entry. An unsustainable industry configuration offers a profitable window for entry which, in an idealized market, can be expected to induce an entrepreneur to produce and thereby alter the industry position.

Cost Efficiency. It has been shown that a feasible industry configuration can be sustainable only if the firms produce the total industry output at the least possible industry cost.[3] Least-cost operation by a firm entails the purchases of inputs at the smallest possible prices, the utilization of inputs without waste, and the choice of input combinations that are cost-minimal for the outputs produced. In an idealized market, firms must operate cost efficiently in order to survive. If a firm were to earn nonnegative profit while producing at greater costs than necessary, an entrant could undercut the firm's prices and earn a positive profit by operating more efficiently. Thus, potential competition from frictionless entrants guarantees that surviving, sustainable firms are cost minimizers.

Moreover, in a sustainable industry configuration, total industry output must be distributed among firms so as to minimize total industry cost. If some rearrangement of output among firms could result in lower total cost, then an entrant whose size reflected some part of that rearrangement could earn a positive profit at prices below the original ones. Thus, frictionless free entry has the power to enforce a cost-efficient industry structure.

These general propositions have important consequences for the case of monopoly. A monopoly enterprise in an idealized market cannot hope to persist, cannot be sustainable, unless it is the least-cost provider of its array of outputs. An industry is said to be a natural monopoly if the cost-minimizing industry structure is a single firm. An enterprise that monopolizes an industry can be sustainable only if it is a natural

---

[2] This definition was introduced and explained in Robert Willig, "Multiproduct Technology and Market Structure," *American Economic Review*, vol. 69 (May 1979).
[3] Ibid.

monopoly. Frictionless free entry provides a market test of whether a monopoly enterprise is actually a natural monopoly; only if it is can it successfully remain alone in its idealized markets.

Cross-Subsidization. An enterprise cannot be sustainable if it engages in cross-subsidization.[4] If any element or category of services and products were noncompensatory, then, by choosing to serve only the compensatory portions of the incumbent's business, an entrepreneur could undercut the market prices and earn a positive profit. Consequently, sustainable prices must all be compensatory, and as such they involve no cross-subsidization.

This general rule has several detailed implications. First, sustainable prices cannot be below the associated marginal costs of production. Otherwise, the last units produced would be noncompensatory, and an entrepreneur could enter profitably by scaling back production of the underpriced goods.

Second, sustainable prices must not be less than the associated average incremental costs. The incremental cost of a product line is the saving in total cost that the enterprise could efficiently achieve by ceasing to produce that product line while continuing to produce all else that it had previously. Given the operating point of the enterprise, incremental cost is the cost that is economically attributable to a product line.

Spreading incremental cost over the number of produced units of the product gives average incremental cost. If the average incremental cost of a product exceeded its price, dropping the product would save more in costs than would be lost in revenues. Thus, an entrepreneur could profitably enter by replicating the incumbent's marketing plan at lower prices, with the exception of the noncompensatory product line.

Third, for every group of products and services, sustainable prices must yield revenues that are greater than or equal to incremental costs. Otherwise, as above, dropping the noncompensatory group of outputs would enable profitable entry. When there are costs that are common to several outputs, this condition is a significant addition to the stipulation that each product line be individually compensatory. In this case, even though the common costs would not be saved by dropping only one product line, they would be economically attributable to the relevant group as a whole. Consequently, the group could be noncompensatory at the same prices that make each product in the group compensatory when viewed alone.

---

[4] See Gerald Faulhaber, "Cross-Subsidization: Pricing in Public Enterprises," *American Economic Review,* vol. 65 (December 1975), pp. 966–77, for the seminal treatment of this topic. The material in this section is based on Panzar and Willig, "Sustainability."

In summary, an enterprise operating in an idealized market must, to avoid inducing competitive entry, levy prices that make all categories, subcategories, and groups of outputs compensatory. In this way, the rigors of frictionless potential competition enforce the absence of cross-subsidization.

However, it should be recognized that completely subsidy-free rates may not be viewed as socially desirable. Because such prices must reflect cost differences, a sustainable price structure may be uncomfortably complex if costs vary over customer groups and service subgroups. Rate-averaging is unsustainable if the uniform price is below the marginal or the average incremental cost of the higher-cost subcategory. Customarily free services such as postal delivery and telephone directory assistance would make the providing enterprise unsustainable in a frictionless market environment. Hence, there is a potential conflict between free competition and intentional elements of cross-subsidization. We shall return to this class of issues later.

The Implications of Sustainable Rates. We have seen that an idealized economic market controls problems 1 and 2 (as listed earlier) in that it forces a surviving enterprise to operate and structure itself cost efficiently and to avoid cross-subsidization. These are necessary conditions for an industry's structure and rates to be sustainable.

In a natural monopoly industry, only a monopoly enterprise can be sustainable. Suppose that a natural monopoly can find and levy sustainable prices. Such prices would earn the enterprise zero economic profit, or, in other words, a normal rate of return on capital. This follows because, by definition, sustainable prices are market-feasible without overall subsidy and because positive profit would allow an entrant to undercut the incumbent's prices and still earn a positive, though smaller, profit.

Further, by definition, sustainable prices deter entry by entrepreneurs who would propose to produce some or all of the same goods or services offered by the incumbent by means of the same technological possibilities available to the incumbent. Thus, while sustainable prices do not necessarily protect a natural monopoly from competitors with improved products or production technology, they do leave a natural monopoly invulnerable to profitable market incursions by those offering nothing new. Such incursions would be socially wasteful in a natural monopoly industry because they would accomplish nothing that the incumbent could not itself effect at a lower total industry cost.

Hence, sustainable prices for a natural monopoly enterprise in an idealized market would solve problems 3 and 4. Sustainable prices would protect the enterprise from socially wasteful duplicative competition without requiring overall subsidies to help defray production costs. Further, a monopoly enterprise in an idealized market that is not a natural monopoly would be unable in the absence of overall subsidies to find sustainable prices and to deter entry, which would decrease total industry costs. Moreover, it seems reasonable to presume that an enterprise in an idealized market would have the survival incentive to attempt to operate in a sustainable manner. Thus, it is tempting to conclude that potential idealized competition does control problems 3 and 4 as well as problems 1 and 2.

Unsustainability. There is a serious impediment, however, to reaching this strong conclusion. The impediment is the possibility that sustainable prices do not exist—even for a natural monopoly producing a set of socially worthwhile products.[5] If this were the case, then the natural monopoly enterprise in idealized markets would be unable to deter socially wasteful duplicative entry, and, further, no industry structure producing the desirable set of products or services would be stable in the face of frictionless entry.[6] Thus, in general, the unsustainability of an enterprise is not proof that it is socially inefficient. And, in general, idealized markets do not guarantee a socially efficient outcome.

For example, consider a natural monopoly enterprise marketing two socially desirable services that are close but imperfect substitutes in demand and that each has product-line-specific increasing returns to scale.[7] Suppose that to maintain an efficient scale of production of each service the monopolist must keep the two demands in balance by setting the two prices at comparable levels. In such a case, the natural monopoly may be vulnerable to uninnovative competitive entry. An entrant may anticipate positive profit from ignoring one of the services, offering the other at a low price, and enjoying the small unit costs achieved by large-scale specialization. Here, the natural monopoly is unsustainable, and no industry structure offering the socially desirable set of services can be stable in idealized markets.

Such an unfortunate scenario is the more likely the stronger the substitution relationships among the enterprise's demands, the weaker the complementarities in production between the outputs, and the greater the product-line-specific returns to scale. These are the elements of the above example that caused frictionless entry to result in social

---

[5] This surprising fact was discovered by Faulhaber and documented in his "Cross-Subsidization."

[6] See Panzar and Willig, "Sustainability."

[7] Examples with this structure were first uncovered in Panzar and Willig, "Sustainability," and are more fully explicated in Willig, "Market Structure."

inefficiency. When these elements are absent, idealized markets have considerable power to effect socially desirable allocations.

The Weak Invisible Hand. Under a set of conditions on the production technology and on market demands, the "weak invisible hand theorem" describes how idealized markets guide a natural monopoly enterprise to a socially (Ramsey) optimal allocation of resources.[8] Given these conditions, sustainable prices for the natural monopolist do exist. Then, presuming that the enterprise in idealized markets has the incentive to survive, it could and would operate in a sustainable manner. Without any overall subsidy, the enterprise would produce cost efficiently, would price without cross-subsidization, and would set rates that make entry by duplicative competitors unprofitable. In short, under the pressure of frictionless potential entry, the unsubsidized natural monopolist would have both the ability and the incentive to solve problems 1–4.

The invisible hand provides yet more guidance for a natural monopoly enterprise. The aforementioned conditions guarantee the sustainability of the set of service offerings, product designs, and prices that are socially optimal under the constraint that the enterprise's sales revenues cover its production costs.[9] (Such constrained social optimality is termed "Ramsey optimality.")[10]

Further, the enterprise can check its prices for Ramsey optimality by making use of economic information (marginal costs and demand elasticities) that pertains only to its current point of operation.[11] While prices and offerings that are not Ramsey optimal may be sustainable, they cannot be so verified without global information on demands and costs at all possible points of operation. Thus, the only way that the enterprise can assure itself with current information of its sustainability is to operate at the Ramsey optimum.

In this case, a natural monopoly in idealized markets has the survival incentive to set socially optimal prices for the socially optimal set of services and product designs. The same invisible hand that forces Adam Smith's perfectly competitive firms, small in their markets, to socially optimal operation also guides a natural monopoly enterprise to

---

[8] This section is based on Baumol, Bailey, and Willig, "Invisible Hand."

[9] The concept of social optimality utilized here is essentially the maximization of the total of consumer's and producer's surpluses. In particular, this concept ignores the distribution of real benefits and costs among economic agents.

[10] The nomenclature honors Frank P. Ramsey, who was the first to study such optimality, in his "Contribution to the Theory of Taxation," *Economic Journal,* vol. 37 (March 1927), pp. 47–61.

[11] For examples of this technique, see Robert Willig and Elizabeth Bailey, "The Economic Gradient Method," *American Economic Review,* vol. 69 (May 1979).

Ramsey optimality. Consequently, under the conditions of the weak invisible hand theorem, idealized markets not only control problems 1–4, they also offer incentives to a natural monopolist to control problem 5: arbitrary and socially inefficient rates.

The sustainable Ramsey-optimal prices will typically have features that are often viewed with discomfort. The Ramsey price structure will generally assign different rates to service categories and groups of customers that have different marginal costs or different elasticities of demand. Because they minimize the allocative distortion caused by the break-even constraint, the Ramsey prices obtain the larger contributions to overhead and common costs from the lower elasticity of demand consumers—those who can less easily escape.

These are the same features exhibited by prices that maximize the excess profit of a monopolist who is unconstrained by regulation and who has a market position that is protected from competitive entry. It is for this reason, I conjecture, that such a "discriminatory" and "exploitative" rate structure is viewed as undesirable. Yet, for an unsubsidized natural monopoly, which is constrained by either frictionless potential entry or by overall profit constraint, such a pattern of prices is best for consumers in the aggregate. Of course, profit-maximizing prices are generally higher than Ramsey-optimal prices. However, both sets of prices have the same pattern, and both fall into the same rate structure.

If the rate-structural flexibility that is required for Ramsey optimality is prohibited to a natural monopoly enterprise, then sustainability may be impossible. In such circumstances, the enterprise may require subsidies or legal protection to stem duplicative and wasteful competitive entry. The weak invisible hand theorem assures that idealized markets control problems 1–5 only if no constraints are placed on the monopoly's rate structure.

The weak invisible hand theorem derives its powerful conclusions from a group of primarily technical assumptions together with two substantive conditions on the production technology. The first of these is globally increasing returns to the entire scale of the enterprise. This means, for example, that if all outputs were increased by 10 percent total (efficient) production costs would rise by less than 10 percent.

The second substantive condition is called transray convexity of production costs. It essentially requires that the economies of scope (that is, the cost saving from joint production of the enterprise's services as compared with their separate production by specialty firms) be stronger than any economies arising from the scale of each of the individual services. Transray convexity is more likely, the larger is the proportion of total cost common to many services and the less important are setup costs specific to subgroups of services.

145

Both overall increasing returns to scale and transray convexity are features of production technologies that can be tested by means of econometric cost studies and by engineering simulations.[12] If the conditions were found to hold, then the weak invisible hand theorem would support the conclusion that idealized markets can control problems 1–5.

New Technologies and Services

Sustainability Theory Extended. In principle, the theory of sustainability can be extended to cover innovations in services, product offerings, and production techniques. As defined and discussed above, sustainability is the ability to deter uninnovative entrants. However, a sustainable natural monopoly may be vulnerable, and perhaps should be vulnerable, to entry by firms with valuable innovations.

In this dynamic setting, new questions arise, such as whether innovators capture the entire market; whether their production facilities entirely supplant the old; whether the incumbent goes into bankruptcy and thereby transfers plant to new owners; whether the incumbent itself adopts innovations; and whether the incumbent devalues its capital equipment, lowers prices, and thereby deters innovative entry.

An analytic approach that is relevant to idealized markets obviates answering questions at that level of detail so as to study more clearly the social efficiency of innovation adoption. This approach ignores the identities of firms and instead focuses on the cost-efficient technology of the entire industry. Consider an industry that includes potential entrants with new production techniques together with an incumbent owning nonfungible capital that embodies old techniques. The cost-efficient industry technology may utilize only the new techniques, or it may utilize only the old equipment whose costs are sunk, or it may call for the utilization of a mixture of the two.

In any case, an industry can be sustainable in idealized markets only if it utilizes the cost-efficient-industry technology, regardless of the institutions that support that utilization. If cost efficiency requires a natural monopoly producing with both new techniques and old nonfungible plant, then sustainability requires that this production structure come about. It is irrelevant from this frictionless viewpoint whether it comes about through the bankruptcy sale of the incumbent's plant to an entrant, through the merger of the incumbent and an entrant, or through the incumbent's purchase of the rights to the new techniques.

Innovations in product design and in service offerings can be viewed

---

[12] For example, see William Baumol and Yale Braunstein, "Empirical Study of Scale Economies and Production Complementarity: The Case of Journal Publication," *Journal of Political Economy*, vol. 85 (October 1977), pp. 1037–49.

in the same way—whether they arise alone or in combination with advances in production technique. All these possibilities can be analyzed together in the context of idealized markets by focusing on the industry technology. This is defined as the collection of techniques and resource utilizations that is cost efficient for the industry, given the set of output quantities to be produced.

Essentially all the material presented in the previous section applies to the broadened concept of industry technology. In particular, the weak invisible hand theorem has yet more powerful conclusions in a dynamic setting. If the entire temporal sequence of industry technologies exhibits overall scale economies and transray convexity, then the industry is an intertemporal natural monopoly. Further, sustainability and survival of the enterprise in idealized markets require that production innovations be adopted at the socially efficient times. Moreover, idealized markets give the enterprise a survival incentive to price and to offer new services and products in accordance with Ramsey optimality.

Unreliable Market Control of Product Innovation. The unsustainability results given earlier also apply in the extended dynamic framework, and here they seem particularly germane to the introduction of new products and services. In particular, when the industry technology encompasses the possibility of developing and producing new goods, it may not exhibit the transray convexity condition that underlies the weak invisible hand theorem.

The stronger are product-line-specific economies of scale in the development and production of a new good, the less likely is transray convexity to be exhibited by the new industry technology. Here, transray convexity can be saved by strong economies of scope between the existing set of products and the new good. Such scope economies would mean that the development and production of the new good by the enterprise already producing the industry's other goods are less costly than would be the introduction of the new good by any other firm. However, if such economies of scope were weak, and if there were significant setup costs to introducing the new good, then transray convexity would be problematic.

In such a case, the conclusions of the weak invisible hand theorem would not be assured, and idealized markets would not necessarily exercise reliable control of problems 1–6. In particular, if innovations were to expand the set of goods and services that could be feasibly produced, the new industry technology over the new set of products would not necessarily be sustainable.

With such unsustainability, any industry structure that marketed the socially optimal set of products would be unstable. Then it could be the case that the incumbent firms would have incentives to avoid introducing socially desirable new products and, further, would have incentives to deter the entry of other firms who would offer the new products themselves. On the other hand, with an unsustainable new industry technology, it could also be the case that new products would unavoidably drive socially desirable old ones out of idealized markets. Or, less extremely, the profitable introduction of new products could drive up the prices of existing ones to the point where the injury to consumers of the preexisting goods outweighs the benefit to those who prefer the new ones.

For an archetypal example, consider this scenario: An existing good is produced with strongly increasing returns to scale, so that the average cost of production rises rapidly as the quantity produced decreases. The price of this good is always equated to average cost, reflecting Ramsey optimality and zero excess profit. A new product is invented that, when priced just above its average cost, is preferred by a small amount to the old one by half the consumers. The other half of the consumers have a strong preference for the preexisting product.

In this scenario, the introduction of the new product would be profitable to an entering firm. Half the consumers would gain small benefits from switching to the new product, enabling the entrant to cover its costs with a small positive margin of profit. As a consequence, however, the other half of the consumers would face a much-increased price for the preexisting product. This price must rise significantly to cover the higher average cost caused by the smaller scale of production mandated by the smaller demand. Thus, in this scenario, the introduction of the new product would appreciably harm those who prefer the preexisting good. Yet, the new product's introduction would yield only small benefit to its consumers and only small profit to its producer. On balance, the harm would exceed the gain, and the innovation's implementation would be socially undesirable. Nonetheless, idealized markets would give entrants a profit incentive to produce and market the new good.

In a somewhat more extreme version of this scenario, the reduction of the market for the preexisting good would drive up average costs to the point where no consumer would be willing to pay a price large enough to compensate the producer for those costs. Here, the old good would be driven from idealized markets, causing potentially unlimited harm to those who prefer it. Yet, the direct social benefit from the introduction of the new good may be quite small. Consequently, idealized markets may cause new goods to displace old ones with concomitant net social losses.

The obverse of these scenarios is possible also. If the development and production of a new good would incur significant fixed setup costs, then the profitable marketing of the good might require significant market penetration. Such widespread switching of consumers from existing products may not occur because of the large production scales, low average costs, and low prices of the old goods. Also, an appreciable fraction of consumers may have a small preference for the old over the new good. Of course, this would make profitable introduction of the new product even more difficult. Yet, it could simultaneously be the case that many other consumers would realize unlimited benefits from the market availability of the innovative good. Here, idealized markets could fail to effect a socially desirable product innovation.

Thus, we are left with the possibility that idealized markets exercise socially unreliable control over problem 6. The extended theory of sustainability has identified two features of the industry technology that are critical to assessing the extent of this market failure. It is likely to be more serious the greater the economies of scale in each product line and the weaker the economies of scope between the old and new products. Moreover, the earlier examples and discussion of unsustainability indicate that, in the absence of transray convexity of industry costs, the closer the demand substitutability of old and new products, the less reliably would markets guide new product introductions.

Directions of Remedy. A related, but different, view of this potential market failure suggests measures that would enhance the social reliability of market control over product introductions. This view focuses on the inability of simple prices that are unequal to marginal costs to reliably signal the intensity of consumers' preferences for products and services.[13] The consequent directions of remedy involve utilizing more complex systems of prices, such as multipart prices, nonlinear outlay schedules, and unbundled rates, to better align social evaluations of product offerings with producers' evaluations of their profitabilities.

This viewpoint can be understood in the context of the archetypal scenarios discussed above. In each case some of the decisions made by entrepreneurs on product offerings lowered the total social value (value to consumers plus profits) of the set of goods marketed. For example, when a new product undesirably drives an old one out of the market, the product introduction causes the social loss of the large value of the old good to those who prefer it intensely, while causing a relatively small social gain to those who weakly prefer the new one. However, if the intensity of consumers' preferences could be more completely reflected in market revenues available to a producer, then the new product would not displace the old one. Instead, the social desirability

---

[13] See A. M. Spence, "Product Selection, Fixed Costs, and Monopolistic Competition," *Review of Economic Studies*, vol. 43 (June 1976), pp. 217–35.

of the old product would mean that its value to consumers exceeded its production cost; hence, producer revenues could cover production cost, and the old good as well as the new one would be offered in idealized markets.

There is a basic reason why market revenues can fail to reflect the intensity of consumer preferences under a simple price system. When faced with a simple price, a consumer has the incentive to purchase enough that the least valuable unit purchased has a value about equal to the price. (Equivalently, the most valuable unit not purchased has a value to the consumer below the price.) Consequently, the price does not reflect the value to a consumer of the more valuable inframarginal units that he purchases and consumes. The total value to a consumer of all the units he purchases is thus greater than the total amount he pays under a simple price system. The net value of the availability of a product, over and above the amount paid, is called the "consumer's surplus."[14] As compared with the unavailability of a good, a consumer's opportunity to purchase all that is desired at the market price is worth an amount equal to the consumer's surplus.

Thus, it is consumer's surplus that reflects the intensity of preferences for a good. But consumer's surplus is not fully reflected in purchasing decisions at market levels of simple prices. For example, two consumers may demand the same quantities at a particular market price and yet have very different evaluations of their inframarginal units. Then, they would have very different levels of consumer's surplus, while expending equal amounts and yielding equal revenues to a vendor in the market. Consequently, a vendor who utilizes a simple price system does not have the incentive (or, perhaps, the information) to respond to intensities of preferences for products.

At the other extreme are hypothetical vendors who could garner the entire consumer's surplus as revenue. Because their incremental profit from each product would equal the incremental social value, their profit-maximizing decisions would perfectly reflect intensities of preferences and would maximize social value.[15] However, such a situation would undoubtedly yield an undesirable distribution of benefits between vendors and consumers. Further, such vendors would require impossibly detailed information about each of their consumers. Nevertheless, this hypothetical case is useful to pursue for the lessons it offers about more realistic pricing mechanisms.

To convert the entire consumer's surplus into revenue, a vendor

---

[14] This discussion glosses over several technical complexities that are treated in Robert Willig, "Consumer's Surplus without Apology," *American Economic Review*, vol. 66 (September 1976), pp. 589–98.

[15] See Spence, "Product Selection."

would have to follow one of two approaches. He could require that each individual pay a personalized fee (set equal to that person's consumer's surplus) for the right to purchase at the going price. Or he could require a different price for each unit purchased and tailor such a special price schedule to each consumer's preferences.

These hypothetical approaches have counterpart pricing mechanisms that are practical, that are free of undesirable distributive consequences, and that permit market revenues to reflect preference intensities more closely than would a simple price system. The most familiar of these mechanisms is a two-part tariff system under which each consumer is required to pay the same entry fee (the first part) for the right to purchase at the going price (the second part).[16] Because the entry fee is standardized for all consumers, a two-part tariff does not enable a vendor to garner all the consumer's surplus. Yet, the entry fee does permit the conversion of some consumer's surplus into vendor revenue. Moreover, regulation or the pressure of frictionless entry in idealized markets can control the levels of a two-part tariff so that they would not earn vendors excess profits.

Practical pricing mechanisms more complex than two-part tariffs can enable market revenues to track consumer's surplus even more closely. One such system, self-selecting two-part tariffs, offers consumers a choice among pairs of entry fee/consumption price combinations.[17] A rather general system faces consumers with an outlay schedule that lists the different outlays required for the purchase of different quantities of the good.[18] The power of each of these mechanisms can be further enhanced by offering different rates, or outlay schedules, to different groups of consumers, provided that the groups can be readily distinguished and that they are known to have differing intensities of preference.

Thus, the more flexible the pricing system, or the more finely the system can sort consumers by their intensities of preference, or the more fully the system permits consumer's surplus to be converted to vendor revenues, the more socially reliable will be the control of product and service offerings by idealized markets. The frictionless entry that characterizes idealized markets ensures that firms utilizing such pricing mechanisms cannot earn excess profits by so doing. It was noted earlier

---

[16] For a recent treatment, see Hayne Leland and Robert Meyer, "Monopoly Pricing Structures with Imperfect Discrimination," *Bell Journal of Economics*, vol. 7 (Autumn 1976), pp. 449–62.

[17] See Gerald Faulhaber and John Panzar, "Optimal Two-Part Tariffs with Self-Selection," Bell Laboratories Economics Discussion Paper (Murray Hill, N.J., 1976).

[18] See Robert Willig, "Pareto-Superior Non-Linear Outlay Schedules," *Bell Journal of Economics*, vol. 9 (Spring 1978), pp. 56–69.

that structural features of industry technologies and demands tend to make market control of product selection unreliable, when simple price systems are utilized. Here, we have seen that in such cases more flexible pricing mechanisms can be at least partial remedies that better enable markets to control problem 6.

Special Social Aims of Pricing

Many regulated prices are consciously kept relatively low to further special social aims.[19] Some well-known examples of such pairings of price categories and social goals are second-class postal services and the dissemination of information, first- and second-class postal services and rural communications, telephone basic monthly charges and universal telephone service, and commuter rail fares and urban environmental quality. Familiar and cogent arguments can support a specially low price for a good or service when its purchase brings diffuse benefits to others.[20] Such benefits are called "externalities" to emphasize that they accrue to people or to firms outside the locus of the purchasing decision.

It should be immediately clear that idealized markets cannot, in themselves, substitute for regulation in furthering special social aims of pricing because externalities, by definition, are not reflected in the market. An unregulated firm is given no incentive by its economic markets to encourage the purchase of a good that happens to yield benefits to people other than the purchaser. Even the weak invisible hand operates only through the market interface between the firm and its customers and must, therefore, be uninfluenced by externalities.

Further, without government intervention, the operation of idealized markets conflicts with the furthering of special social aims through market prices. A market price that is kept relatively low to reflect beneficial externalities would cause a cross-subsidy if it were below the marginal cost or below the average incremental cost of the product or service. And, as noted, such an internal cross-subsidy prevents an enterprise from being sustainable. In idealized markets, an internal cross-subsidy makes uninnovative entry appear profitable to an entrepreneur planning to replicate some of the incumbent's offerings, while refusing to compete for the cross-subsidized goods or services. Of course, not only would such entry wastefully raise total industry costs; it would also make infeasible the continuation of the purposeful cross-subsidy.

---

[19] In fact, it has been argued that this may often be the principal motivation for regulation. See Richard A. Posner, "Taxation by Regulation," *Bell Journal of Economics,* vol. 2 (Spring 1971), pp. 22–50.

[20] See Peter Diamond, "Consumption Externalities and Imperfect Corrective Pricing," *Bell Journal of Economics,* vol. 4 (Autumn 1973), pp. 526–38.

Even if a price to further a special social goal were not so low as to be exceeded by marginal or average incremental cost, it could still cause unsustainability. The conditions of the weak invisible hand theorem assure the sustainability of only the prices that are Ramsey optimal from the viewpoint of the purchasers of the enterprise's products. In contrast, prices that optimally reflect externalities (given the profit constraint) may not be invulnerable to duplicating entry. And the market signals that can guide an enterprise to the sustainable Ramsey-optimal set of prices provide no guidance on the sustainability or unsustainability of prices that attempt to correct for externalities.

Thus, idealized markets cannot, in themselves, provide intentional cross-subsidies to further special social goals. Nor can market forces lead an enterprise to prices that would reflect the values of the goods and services to those other than the purchasers.

On the other hand, appropriate government intervention could, in principle, achieve the desired low levels of selected prices without impeding the operation of idealized markets. The crucial criterion is that the intervention affect in an equal manner the opportunities of all firms, both incumbents and potential entrants alike. Only then would market incentives for entry, and the concomitant market control over incumbents, be left undistorted.

For example, consider a subsidy payment that is offered by the government to any firm, on the basis of the quantity of a particular good or service that the firm is able to sell. Suppose that the subsidy funds are raised by excise taxes levied on the sales of some other of the industry's products, again regardless of the identity of the firm making the sale. Such a system of taxes and subsidies can duplicate the effects of intentional, internal cross-subsidies and can cause consumers' prices of selected goods to be especially low. Yet, because the subsidies and taxes affect all firms indiscriminately, they do not impede the operation of idealized markets the way internal cross-subsidies do.

Recall that internally cross-subsidizing products are priced so that revenues exceed stand-alone cost. Consequently, an entrant would be able to undercut these prices and operate profitably, even if he were somewhat less efficient than the incumbent. However, when the cross-subsidy is not internal but is instead evenhandedly enforced by excise taxes on all vendors of the subsidizing goods, then this source of inefficient advantage to entrants is eliminated.

Obversely, internally cross-subsidized products are priced so that revenues fall short of incremental cost. Consequently, an entrant would be unable to meet these prices profitably, even if his total cost were somewhat below the incremental cost of the incumbent. Were the subsidy offered evenhandedly to any firm, instead of internally to the incumbent firm, then this source of inefficient advantage to the incumbent would be eliminated. Thus, in principle, explicit subsidies and taxes that are tied to particular goods or services, regardless of the vending firm, can succeed in causing prices to reflect special social aims, while they permit idealized markets to operate unimpeded.

Nonetheless, there do seem to be some endemic problems with this approach. Entrants would have incentive to claim that their goods, although differentiated, are enough like those of the incumbent that are subsidized to themselves warrant subsidization. And they would also have incentives to attempt to avoid the excise taxes with claims that their products are sufficiently different from those of the incumbent that are taxed. Incentives aside, new product varieties with varying degrees of similarity to the incumbent's goods may well arise and therefore require assessment as to eligibility for taxes or subsidies. Consequently, such a system would require that some government body decide questions of product or service definition and degree of differentiation. These necessarily arbitrary nonmarket decisions would potentially determine the fates of new product varieties, of old offerings of the incumbent, and of the entering firms themselves.

This problem with a system of explicit taxes and subsidies would be the more serious, the more complex the system and the subtler the distinctions among products or services that receive different treatments. Surely, only very simple systems that rest on extremely clear product definitions could be implemented without the needed nonmarket decision making becoming more controlling of overall outcomes than the economic market itself.

To summarize, then, in the absence of government intervention, there are conflicts between the operations of idealized markets and the furthering of special social aims through market prices. In principle, such conflicts could be avoided with government intervention that was evenhanded in its effects on incumbent firms and on potential entrants. In a dynamic environment, however, there is a danger that such government intervention would require frequent nonmarket decisions that would prove to have more influence over industry performance than the operation of the idealized markets themselves.

Frictions and Economic Entry Barriers

Actual economic markets may be quite different from the idealized markets that have provided the abstract centerpiece of this analysis. Idealized markets provide useful benchmarks for policy analysis only to the extent that their properties are approximated by the essential features of the markets of the industry in question. In particular, frictionless free entry is the crucial property of idealized markets that is most likely to be at variance with reality.

The more important are frictions and entry barriers, the less able is the discipline of potential entry to control the performance of an incumbent enterprise. To trace most clearly the implications of frictions and entry barriers, suppose that their full effect can be represented by entry costs that must be borne by any entrant but that were not incurred by the incumbents.[21] Then, potential entry limits the profit of an incumbent to the level of the entry costs. With frictionless free entry, those costs are zero so that, as discussed earlier, idealized markets control profits to normal levels. However, markets with entry barriers would not generally control profits so tightly and instead would only assure that the profit of an incumbent not exceed entry costs.

A profit-maximizing firm in such a market would attempt to capture the full entry costs as profit or rent. In so doing, it would have profit incentives to operate cost efficiently, to avoid cross-subsidization, and to set prices that deter entry. Further, under the conditions of the weak invisible hand theorem, the firm would have incentives to establish the prices and product offerings that are Ramsey optimal—given the maximal level of profit permitted by the entry barriers. Thus, even in the absence of idealized markets, potential entry does exercise some beneficial control over firms, provided that they are devoted to profit maximization. However, the larger the entry costs, the greater are the excess profits of such incumbents, the higher is the level of industry prices, and the lower are both consumer and total welfare.

Moreover, entry barriers permit incumbent firms discretionary behavior and the choice to forgo profit maximization. As such, incumbents could operate with cost inefficiencies up to the level of entry costs without necessarily provoking competitive entry. Similarly, a firm could cross-subsidize while remaining invulnerable to entry by holding the shortfall between revenues and incremental cost below the associated entry cost. Also, a firm's rate structure can deviate from Ramsey optimality. As noted above, none of these behavioral patterns is consistent with profit maximization. Nevertheless, entry barriers allow firms the freedom to adopt such patterns. In contrast, since they offer at most zero profit, idealized markets force firms to maximize profit in order to survive. By so doing, idealized markets control firms to cost efficiency, to the avoidance of cross-subsidy, and to the solutions of many facets of problems 1–6.

Thus, the effectiveness of the control on firm performance exercised

---

[21] To my knowledge, this analytic approach was first employed in Baumol, Bailey, and Willig, "Invisible Hand." Many of the results stated below are proven there.

by potential entry is inversely related to the size of the entry costs, where these serve as a useful measure of the importance of frictions and entry barriers. Therefore, it is important to have an understanding of the structural features of industries that determine the size of entry costs. Of course, a large part of the economics literature on industrial organization has been addressed to the subjects of entry barriers, their causes, their measurement (by proxies), and their correlates. [22] Hence, I will limit myself here to selected cursory remarks.

In my view, the principal barriers to entry (other than legal restrictions) can be ascribed to the risk perceived by potential entrants of losing nonrecoverable costs that they would have to incur in order to enter. Then, what I have been calling entry cost is the certain dollar flow equivalent to the difference between the potential entrant's perceived risk and the risk already accepted by the incumbent. The former may be larger than the latter simply because the entrant knows that competition with the incumbent is inevitable, while the incumbent may have enjoyed a less competitive environment and may have discounted the possibility of later competitive encroachment.

In any case, it is clear that entry barriers are lower and entry costs are smaller, the smaller the nonrecoverable start-up costs. Some of the major categories of start-up costs are associated with litigation, marketing, and the establishment of production facilities. Litigation may be required for entry into an industry because of government regulation, patented technologies, or a host of other reasons. Such litigation would cause a potential entrant to incur direct costs, and indirect costs from the concomitant delays, that would be nonrecoverable; that is, they would be entirely lost if the entrant later decided to exit because of the unprofitability of continued operation. Similarly, advertising and other marketing investments would retain no value for a firm that entered and then exited an industry. Faced with the possibility of such losses, a potential entrant would need better prospects than otherwise to attempt entry at all. Consequently, the need for such nonrecoverable start-up costs is an entry barrier.

The establishment of production capability may or may not require that significant nonrecoverable start-up costs be incurred. If needed capital facilities were fungible, with high value in other uses by the entrant, or with high resale value, then setup production costs would be largely recoverable and would thus be little barrier to entry. If the

---

[22] For particularly insightful treatments, see Joe Bain, *Barriers to New Competition* (Cambridge, Mass: Harvard University Press, 1965); F. M. Scherer, *Industrial Market Structure and Economic Performance* (Chicago: Rand McNally, 1971); and R. E. Caves and M. E. Porter, "From Entry Barriers to Mobility Barriers," *Quarterly Journal of Economics,* vol. 91 (May 1977), pp. 241–62.

start-up costs are for labor or for other services on a flow basis, then, although they may be appreciable, they need not be a barrier to entry inasmuch as their flow can be halted with the cessation of production. Hence, production technologies with economies of scale, fixed costs, or setup costs need not present entry barriers unless significant expenditures must be undertaken prior to production that are not recoverable if production is ceased.

Thus, to summarize, frictions and entry barriers are the principal reasons why actual markets need not exercise the strong control over the performance of incumbent firms that theory suggests would be exercised by idealized markets. A useful conceptual indication of the laxness of control is the level of entry cost. This can be defined as the certain dollar flow equivalent to the difference between the potential entrant's perceived risk and the risk already borne by the incumbents. Such entry cost is larger, the more the potential entrant fears competitive responses from the incumbents and the greater are the nonrecoverable start-up costs. Where entry costs are sufficiently low, actual markets can be expected to provide the control that the analysis has ascribed to idealized markets.

What Can Markets Control?

The preceding analyses have been attempts at assessing the abilities of markets to control the generic problem areas that were listed at the start of this paper. The basic question—What can markets control?— has been reduced to a series of narrower questions about the industrial structure by means of logical propositions that connect various structural features to the elements of market control. Most of these propositions focus on the properties of idealized markets. The analysis in the preceding section indicated that entry barriers limit both the applicability of these results and the power of markets to control performance. Consequently, an investigation of whether markets can control postal services, or any particular industry, naturally begins with questions concerning entry barriers.

Without such legal restrictions as those contained in the private express statutes, would there be important barriers to entry into markets for postal services? This narrower version of the question is suggested by the preceding discussion: Would the provision of postal services require significant nonrecoverable start-up costs? One approach to answering these questions would be to study the private delivery firms that have been entering second-class mail markets. A simpler (and too glib) approach would be to argue that since payroll constitutes a large portion of postal costs, nonrecoverable capital costs must not be significant for an entrant. Alternatively, one could cite the argument of Charles Jackson (Chapter 7 herein) that the capital equipment required for electronic mail will soon be widely in place for reasons other than the provision of postallike services.

In any case, my purpose here is not to attempt to answer these questions, and those that follow, but rather to identify some of the information that could be brought to bear on the issue of whether to leave postal services to market control. Hence, let us suppose that entry barriers have been found to be sufficiently low to warrant proceeding with analyses based on the benchmark of idealized markets.

Then, as detailed above, incumbent firms that survive the competition from potential entrants would produce the outputs of the industry cost efficiently and would price them without internal cross-subsidization. The important question that must be raised here is whether society is willing to accept the end of long-entrenched postal cross-subsidies. Systematic cross-subsidies need not impede the operations of free markets, as long as the subsidies and taxes are offered and levied evenhandedly by government agencies. It seems plausible, however, that such intervention could dominate market forces if the bureaucratic apparatus were charged with maintaining networks of cross-subsidies as pervasive and complex as those embedded in current postal prices. One might conclude that markets can control the postal industry only if society is willing to face rates that for most postal services, locations, routes, and other categories cover the associated incremental costs.

Even with such subsidy-free rates, open postal markets can be assured to provide the traditional set of services stably and efficiently only if sustainable prices exist. Unsustainability is unlikely unless there are some services with significant product-line-specific returns to scale that are close substitutes in demand. Whether or not these potentially troublesome conditions obtain is a question that can be investigated with either casual empiricism or formal demand and cost studies.

If cost studies indicate that postal services can be efficiently produced with overall scale economies, with strong economies of scope, and with relatively insignificant returns to the scale of each product line, then it is likely that the weak invisible hand theorem would pertain. It could be inferred that free markets would reliably control the performance of the natural monopoly producer of postal services and would provide private incentives for socially optimal prices and service offerings.

The most serious challenges to market control are presented by technological advances and product innovations like those associated with electronic mail. Although free markets are probably most conducive to dynamic progressivity, they may not reliably channel advances along socially efficient paths. When innovative services are substitutes for traditional ones, their profitable introduction might be unprofitable. Such inefficiencies are more likely, the greater the returns to scale in providing the new services and the weaker the economies of scope between the new and old services. These criteria identify important questions about the new communications technologies and their relationships to the traditional ones.

If the answers to these questions indicate that forthcoming communications innovations are likely to cause appreciable social inefficiencies, then the remedies presented here should be seriously considered. They involve a rate structure that is far more flexible, more differentiated, and more discriminating among consumers than the traditional structure of postal rates. Such patterns of rates could increase static consumer welfare as well as ameliorate dynamic inefficiencies. Under the conditions of the weak invisible hand theorem and with complete rate freedom, the vendor of postal services would be provided with incentives to implement such a price structure by idealized markets.

Hence, the last of the questions emerges: Would society be willing to grant complete rate freedom to firms in open markets for postal services? The analysis has indicated that only then could markets reach their full potential for the control, as well as the stimulation, of technological change. And only then could markets control all the postal problem areas listed at the start of this paper.

Commentary

Leland L. Johnson

In delineating the limits of socially desirable competition, Robert Willig
draws implications from the sustainability literature for the future development and operation of electronic message services. In my mind,
his paper raises the basic question: How useful is the sustainability
literature to policy decision making? It is to this question that I will
direct my comments.

This literature provides an interesting theoretical construct of the
effects of competition in the presence of natural monopoly and is useful
in posing questions about economic efficiency that policy makers should
confront. But the underlying assumptions are too heroic to permit us
to take the literature seriously in today's policy deliberations. In de-
fending this view, let us recapitulate very briefly Willig's argument.
First, he postulates the presence of an incumbent, like the Postal Service, with economies of scope where joint production of multiple services
involves a lower total cost than that arising from separate production
of each service. He assumes the incumbent firm to operate at minimum
cost for any given output. Thus, it enjoys perfect management, it suffers
no X-inefficiency, and, presumably, it undertakes the optimal rate of
technological innovation.

Second, Willig postulates the entrance of competitors with a new
technology, in this case electronic message service (EMS), with the
following characteristics: (1) economies of scale reflecting high start-up
costs for the new service; (2) weak economies of scope between this
new service and existing postal services reflecting new and unique production input requirements; and (3) strong cross-elasticities of demand
between the new and old services. Given these conditions, Willig suggests that wasteful competition could arise between EMS and conventional postal services. According to the sustainability literature,
competitors supplying EMS might survive in competition with the incumbent firm even though their costs are higher than those that would
be incurred by the incumbent.

160

The problem is, of course, that the sustainability literature assumes away all possibilities of competition spurring more efficient behavior by the incumbent firm, or stimulating innovation and the introduction of new services, or improving management effectiveness. Because the fundamental potential advantages of a competitive environment are not taken into account, within the confines of the literature, one can easily conclude that competitive entry of electronic services may lead to economic waste.

The situation described by Willig is reminiscent of the competitive positions of basic telephone service and postal service, in terms of both service characteristics and the public policy issues involved. To illustrate, let us suppose that we were discussing these same kinds of issue soon after World War I, on the heels of the tumultuous early history of the telephone's development. What would the sustainability literature have told us at that time? Willig's description and analysis of electronic message communications vis-à-vis the Postal Service is remarkably similar to what he might have described at that earlier time. Then, too, telephone service was highly cross-elastic with postal service. Indeed, the inroad made by telephone service over the subsequent decades on first-class mail has contributed heavily to the financial plight of the Postal Service. Moreover, as in the case of electronic message services, telephone service shows weak economies of scope with respect to postal service since rather little cost would be saved by combining the two. Finally, telephone service, like electronic message services, would have economies of scale reflecting substantial start-up costs. Thus, for the same reason that Willig suggests that competition might lead us in the wrong direction with respect to postal and electronic services, we might also have concluded on the basis of sustainability literature fifty or sixty years ago that the telephone industry itself should be integrated with the postal service. Indeed, many countries have adopted this solution. Although we cannot say for sure what would have happened had the United States moved in that direction fifty or sixty years ago, I, for one, would have misgivings.

In conclusion, I find the sustainability literature challenging as a new thrust in microeconomic theory dealing with issues that raise important relationships among firms, some of which have monopoly markets and others of which do not. But to make this analysis relevant to policy making would require further substantial development, including relaxation of the perfect-behavior assumptions that underlie the work to date. In particular, a worthwhile elaboration to test sensitivity of results would involve estimating the quantitative degree to which the incumbent firm would need to exhibit X-inefficiency to equalize competitive and monopoly outcomes.

9

The Postal Service and Electronic Communications: Various Legal Issues and Sundry Open Questions

Kenneth Robinson

Youth culture, wood-sided station wagons, and the legal implications of virtually any commercial development are standard and traditional American preoccupations.[1] The U.S. Postal Service is one of our oldest national institutions and uses Jeeps, not station wagons, in conjunction with delivery operations, but its probable diversification into electronics does have the expectable legal implications.

Since at least the early 1960s the Postal Service has been skating on the brink of a calamitous visitation. In the public's imagination, it is a perennial institutional *Titanic*. And it is generally assumed that with the advent of electronic mail services—a generic term used by technological primitives—the days of traditional document delivery services will essentially be ended.

Socially, the potential demise of the Postal Service as we now know it has very serious implications. The organization employs, for example, some 600,000 people; it is one of the largest single work forces in the nation. As postal union leaders correctly point out, these individuals will either work and be paid for certain services performed, whether well or poorly, or they will simply be moved to the transfer payments roster to collect funds as they are retired, are retained, or, in a period of serious general unemployment, await other forms of employment.

The views and opinions expressed by the author, a communications lawyer currently employed by the Antitrust Division of the U.S. Department of Justice in Washington, D.C., should not be construed as reflecting those of the division, the department, or any other federal agency.

[1] See Robert Hargreaves, *Superpower: A Portrait of America in the Seventies* (New York: St. Martin's Press, 1973), p. 429; Eugene S. McCarthy, *America Revisited: 150 Years after Tocqueville* (Garden City, N.J.: Doubleday, 1978), p. 17.

Whether this is "good" or "bad" is somewhat beside the point; one way or another a large number of current postal workers for the perceivable future are going to cost taxpayers a substantial sum of money.

Politically, one of the proposed salvations for the Postal Service—substantial diversification into electronic communications—has other serious implications. The United States is unique among major nations in that our electronic communications systems are now owned and operated primarily by the private sector. Large and very profitable private firms including AT&T appear relatively unconcerned at the prospect of Postal Service diversification, provided it is somehow limited to performing services complementary to their own—the physical delivery of hard-copy messages transmitted electronically, for example. These firms and many government policy makers are concerned, however, by the prospect of any full-line diversification by this "independent federal establishment" into all facets of electronic mail, with all the implications that the catch phrase "nationalized communications system" necessarily entails.[2]

To those not well steeped in postal lore, some background information may be helpful as general context for the legal implications of electronic mail. The U.S. Postal Service, basically, is an "independent establishment" of the federal government, with substantial annual revenues aggregating some $17 billion this year. The Postal Service is a constitutionally sanctioned, labor-intensive, nationwide "record" or "hard-copy" communications system—essentially a large and relatively expensive federal utility.[3]

The Postal Service was legislatively reorganized in 1970, by the same 91st Congress that brought us Amtrak[4] and devised the baroque way federal workers' salaries automatically and annually are raised without any politician appearing to be really responsible.[5] The overriding objective of the 1970 Reorganization Act was to render the Postal

[2] U.S. Congress, House, Committee on Post Office and Civil Service, *Report on H.R. 7700: Postal Reorganization Act Amendments of 1977,* November 1977, pp. 13–14.
[3] See generally U.S. Constitution, Article 1, section 8, clause 7 (House Document no. 92–250, 92d Congress, 2nd session, 1972, p. 6); Postal Reorganization Act of 1970, P.L. 91–375, 84 Stat. 720 (August 12, 1970), 39 *U.S. Code,* sections 101 ff. (1976). See also "The Postal Reorganization Act: A Case Study of Regulated Industry Reform," *Virginia Law Review,* vol. 58 (1972), pp. 1031–70.
[4] Rail Passenger Service Act of 1970, P.L. 91–518, 84 Stat. 1328 (October 30, 1970), 45 *U.S. Code,* sections 501 ff. (1976). See also James C. Miller III, "What's to Be Done about Amtrak?" *Wall Street Journal,* August 25, 1978, p. 8; Edward R. Fried, Alice M. Rivlin, Charles L. Schultze, and Nancy H. Teeters, *Setting National Priorities: The 1974 Budget* (Washington, D.C.: Brookings Institution, 1973), pp. 238 ff.
[5] Federal Pay Comparability Act of 1970, P.L. 91–656, 84 Stat. 1946 (January 8, 1971), 5 *U.S. Code,* section 5305 (1976).

Service independent of partisan politics, and in this regard the act has been remarkably successful. One will rarely find any elected or appointed official, for example, who claims to exercise any control, political or otherwise, over current U.S. Postal Service operations.

Although the Postal Service is technically exempted from partisan direction, it is nonetheless a political undertaking because it employs a large number of well-paid, well-organized people, 550,000 represented effectively by three large AFL-CIO member unions. The Postal Service as operated at present, moreover, disburses substantial annual subsidies to significant elements of the national press. Suburban and rural newspapers—second-class mailers—that do not employ carriers, for example, rely on Postal Service delivery. Major magazines such as *Time* similarly benefit from subsidies both appropriated directly by the Congress and generated internally under current postal rates.

As systems go, the U.S. Postal Service is not cheap. It hypothetically costs the typical American family some $220 annually. This is about half the hypothetical annual "contribution" per family to AT&T's revenues, however. And compared with federal expenditures for MX missile systems or B–1 bombers, for example, the Postal Service receives merely the proverbial drop in the bucket.[6] Moreover, while the Postal Service enjoys a reputation for wild inefficiencies—not necessarily substantiated by the facts—our mail delivery system apparently is genuinely "the best mail service in the world."[7]

From a public relations perspective, the Postal Service has a reputation only slightly better than the Arkansas Department of Prisons. Its operations have been described, probably unfairly, in the words of Dr. Johnson about a "dog walking on his hinder legs—it is not done well; but you are surprised to find it done at all."[8] Nor have the Postal Service's efforts at modernization necessarily captured the public's imagination, at least not in any affirmative sense. The Postal Service, according to the 1970 Reorganization Act's proponents, was supposed to be capable of yielding a $1 billion annual taxpayers' bonus through

---

[6] See generally "Communications," *Standard and Poor's Industry Surveys,* December 29, 1977, p. C–61.

[7] See, for example, U.S. Congress, House, Subcommittee on Postal Service of the Committee on Post Office and Civil Service, *Hearings on H.R. 2445: Postal Reorganization Act Amendments of 1975,* 94th Congress, 1st session, February 1975, p. 100 (testimony of James H. Rademacher, president, National Association of Letter Carriers, AFL-CIO); Letter to Donald M. Frazer from Victor L. Lowe, director, General Government Division, General Accounting Office (ref. B–114874), dated December 11, 1975, reprinted in U.S. Congress, Senate, Committee on Post Office and Civil Service, *Hearings on S. 2844: Postal Amendments,* 94th Congress, 2nd session, January 1976, p. 93.

[8] Austin H. Kiplinger and Knight A. Kiplinger, *Washington Now* (New York: Harper and Row, 1976), p. 508.

adoption of much-touted "modern business methods."[9] Of course, this bonus has not yet materialized.[10] Because the 1970 act was probably oversold as a universal panacea, and postage rates have a direct and immediate impact on the public, this failure to achieve self-sufficiency and a tax saving has attracted attention, despite the fact that other political promises—the post-Vietnam peace dividend, gains from zero-based budgeting and government reorganization, and benefits from deficit-laden full employment budgets, for example—are also yet to be fulfilled.[11]

To a considerable extent, a key to understanding present Postal Service motivations may well be some underlying work-force employment imperative. The 1970 act has been described as schizophrenic. On the one hand, postal management was admonished to "be efficient." On the other, however, stringent employment safeguards were imposed and have been continued in subsequent negotiated contracts. Well over 80 percent of total Postal Service costs reputedly are labor costs and are therefore largely beyond effective management control. As a result, not only is postal management intensely concerned about returning some revenue from the "fixed costs" this work force represents, but it also seems very concerned with assuring that there will be enough demand for its services to keep this substantial work force at least moderately busy.

The Postal Service and Electronic Diversification

The Postal Service's management, some congressional allies, and the well-organized work force appear motivated to push the Postal Service into electronic mail for many of the same reasons another well-known nationwide utility—AT&T—is now diversifying into computers and various data-processing-related activities. In brief, these parallel developments seem to reflect institutional desires to (1) recoup commercial losses in traditional markets occasioned by at least partly self-induced

[9] See Theodore C. Sorensen, "Improper Payments Abroad: Perspectives and Proposals," *Foreign Affairs,* vol. 54 (July 1976), pp. 719–33; James North, "The Economics of Extortion," *Washington Monthly,* vol. 10 (November 1978), pp. 29–34; Arnold A. Rogow, *The Dying of the Light* (New York: G. P. Putnam's Sons, 1975), p. 83.

[10] Kappel Commission Report, quoted in U.S. Government, *Report of the Commission on Postal Service,* vol. 1 (April 1977), p. 1.

[11] See generally Robert H. Hartman, "Multiyear Budget Planning," in *Setting National Priorities: The 1979 Budget,* ed. Joseph A. Pechman (Washington, D.C.: Brookings Institution, 1978), p. 307; Herbert Kaufman, "Reflections on Administrative Reorganization," in *Setting National Priorities: The 1978 Budget,* ed. Joseph A. Pechman (Washington, D.C.: Brookings Institution, 1977), p. 391.

outside competition; (2) participate in the development of very rapidly growing commercial sectors under the umbrella of "the office of the future"; and (3) in this way secure revenues so that AT&T's more than $86 billion in rate-base capital investment and a postal work force of about 600,000 can be financially sustained, indeed well nourished, in the future.

The Postal Service and AT&T's parallel interests and desires are understandable, since both organizations confront analogous competitive predicaments. Both AT&T and the Postal Service, for example, have traditionally concentrated on offering the public broadly standardized or "shelf item" services. These offerings were salable when demand was relatively fungible and easily predictable. Today, however, technology is producing a plethora of goods and services. And this diversification in supply is occurring at the same time that AT&T and Postal Service traditions of administering discriminatory prices are demonstrably driving customer groups to seek out the increasingly available technological alternatives. Price discrimination does not work well when the targets of that discrimination have alternatives available. Both AT&T and Postal Service management are being required to deal with this commercial reality. [12]

Since the 1940s, moreover, economic concentration in the economy generally has steadily increased. This means that, even more than in the past, small, relatively discrete customer groups account for very large chunks of both Postal Service and AT&T revenues. It is difficult to obtain reliable AT&T figures, though perhaps 100 major U.S. corporations account for as much as 40 percent or more of AT&T's business. In the case of the Postal Service, it has been estimated that 86 percent of all revenues derive from about 10 percent of U.S. corporations. [13] When so much of a firm's business is accounted for by so few large and sophisticated customers, relatively small changes in price or service levels can trigger very rapid shifts in firm revenues.

Both AT&T and the Postal Service traditionally have employed variants on "value-of-service" pricing. Often, and particularly in the case of first-class mail (or its telephone-industry equivalent, message toll service), there are substantial differentials between price and actual

---

[12] See, for example, *AT&T Private Line Case*, 65 F.C.C.2d 295 (1977); *National Association of Greeting Card Publishers* v. *U.S. Postal Service*, 569 F.2d 570 (D.C. Cir. 1976).

[13] Konrad K. Kalba, Marvin A. Sirbu, Jr., Ithiel de Sola Pool, and Janet Taplin Thompson, "Electronic Message Systems: The Technological Market and Regulatory Prospects," report prepared for the Federal Communications Commission by Kalba-Bowen Associates and the Center for Policy Alternatives, Massachusetts Institute of Technology, in fulfillment of FCC contract no. 0236 (April 1978), p. 122.

costs of providing service. Major users, perhaps pinched by inflation, have become more sensitive to these differentials, and this sensitivity has been enhanced as electronic technology brings forth cheaper and more cost-effective alternatives. AT&T has found, for example, that its traditional long-distance-service pricing policies and its terminal-equipment leasing charges have been very effective in inducing new competitive entry into both these communications market sectors. The prices the Postal Service charges first-class users for transaction mail—billing and similar commercial traffic—appear to have not only induced private competition from couriers but also contributed to development of alternatives such as electronic fund transfer systems (EFT). [14]

At the same time that the Postal Service and AT&T by relative neglect of their prime customer vineyards have contributed to the emergence of increasingly viable competitors, the American office has become something of the equivalent of a great, new, unexploited commercial frontier. The capital investment per agricultural worker, for instance, ranges around $70,000, more or less. Such investment per manufacturing or similar worker runs in the neighborhood of $20,000 to $50,000, depending on circumstances. By contrast, the capital investment per American office worker is much less—only around $3,000, according to some calculations. As Xerox Corporation radio commercials remind us, most modern-day office environments would be reasonably compatible to any revisiting nineteenth-century scrivener. Rising payroll taxes and worker fringe benefits are making labor dearer. Simultaneously, steady inflation is pressuring corporate management to reduce administrative and operating overhead and ratchet up labor productivity—to get the same or a bigger sales bang for lower production costs.

Computers and electronic communications systems, of course, appear to promise substantial operating efficiencies, and the sales force of the burgeoning electronics industry is pointing out these potential savings to corporate managements. As a consequence, more equipment of greater sophistication is being deployed throughout American offices, especially those of the major firms who represent a significant portion of demand for mail delivery and telephone services. This new equipment—the computerized typewriters, word processors, facsimile machines, and other devices a nineteenth-century scrivener would be amazed to see—often consists of little more than some of the components that can be pieced together to yield an electronic mail system.

---

[14] See generally Donald R. Ewing and Roger K. Salaman, "The Postal Crisis: The Postal Function as a Communications Service," U.S. Department of Commerce, OT Special Publication 77–13 (January 1977), p. 17.

Should the Postal Service Enter?

The computer business and the communications business are both over-whelmingly dominated by monolithic firms—IBM and AT&T. The Postal Service is an obvious candidate for entry into the electronic mail field that essentially bridges these twin monopolized camps. Tradition-ally, with few exceptions, competition policy has favored new entry into highly concentrated commercial fields.

There are many reasons, and reasons with some merit, for barring the Postal Service from entering altogether, not the least being the likely public reaction to any such venture—"From the people who brought you the package-mangling machines, now, electronic mail!"

First, there are certain residual prejudices to any expansion in gov-ernment enterprise, reflected in the perennial debate between investor-owned and consumer-owned electric utilities. In theory at least, the United States relies to the maximum extent possible on the private sector—aided by the investment tax credit and other assists—to satisfy public needs. Second, there is, to the dismay of some academic econ-omists perhaps, an equally prescientific belief held fairly widely that publicly franchised, utilitylike organizations should not be allowed to diversify but should be kept in their "proper" place.

Much of the literature suggests that expansive government enter-prise contributes to the erosion of the entrepreneurial spirit, socialism, and other presumed ills. [15] Less doctrinal objections include the fact that government enterprises result in taxes forgone, contribute to more of our gross national product filtering through a public bureaucracy, result in confused signals to the private sector and investors, and the like. [16]

The question whether the Postal Service should diversify into elec-tronics, and to what extent, is not much different from the question considered by the recent National Commission on Electronic Fund Transfers, one of the more specialized and obscure of recent government study efforts. [17] There the issue was somewhat different—the Federal Reserve System by most measures is one of the most successful of

---

[15] Albert S. Abel, "The Public Corporation in the United States," in *Government Enterprise: A Comparative Study*, ed. W. G. Friedman (New York: Columbia University Press, 1970), p. 181.

[16] See W. A. Robson, "Ministerial Control of the Nationalized Industries," in Friedman, *Government Enterprise*, pp. 79–82.

[17] See Donald Lambro, *The Federal Rathole: How to Save Billions by Abolishing over 1,000 Nonessential Government Agencies, Offices, Bureaus, Boards, Commissions, Coun-cils, Committees, Administrations, and Other Federal Programs* (New Rochelle, N.Y.: Arlington House, 1975), p. 125.

government monopolies. The Federal Reserve currently operates the manual and the heavily computerized paper-check-clearing process that the fabled electronic fund transfers (EFT) systems are supposed to replace. Moreover, in a technical sense the Federal Reserve System is literally "owned" by the nation's leading banks and has some tradition for being responsive to its putative owners' service needs and requirements.

Despite the fact that this government enterprise is highly competent in performing its current tasks, heavily involved in the threshold markets, and traditionally responsive to potential customers, the banks, the EFT commission opted for a policy of at least modified exclusion. The commission argued in this respect that the "premature entry" of the Federal Reserve into EFT "would tend to freeze current technology and stifle incentives for innovation in this rapidly evolving area. Even if the Government operated its . . . facility free of subsidies," the commission asserted, "its very presence would dampen private sector investment and deter entry by new competitors."[18]

These arguments seem ideological, as distinguished from firm or fact-based. Although they are germane to the Postal Service diversification issue, it is not clear that they are dispositive or even persuasive. Many if not most of the basic advances in communications technology since World War II, for example, are the direct result of federal—not private—adventuresomeness and funding (quite apart from the fact that most private research activities might be counted as government since they are financed through tax expenditures). Space satellites, mobile radio systems, and the electronic switching systems developed by Western Electric for Project Safeguard and now being deployed commercially by AT&T are examples of this phenomenon. Indeed, by financing the early efforts of an itinerant West Point graduate turned Capitol mural painter and then electronics fiddler, Samuel F. B. Morse, the Postal Service is in some sense responsible for the birth of electronic communications.

The record of federal underwriting and commercial sponsorship could be much better, and the Postal Service is not literally required to employ standard competitive procurement techniques. Nonetheless, the government does have perhaps a better record than other large bureaucratic operations for fostering, not "chilling," small business innovations in particular. In any technologically intensive environment, more is almost always better, and an argument can be advanced that

---

[18] "EFT in the United States: Policy Recommendations and the Public Interest," *Final Report of the National Commission on Electronic Fund Transfers* (October 1977), p. 216.

a Postal Service electronic mail system would further this desirable objective—not necessarily "stifle innovation" so much as, perhaps, encourage it. [19]

If ideological objections are just that—ideological—one should nevertheless not overlook the strong objections usually advanced to diversification by large, monopolistic utility operations. The current debate surrounding AT&T's diversification into the data-processing business provides ample evidence of those objections. The Rostow task force, now often cited by AT&T for other propositions, concluded that the Bell System companies should be flatly barred from the data-processing business because "the economic strength of a protected market should not be used to gain advantage in tenuously related competitive markets." [20] Other related views and arguments include the opinion that regulated firms ought to eschew diversification and concentrate instead on improving the quality of their existing services; [21] that utility diversification may result in a diversion of resources better employed, again, in improving the quality of franchised offerings; [22] that firms offering basic services should not diversify because then competitors will be in the position of trying to compete with their own wholesale suppliers; [23]

---

[19] The literature suggests, for example, that medium-sized firms with perhaps $200 million in annual sales have higher research and development intensity (R&D as a ratio of sales) than either larger or smaller firms and that industries that have a medium amount of concentration (a four-firm concentration ratio of about 50–55 percent) have higher R&D intensities than industries that are either more or less concentrated. See Arthur D. Little, Inc., "The Relationship between Market Structure and the Innovation Process," report prepared for American Telephone and Telegraph Co., January 1976 (Bell Exhibit no. 52, FCC Docket no. 20003 [*Economic Impact of Competition*]), app. C, "A Survey of the Economic Literature Relating Innovation and Market Structure," p. C-7. See also John K. Galbraith, "The Government vs. Small Business," *Washington Monthly*, vol. 10 (September 1978), pp. 42–46.

[20] *Report of the President's Task Force on Communications Policy* (1968), chap. 6, pp. 30–31.

[21] See, for example, *National Courier Association* v. *Federal Reserve Board*, 516 F.2d 1229, 1232 (D.C. Cir. 1975); *Independent Bankers Association of Georgia* v. *Federal Reserve Board*, 516 F.2d 1206, 1221 (D.C. Cir. 1975); *Martin-Trigona* v. *Federal Reserve Board*, 509 F.2d 362 (D.C. Cir. 1975).

[22] See generally U.S. Congress, House, Subcommittee on Special Investigations of the Committee on Interstate and Foreign Commerce, *Hearings on the Penn-Central Transportation Company: Adequacy of Investor Protection*, 91st Congress, 2nd session, 1970; U.S. Congress, Senate, Committee on Banking and Currency, *Hearings on One-Bank Holding Company Legislation*, 91st Congress, 1st session, 1970, part 1.

[23] See, for example, *National Association of Regulatory Utility Commissioners* v. *Federal Communications Commission*, 525 F.2d 630, 634 (D.C. Cir. 1976); *Authorized Users*, 4 F.C.C.2d 421 (1966), reh. denied, 6 F.C.C.2d 511 (1967). See also *Bell Telephone Co. of Pennsylvania* v. *Federal Communications Commission*, 503 F.2d 1250 (3d Cir. 1974); *ITT Worldcom, Inc.* v. *New York Telephone Co.*, 381 F. Supp. 113 (S.D.N.Y. 1974).

and that, by any legitimate standard, utility diversification and competition with nonutility firms is just "basically unfair."[24]

Most traditional objections boil down to some variant on familiar themes involving predatory pricing. Although the Postal Service may be an institutional *Titanic,* this $17 billion operation poses some genuine threats to many firms. Certainly one must pay some attention to "deep-pocketing" objections, given the Postal Service's record of strategic pricing and creative accounting and the fact that the Postal Rate Commission and other bodies have only the vaguest notion of underlying mail service costs.[25]

As a federal enterprise, the Postal Service like many other government agencies is relatively independent of ordinary systems of financial and economic control. It is not clear that the Postal Service is amenable to control processes including application of the antitrust laws. Indeed, the Postal Service recently succeeded in being declared independent of the rest of the government basically for procedural purposes surrounding the Department of Justice's AT&T antitrust case. The Supreme Court has in recent years sharply limited the "sovereign immunity" enjoyed by state governments, however, and the courts have ruled that the Postal Service does not enjoy sovereign immunity from suits in certain kinds of civil actions, ordinary contract, and wage garnishments, for example.[26] These decisions notwithstanding, it seems reasonably certain that the courts would hold the Postal Service itself exempt or "immune" from virtually all types of traditional antitrust suits.[27]

Despite all the downside risks associated with Postal Service div-

---

[24] See, for example, *Mayor and Common Council of Georgetown v. Alexandria Canal Co.,* 37 U.S. (12 Pet.) 91, 95, 99 (1838); *New Orleans, Mobile, and Texas R. Co.* v. *Ellerman,* 105 U.S. 166, 174 (1882); *Tennessee Electric Power Co.* v. *Tennessee Valley Authority,* 306 U.S. 118 (1939).

[25] See, for example, *National Association of Greeting Card Publishers* v. *U.S. Postal Service,* 569 F.2d 570, 590, and n. 81.

[26] See *Goodman's Furniture* v. *U.S. Postal Service,* 561 F.2d 462, 464–65 (3d Cir. 1977), and citations therein. In recent years, the Supreme Court has narrowed the immunity from antitrust attack that might have been previously enjoyed by states and local governments and their agencies. See, for example, *City of Lafayette* v. *Louisiana Power and Light Co.,* 435 U.S. 389, 1978–1 CCH Trade Cas., para. 61936 at p. 73966 (decided March 29, 1978); *Bates* v. *State Bar of Arizona,* 433 U.S. 350 (1977); *Parker* v. *Brown,* 317 U.S. 341 (1943). These rulings notwithstanding, it seems unlikely the federal courts would entertain an action against the Postal Service on antitrust grounds. But compare, for example, *Nader* v. *Allegheny Airlines,* 426 U.S. 290, 299 (1976).

[27] Although the U.S. Postal Service as such may be immune from antitrust suit, this immunity does not necessarily extend to the individual actions of Postal Service employees. See, for example, *Kurek* v. *Pleasure Driveway and Park District,* 557 F.2d 580, 589–90 (7th Cir. 1977); *Duke and Co., Inc.* v. *Foerster,* 521 F.2d 1277 (3d Cir. 1975).

ersification, and the meritorious arguments that can be marshaled against it, the probabilities seem to favor it. A substantial and politically potent work force appears to favor such diversification. There are significant congressional pressures encouraging the Postal Service management to "do something" to stave off institutional decline.[28] Few politicians are prepared to state publicly that the Postal Service should proceed to diversify into all segments of the electronic communications field, but even fewer are prepared to assert that Postal Service management should not be "allowed" to make use of new electronic technology to improve the speed and quality of mail service. As a consequence, the Postal Service is now planning fairly significant diversification efforts—the so-called candidate system, for example, which reputedly will entail some $1.5 million in capital investment (which seems high) and some eighty-seven "stations" (which seems low). When political leadership for various reasons is unwilling to take a "go" or "no-go" position, the result is to cede the initiative to other forces. In the case of electronic mail services, postal management seems to have picked up the ball and proceeded quietly to move forward with it.

Issues Posed by Postal Service Entry

Much of the public policy debate has swirled about fundamental questions, such as whether the Postal Service should enter the electronic field at all. Given the current conditions, these past arguments seem irrelevant or naive.

> The function of politics [and lawyers] is to react to real situations, and not to line up realistic situations, side by side, and on a footing of equality, with pipe dreams. If a waiter asks you to choose between spaghetti and potatoes, there is no point in saying that you prefer caviar. The question is, spaghetti or potatoes; and nothing else. In politics, as in the kitchen, one may dream of circumstances in which the fare offered would be more palatable; but to dream is not the same as to act in accordance with a given reality. . . . For, politically speaking, to make a decision because of, or in favor of, something that will never happen, is the same as making no decision at all.[29]

The first range of legal issues presented by the current menu raises the question of how the Postal Service should enter—independently or via

---

[28] See, for example, U.S. Congress, House, Subcommittee on Postal Service of the Committee on Post Office and Civil Service, *Hearings on Cutbacks in Postal Service,* 94th Congress, 2nd session, May 1976, p. 22 (remarks of Chairman James M. Hanley).

[29] Jean-Francois Revel, *Without Marx or Jesus: The New American Revolution Has Begun* (Garden City, N.Y.: Doubleday, 1970), pp. 43–44.

joint venture. The second range of issues is concerned with the question of whether the role of the Postal Service in electronics can be artificially limited to certain processes. And the third range of questions deals basically with downside risk-anticipation procedures—what can reasonably be done to achieve at a minimum some level of damage control.

The recent Commission on Postal Service addressed some of the first range of questions presented, and concluded (as have others) that the best way for the Postal Service to enter electronics is to undertake one or more joint ventures—similar to the present Mailgram and the proposed enhanced Mailgram or ECOM (electronic computer-originated mail) undertaken with one of our most durable regulated utilities, Western Union. As this special study commission concluded:

> The Postal Service must understand the communications needs of the public. Cooperative joint venture with the private sector would help achieve this goal. Joint venture experiments can minimize capital investment, reduce risk, and utilize the unique collection and delivery network and trained workforce of the Postal Service. Immediate participation would help to establish credibility and demonstrate a commitment to preserve the Postal Service. The Postal Service should not be deterred from immediate entry into the electronic communications field. [30]

From postal management's perspective, a joint venture with a private firm has these and other advantages. It might tend to neutralize otherwise virulent private-sector opposition to Postal Service entry to begin with. A joint venture might also contribute to some extent to ameliorating overall system costs. To piece out a full electronic mail system, for instance, would require the Postal Service to develop an internal management capability that it may not now have. Adding personnel to a payroll already burdened may entail both unnecessary start-up and longer-term service costs, whereas these costs should be minimized if one assumes regulators will require them to be unbundled and reflected in electronic service prices. Though even the most inefficient electronic mail system is likely to display costs significantly below conventional mail-handling systems, if one assumes that the electronic mail environment in the future will be at least workably competitive and that the Postal Service intends to compete, some effort at minimizing diversification costs would seem important.

Legally, any joint venture at this time seems subject to some, if not substantial, questions. Recently, for example, the Court of Appeals for the District of Columbia Circuit overturned a Federal Communi-

---

[30] *Report of the Commission on Postal Service,* vol. 1, p. 24.

cations Commission ruling approving without hearing a joint venture between two likely independent entrants into the domestic communications satellite field, Comsat and IBM. In that landmark decision, which the parties are currently appealing, the court seemed to suggest that a joint venture between such entrants was inherently suspect, unless it could be shown that the joint venture was "essential." [31]

Any simple survey of potential Postal Service joint venture partners—Western Union, RCA, Comsat, or IBM, for example—may give rise to analogous challenges. This would be particularly true, it would seem, not only because the Postal Service is a likely independent entrant in addition to these and other firms, but also because it currently controls such a massive volume of potential electronic message traffic that it plus its selected joint venture partner would enjoy, at least at the outset, some significant advantage over many other entrants.

In the current FCC-regulated communications world, firms are permitted, indeed encouraged, to protest any new, competitive entry on virtually any ground. Among the most fruitful grounds, in terms of generating large fees for the organized bar,[32] are antitrust questions, including whether joint ventures threaten rights of "reasonable access" or will lead to "entrenchment."[33] Given the state of present law, these questions and the ability of private parties to interpose them to achieve self-serving delays are largely beyond the control of regulatory agencies. Although a comprehensive revision in present communications laws has been recently proposed that, if enacted, might lessen current institutional and privately erectable barriers to entry via joint venture (or otherwise), about all that can be said with any certainty at this stage is that the joint venture option advanced by the Postal Service Commission seems very amenable to private challenges.

Some public policy spokesmen have suggested postal joint ventures with the private sector as a means, apparently, of limiting the Postal Service's role in electronic services. Typically, electronic mail services are broadly classified into three groups: post office to post office; source to post office; or all of the foregoing plus some kind of source-to-source capability. The view is advanced that it should be possible to limit the

---

[31] See *Satellite Business Systems*, 62 F.C.C.2d 977 (1977), rev'd sub nom., *United States v. Federal Communications Commission*, __F. 2d.__, 44P. & R. Radio Reg. 2d. 59 (D.C. Cir., August 29, 1978)(Reconsid. *en banc* pending).

[32] See generally Mark J. Green, *The Other Government: The Unseen Power of Washington Lawyers* (New York: Grossman Publishers, 1975), p. 8; Fred Rodell, *Woe unto You, Lawyers* (New York: Reynal and Hitchcock, 1939), p. 274.

[33] See, for example, *United States* v. *Southwestern Greyhound Lines, Inc.*, 1953 CCH Trade Cas., para. 67740 (N.D. Okla. 1953); *Gamco, Inc.* v. *Providence Fruit and Produce Building, Inc.*, 194 F.2d 484 (1st Cir. 1952); *United States* v. *Penn-Olin Chem. Co.*, 378 U.S. 158 (1964); *Federal Trade Commission* v. *Procter and Gamble Co.*, 386 U.S. 568, 578 (1967).

Postal Service to its traditional functions—local delivery of some kind of hard or record copy—while reserving to private carriers the prerogative of performing the actual electronic transmission.

Whether these distinctions are currently relevant or, over time, sustainable given the technological and commercial dynamics of this market is an open question. Careful differentiation of charter and scheduled air service has proven unsustainable in that dynamic environment. The intermodal transportation controversies currently confronting both the Interstate Commerce Commission and the Federal Maritime Commission suggest that piecing out parts of an overall transportation system and reserving them to certain designated entities will not work over time. Certainly, in the telecommunications field, the Federal Communications Commission's valiant, and unsuccessful, efforts artificially to confine specialized carriers to providing "private line" services suggest that regulatory boundaries will tend to be breached.[34]

Whether artificial restrictions *should* be placed on Postal Service activities in the field of electronics is perhaps the better question. Presumably any decision to permit the Postal Service to enter electronic communications would reflect the judgment that this major institution should be allowed to make use of new technologies and should be permitted to participate in a field as its current line of business is eroded. A further presumption is that we should not adopt the so-called Curtis LeMay approach of relegating the Postal Service to what is, by comparison with new electronic services, a Stone Age technology. If the Postal Service does in fact enter electronic mail services to any significant extent, it seems to make little sense to endeavor to hedge that technology with standards and classifications that may themselves be shortly overcome by subsequent technological advances.

If one assumes that the Postal Service will enter electronics, whether in a joint venture or independently, and that it will offer some range of services up to and including the full range of electronic mail, then a third range of issues should be confronted—the operational details. Among the topics of current debate is, of course, the regulatory issue—which of two agencies, the FCC and the Postal Rate Commission (PRC), will actually be in charge, and who will be able to do what, when, and to whom. Associated with these issues, moreover, is the question of the implications—real or perceived—of the famous private express laws.

The Federal Communications Commission, in all likelihood, will assume overall regulatory leadership in this emerging field, for it is both historically the most aggressive, indeed imaginative, of the two agencies

---

[34] See *MCI Telecommunications Corp.* v. *Federal Communications Commission,* 561 F.2d 365, 380 (D.C. Cir. 1977).

and by far the best endowed with resources. At present, for example, the FCC continues to pursue the same expansive and elastic jurisdictional theories that allowed it to ensnare the entire cable television industry by virtue of ingenuous arguments of ancillary jurisdiction. As one former FCC commissioner has put it, FCC policy seems to be that "if it moves, regulate it. And if it doesn't move, kick it until it moves, and then regulate it."

Recently the FCC developed, and sustained in the courts, the theory that the 1934 Communications Act compels the agency to assert "pervasive jurisdiction" over firms and entities that lease bulk capacity from regulated common carriers and "add value," broker, or otherwise resell that bulk capacity.[35] The Rostow Task Force observed that the 1934 Communications Act had almost "constitutional flexibility." In conjunction with the FCC's *Resale and Brokerage* decision, a number of parties questioned the logic of extending regulation to reach brokers, when the services involved were provided under tariff by fully regulated carriers and those services were offered under competitive conditions. Customers dissatisfied with brokers' services, of course, have readily available to them reasonable alternatives retailed by large public utilities including AT&T. Nonetheless, the FCC reached forth its regulatory hand and grabbed this new ancillary business—not an unexpected assertion of authority for the same agency that shortly beforehand developed and imposed an elaborate scheme for the licensing of "receive-only" satellite earth station antennas. Certainly, therefore, the FCC will seek to impose some kind of regulation on electronic mail services. Indeed, should the Postal Service choose AT&T as one of its electronic mail partners, that probability is enhanced, since that firm is constrained by consent decree generally from offering other than "regulated communications services."[36] Although the Postal Service can be expected institutionally to resist any such assertion of FCC authority at the start, it should not take too long for it to grasp the happy fiscal realities, from a historical standpoint, of "pervasive FCC regulation," as spokesmen for the television, telephone, even telegraph companies can readily attest.

What role the Postal Rate Commission might play in this soon-to-be-unfolding drama is not completely clear, though this agency has

---

[35] *Resale and Shared Use of Private Line Facilities*, 60 F.C.C.2d 261 (1976), aff'd sub nom., *American Telephone and Telegraph Co.* v. *Federal Communications Commission*, 572 F.2d 17 (2d Cir. 1978).

[36] See *Report of the President's Task Force on Communications Policy* (1968), chap. 6, pp. 43–44; *United States* v. *Western Electric Co. et al.*, 1956 CCH Trade Cas. para. 68246 (D.N.J. 1956). See also *Dataspeed 40/4 Device*, 62 F.C.C.2d 21 (1977), aff'd sub nom., *International Business Machines* v. *Federal Communications Commission*, 570 F.2d 452 (2d Cir. 1978).

commenced a major proceeding into one proposed new Postal Service offering, denominated electronic mail. At present, the PRC differs from other regulatory bodies in that its actions are dependent largely upon the initiative of its sole regulatee, the Postal Service, and are more circumscribed than is superficially apparent in other regulatory forums.[37] Presumably the PRC would have some legal authority if only to subtend Postal Service prices, service classifications, and cost allocations associated with any electronic mail offerings. It would also seem that the PRC could assert some generalized regulatory authority over Postal Service plans in this area, insofar as it is obliged to ensure that there are no undesirable diversions of resources or facilities to auxiliary electronic enterprises. This kind of ancillary jurisdiction—the regulatory variant on civil court "long-arm" jurisdictional assertions—should be familiar.[38] In comparison with other regulatory agencies, however, the PRC is relatively toothless; it has few credible sanctions available to it. Indeed, decisions of the PRC are ordinarily subject to some review by the Board of Governors of the U.S. Postal Service (including, incidentally, PRC budget requests, evidently). In short, while it seems likely that the Postal Rate Commission will play some regulatory role in the electronic mail business, the level and intensity of its scrutiny remain today basically an open question.

The Private Express Laws Connection

The U.S. Postal Service is different from most commercial operations in that it has enjoyed since early in the nineteenth century a monopoly buttressed by both civil and criminal statutes. These statutes, referred to as the private express laws, essentially bar private delivery of things denominated "letters." Most experts consider these laws the chief source of economic clout currently enjoyed by the Postal Service.[39]

The express laws historically can be traced back to Elizabethan times. Then, it has been suggested, their chief utility was that they afforded the sovereign a control process that facilitated snooping on

---

[37] See, for example, U.S. Congress, House, Subcommittee on Postal Operations and Services and Subcommittee on Postal Personnel and Modernization of the Committee on Post Office and Civil Service, *Joint Hearings on H.R. 7700: Postal Service Act of 1977,* 95th Congress, 1st session, September 1977, p. 263 (statement of Donald R. Taub, National Association of Greeting Card Publishers).

[38] See, for example, *United States* v. *Montreal Trust Co.,* 358 F.2d 239, 249 (2d Cir. 1966); *Federal Maritime Commission* v. *Seatrain Lines, Inc.,* 411 U.S. 726, 745 (1973); *Ambassador, Inc.* v. *United States,* 325 U.S. 317, 323–25 (1945).

[39] See generally John Haldi, *Postal Monopoly: An Assessment of the Private Express Statutes* (Washington, D.C.: American Enterprise Institute, 1974); U.S. Department of Justice, *Changing the Private Express Laws: Competitive Alternatives and the U.S. Postal Service* (January 1977).

potentially rebellious or troublesome subjects' writings. In recent years, according to private delivery services, the Postal Service has construed these archaic statutes expansively, an allegation that the Postal Service not unexpectedly denies. [40]

There have been only a few civil or criminal prosecutions over the past century under the private express laws. These court cases usually involved private activities that were basically identical to those performed by postal workers, except for the wearing of gray uniforms. Recent decisions reflect some considerable scrambling of legal and economic concepts. In the principal case ordinarily cited as upholding the Postal Service's interpretations—the so-called Christmas cards case—one of the postal unions, not the government, successfully obtained an injunction against an almost identical, overlapping private delivery service. There the Oklahoma court reasoned that the private firm's activities "would reduce gross postal revenues. And reduced postal revenues would inevitably have an adverse effect on the general employment status of the plaintiff's members." [41] When a sister union endeavored to enjoin the same firm in another circuit, however, the panel (which included the present solicitor general) concluded that the union lacked standing and dismissed the action. [42]

It is curious to see, in these decisions, that the loss of *gross* revenues is equated to the loss of employment opportunity for postal workers and then to injury to the "public interest." These components are not always or even usually connected. The 1970 Reorganization Act, for example, does contain elaborate job security provisions, but it is not clear that Congress equated maintenance of postal worker positions with the public interest. Similarly, the absence of a U.S. Postal Service local distribution system does not necessarily mean that the public interest will be adversely affected. Logically, on the assumption that there is a public demand for such service, the local system of the Postal Service would decline only as people shifted to another system that, presumably, they would find more satisfactory. As the courts have noted in other situations where one firm's services may be complemented or, indeed, displaced by another's, "the public is not concerned with whether it gets service from A or B or from both combined. The public interest is affected [only] when service is affected." [43]

---

[40] Haldi, *Postal Monopoly*, p. 4.

[41] *National Association of Letter Carriers, AFL-CIO* v. *Independent Postal Service of America,* 470 F.2d 265, 271 (10th Cir. 1972).

[42] See *American Postal Workers, AFL-CIO* v. *Independent Postal Service of America,* 481 F.2d 90 (6th Cir. 1973).

[43] *Carroll Broadcasting Co.* v. *Federal Communications Commission,* 258 F.2d 440, 444 (D.C. Cir. 1958); *MCI Telecommunications* v. *FCC,* 561 F.2d 365, 380, and n. 71.

The 1970 Reorganization Act, moreover, explicitly directs the Postal Service to render "efficient services."[44] Worker positions and efficient operation are necessarily conditional upon maintaining gross postal revenues. A firm may become more efficient, for example, by relinquishing low-profit–high-cost operations to other enterprises and concentrating resources, including employees, on higher-profit–lower-cost operations. The Postal Service has maintained that it loses money on local residential delivery operations, for example. Yet, in the Oklahoma case mentioned earlier, it joined with the union in seeking to enjoin a competing local residential delivery operation. Ordinarily one would not assume that efficiency is furthered by preserving a firm's opportunity to continue to lose money, yet there the court did essentially that.

It is conventional legal teaching that statutes should be construed to achieve the public interest which is the purpose of the law.[45] The regulatory world is filled with examples in which agencies engage in construing statutes as oblique, often, as the private express laws. The Federal Reserve Board and the comptroller of the currency, for example, determine what activities are "closely related to banking," often on an ad hoc basis.[46] The Interstate Commerce Commission determines what exactly qualifies for the "agricultural commodities" exemption from standard motor carrier regulations—making, for instance, the classic differentiation between iced, speed-chilled, and frozen broilers. Agencies including the Civil Aeronautics Board and the Federal Maritime Commission determine what kinds of business activities are integral to regulated air or ocean transportation and thus eligible for antitrust immunity grants.[47] The institutionalized champion of free enterprise competition—the Antitrust Division—routinely undertakes to determine the status and eligibility of activities under its extensive repertoire of consent decrees and for other purposes. Recently, for ex-

---

[44] See 39 *U.S. Code*, section 101(*a*)(1976); and *Association of American Publishers, Inc.* v. *Governors, U.S. Postal Service*, 485 F.2d 768, 776 (D.C. Cir. 1973).

[45] See, for example, *Oregon* v. *Mitchell*, 400 U.S. 112, 131 (1949) and 246–49 (separate opinion of Brennan, White, and Marshall, JJ.); *American Commercial Lines, Inc.* v. *Louisville & Nashville R. Co.*, 392 U.S. 571, 589–90 (1968). See also *Citizens to Preserve Overton Park* v. *Volpe*, 401 U.S. 402, 412–13 (1971).

[46] 12 *U.S. Code*, section 1843 (*c*) (1976). See also *Association of Data Processing Service Organizations, Inc.* v. *Camp, Comptroller of the Currency*, 279 F. Supp. 675, 677 (D. Minn. 1968), aff'd, 406 F.2d 837 (8th Cir. 1969), rev'd, 397 U.S. 150 (1969); *Investment Company Institute* v. *Camp, Comptroller of the Currency*, 401 U.S. 617 (1971). See generally *State ex rel. Colorado State Banking Board* v. *First National Bank of Fort Collins*, 540 F.2d 497 (10th Cir. 1976); *Independent Bankers Association* v. *Smith, Comptroller of the Currency*, 534 F.2d 921 (D.C. Cir. 1976).

[47] See 49 *U.S. Code*, section 1384, 1976; 46 *U.S. Code*, section 814, 1976; *Consolidated Airline Purchasing Organization*, 40 C.A.B. 986, 933 (1964); *Federal Maritime Commission* v. *Aktiebolaget Svenska Amerika Linien*, 390 U.S. 238 (1968).

ample, the division undertook proceedings to determine the status of "ranch-raised broilers" during the "grow-out" phase for the purposes of the Capper-Volstead antitrust exemption for certain farmers' cooperatives. [48] In virtually all of these proceedings, legal concepts and economics are elaborately considered, and usually considerable attention is given to the consequences of interpretations on both actual and potential competition of all sorts and kinds. [49]

Private express law interpretation differs from these familiar regulatory operations in at least four significant ways. First, the Postal Service itself, not the Postal Rate Commission, currently has authority to interpret these monopoly statutes. Indeed, only this year the Postal Service proposed, in connection with legislation aimed at clarifying the scope of the express laws, that a special administrative enforcement mechanism or "postal court" system be created. The courts for many years have ruled that those with a substantial and obvious pecuniary interest in the outcome of legal proceedings should not adjudicate such disputes. This would seem to be particularly true where the would-be adjudicatory agency is also the potential victim of possibly unlawful conduct. [50] Paradoxically, at the same time that the Postal Service was recently urging enactment of a special postal court it was also arguing that it was not a government agency for the purposes of discovery requests in conjunction with the current antitrust suit against AT&T. [51]

Second, private express law is interpreted by the Postal Service ordinarily without taking any apparent account of economic considerations. The traditional doctrine of the "least anticompetitive alternative" reflected in almost any other analogous regulatory interpretation appears to be completely ignored in Postal Service interpretations. Economics or dollar figures virtually never appear, making it difficult to ascertain whether there has been any considered balancing of competitive factors. This is quite different from other situations, where the courts have generally insisted that regulatory bodies set forth with some

---

[48] *National Broiler Marketing Association* v. *United States,* 436 U.S. 816, 1978–1 CCH Trade Cas., para. 62074 (decided June 12, 1978). See also *American Waterways Operators, Inc.* v. *United States,* 386 F. Supp. 799 (D.D.C. 1974); *Colorado Interstate Gas Co.* v. *Federal Power Commission,* 324 U.S. 581, 608 (1945).

[49] See, for example, *Gulf States Utility Co.* v. *Federal Power Commission,* 411 U.S. 747 (1973); *United States* v. *Federal Communications Commission, supra.*

[50] See, for example, *Gibson* v. *Berryhill,* 411 U.S. 564, 579 (1972); *Tumey* v. *Ohio,* 273 U.S. 510 (1927).

[51] See *United States* v. *American Telephone and Telegraph,* 461 F. Supp. 1314, 1978–2 CCH Trade Cas., para. 62247 at p. 75554 and n. 49, 75559 and n. 65 (D.D.C. September 11, 1978).

clarity the economic factors they considered in order to aid reviewing courts in determining whether agencies balanced correctly.[52]

Third, the principal target of existing express law interpretations and enforcement activities appears to be not private carriers but rather those who may patronize such commercial operations. In the special postal court legislation that was proposed, for example, only users, not private couriers, would have been potentially subject to the imposition of substantial sanctions. This is understandable, if hardly defensible, inasmuch as individual customers are more likely to acquiesce and less likely to appeal to the courts as a consequence of Postal Service actions. Individuals, obviously, are much more subject to pressures than, for example, very large commercial carriers—United Parcel, Purolator, Brink's, and the like—who have the resources and the clear incentive to contest Postal Service actions that may adversely affect them commercially. It is not conventional enforcement policy at most regulatory agencies, however, to concentrate efforts on members of the public who may use a service to the virtual exclusion of the firms that are engaged in offering that service to the public.

Fourth, some private express law interpretations strike many critics of these statutes as bizarre, to say the least. Generally, the express laws are written to prohibit the private carriage of things denominated "letters"; sometimes the archaic term "packets" also appears. "Letters" ordinarily are considered to be handwritten or typescripted documents that are sealed in envelopes and addressed to particular persons. The Postal Service has apparently construed the term "letter" to include, however, such items as payroll checks, fishing licenses, Mickey Mouse posters, San Francisco Forty-niners tickets, punch cards, blueprints, data-processing tapes, computer programs, credit cards, advertising included in boxes of merchandise, intracompany correspondence—in short, as one district court ruling now on appeal suggested, virtually anything "properly transmittable" through the U.S. Postal Service's delivery system other than newspapers or parcels classified as fourth-class mail.[53]

The Postal Service adheres to the theory that the private express laws (which are designed to protect revenues) should be construed in-

[52] See, for example, *United States* v. *Third National Bank in Nashville,* 390 U.S. 171, 188–89 (1968); *United States* v. *Phillipsburg National Bank,* 399 U.S. 350, 369–71 (1970); *Marine Space Enclosures, Inc.* v. *Federal Maritime Commission,* 420 F.2d 577, 589 (D.C. Cir. 1969). See also *Shelton* v. *Tucker,* 364 U.S. 478, 488 (1960).

[53] See generally Lawrence L. Hillblom and James I. Campbell, Jr., "A Practical Guide to the United States Postal Monopoly for Businessmen Who Use Private Express Companies to Deliver Documents" (Washington, D.C., 1978, processed).

dependently of the mail classification laws (which are designed to generate the revenue to be then protected). [54] It is commonly thought, for example, that the express laws and the Postal Service monopoly only prohibit the private carriage of documents that would be classified as first-class mail. The Postal Service, however, has traditionally disputed that easy convention. Not only does this contribute to the widespread confusion among mailers as to what exactly may be within or without the Postal Service monopoly, but some of the Postal Service's interpretations generate some private-sector trepidation. Recently, for example, the Michigan Department of Agriculture distributed special emergency kits to dairy farmers in the state to combat the widespread contamination of dairy cattle with polybrominated biphenyl (PBB). The kits were distributed via United Parcel Service, one of the major private carriers. The Postal Service subsequently advised that the directory of special veterinarians, the forms to be filled out showing absence of milch cow contamination, an emergency instructions pamphlet, and copies of the relevant state statute all were "letters" and that their carriage by UPS was thus in violation of the express laws. Only the plastic vials for tissue samples and the gummed blank labels that were sent were de-

---

[54] Ordinarily, the standards applied for one purpose are considered relevant to standards applied for related purposes. As the Supreme Court has observed in requiring coincidence of employment rules, "Good administration of the Act and good judicial administration alike require that the standards of public enforcement and those for determining private rights shall be at variance only where justified by very good reasons." *Skidmore* v. *Swift and Co.,* 323 U.S. 134, 140 (1944). See also *TelePrompter Cable Systems, Inc.* v. *Federal Communications Commission,* 543 F.2d 1379, 1385 (D.C. Cir. 1976). Fundamental due process ordinarily requires that agencies not conjure up distinctions, adopt variegated standards, or treat similarly situated parties very differently. See *Moog Industries, Inc.* v. *Federal Trade Commission,* 355 U.S. 411, 413 (1958); *Automobile Club of Michigan* v. *Commissioner, Internal Revenue Service,* 353 U.S. 180, 185–86 (1957); *International Business Machines* v. *United States,* 343 F.2d 914, 919, 923 (Ct. Cl. 1965). It is not unusual, however, for the Postal Service to decline to acquiesce in rulings. The Postal Service, for example, litigated the issue of whether it was immune from state garnishment laws in nineteen federal district courts and appealed the issue six times to the U.S. courts of appeals sequentially and unsuccessfully, a record of tenacity, if nothing else, very nearly unparalleled in recent judicial history. See *Goodman's Furniture* v. *U.S. Postal Service,* 561 F.2d 462, 463. As Judge Weis noted, concurring, "The issue here is a simple statutory interpretation which was first decided by a distinguished panel of the Court of Appeals for the Seventh Circuit in Standard Oil Division, *American Oil Company* v. *Starks,* 528 F.2d 201 (7th Cir. 1975). At that point, the postal authorities could have sought certiorari by the Supreme Court or asked Congress to change the statute. They did neither, but instead refused to accept the decision and continued to litigate in other federal courts. That course of action by the Government is unseemly. The practice of fomenting inconsistency among various courts of appeals by Government officials is unsettling to the course of justice. It is disrespectful toward the courts and hinders efficient judicial administration" (*Idem.* at 465).

clared not to be letters.[55] Such interpretations do not necessarily promote public confidence in the reasonableness of the Postal Service's enforcement processes.

Three years in law school are not required to appreciate that there is a certain looseness in the express laws and their interpretation for electronic mail. Most versions of electronic mail, for example, at one stage or another involve the use of hard copy. Although the Postal Service would presumably not seek to construe these elastic laws to encompass electronic waves or digital blips, hard copy, of course, is quite another question. The Postal Service denies that it would expand the definition of "letter" to encompass electronics. Of course, electronic mail systems do not now exist that would threaten gross Postal Service revenues, nor, except for the very small Mailgram program, does the Postal Service currently offer its own electronic system that might be affected by private competition.

Historical experience suggests that the private sector is not always best advised to rely upon official disclaimers of regulatory impotence. In 1966, for example, the Federal Communications Commission sought legislation to enable it to regulate cable television, maintaining that otherwise it would lack the ability to protect broadcaster profits from cable competition. Subsequently, of course, the FCC's attorneys were able to discover and sustain a convenient theory of "ancillary jurisdic-

---

[55] See memorandum from Jack T. DiLorenzo, assistant general counsel, Opinions Division, U.S. Postal Service, to the regional chief inspector, Central Region (ref. PES 78–3), dated January 31, 1978, p. 4. State governments and their agencies appear to be a particularly troublesome area of private express law interpretation. The Postal Service has ruled, for example, that the Georgia Department of Transportation may not transmit contracts to county commissioners via private courier, and only project blueprints if they are bound and have more than twenty-four pages, at least twenty-two of which are printed (PES 75–25, July 9, 1975). The Kentucky Department of Drivers Licensing was instructed that it could not ship renewal and original licenses from Frankfort to county clerks for pickup by the public using United Parcel, unless applicable postage was paid (PES 75–2, January 3, 1975). The North Carolina Department of Administration was allowed to use state couriers to deliver items between state agencies and to counties; state couriers were forbidden, however, to deliver items from counties to other counties (PES 76–9, May 6, 1976). The University of Virginia was instructed that it could use a private courier to take its payroll tapes to Richmond for processing, but the paychecks evidently could not be brought back to Charlottesville if it took more than twelve hours (PES 76–24, November 24, 1976). And the Iowa Department of Social Services was told its payroll computer tapes could be sent from local offices to Des Moines via private courier, but use of a courier to deliver welfare case files among offices was forbidden—unless, of course, the department remitted the requisite postage to the Postal Service (see PES 77–7, February 1, 1977). As Representative Trent Lott has pointed out, these rulings are, of course, tantamount to the imposition of a postal "tax" on state government agencies. The federal government and its agencies generally are not subject to the express laws or Postal Service regulations in this regard.

tion" and proceeded to enshroud this new, competitive industry with a maze of wildly anticompetitive regulations. [56]

In regard to document delivery services, it is perhaps instructive to consider the recent experience of special courier operations. For many years, private courier activities seem to have escaped the application of the private express laws. These private activities provided delivery services the Postal Service (or the Post Office Department) neither offered nor seemed prepared to offer. Such operations are not clearly subject to at least some of the applicable statutes. The delivery of twenty-five or fewer letters or packets, for example, would seem to be explicitly exempted from the application of the express laws. [57]

The advent of the Postal Service's own "express mail" offering, however, appears to have aroused enforcement interests. Private courier companies have complained of Postal Service inspectors visiting customers to discuss the private express laws with subsequent visits from Postal Service marketing personnel. Publications, including the Postal Service's *Competition Watch,* have appeared, reminiscent of those AT&T distributed to its personnel in conjunction with that firm's notorious efforts to eliminate its competition. The Postal Service has reportedly threatened shippers with both criminal and civil prosecutions. As the sponsor of legislation that was passed by the House of Representatives April 6, 1978 (384 to 11), explained,

> The Postal Service's interpretation of the private express statutes has justifiably aroused a great deal of rancor within the business community. There are a number of reasons for this concern:
>
> First. The most recent interpretation of a "letter" has included intracompany communications and data processing materials.
>
> Second. Statutes are so unclear and unwieldy that compliance is difficult at best. Recent interpretations have lumped everything from IBM cards to engraved tombstones under the same heading requiring the item be placed in an individually addressed envelope, sealed, and stamped.
>
> Third. Present requirements are wasteful and inflationary. Thousands of man-hours are lost annually when interoffice communications and data processing materials qualifying as so-called "letters" must be segregated then addressed, sealed and stamped.
>
> Fourth. The Postal Service's capricious interpretation of the

---

[56] See Paul W. MacAvoy, ed., *Cable Television Deregulation* (Washington, D.C.: American Enterprise Institute, 1977).

[57] See 18 *U.S. Code,* section 1696(*c*) (1976).

law and the penalties that await violation require businesses to have a "lawyer" in every shipping room to determine whether such items as data disks or bills of lading qualify as "letters" and are subject to the postal "tax."

Fifth. Finally, .the Postal Service cannot provide rapid and reliable service such as same-day or overnight delivery. Companies are therefore forced to seek a more costly alternative for delivery of this vital correspondence. The effect has been to pass these additional costs to the consumer.

It is clear that something can and should be done. [58]

Other concerns have been advanced that the Postal Service's interpretations have the effect of negating the actions of other federal agencies. Virtually all private courier activities and private delivery services, for example, hold permits issued by the Interstate Commerce Commission or by the Civil Aeronautics Board to transport exactly those items the Postal Service maintains cannot be carried without impinging upon its delivery monopoly. Further concerns have arisen about Postal Service pricing policies. According to the chief administrative law judge of the Postal Rate Commission, for example, United Parcel Service has been the target of overtly predatory pricing tactics, with the Postal Service seeking to maintain its dwindling share of fourth-class-mail traffic by "selling below cost and placing the resulting cost burden on first class mailers." [59] United Parcel has, of course, complained about this practice for several years, as has its employee union, the International Brotherhood of Teamsters, Warehousemen, Chauffeurs, and Helpers. The Postal Service having sunk tremendous capital costs into the well-known bulk-mail facilities, the Congress until recently appeared to wink at these pricing tactics. [60]

The concern has been voiced that the Postal Service will diversify into all or part of the electronic mail business, seek to secure a meaningful market share by pricing services below legitimate cost levels, invest a substantial amount of money in such a system, and then energize its private express enforcement mechanisms so as to hobble or eliminate its electronic mail competitors. This may well be, of course, simply overimaginative forecasting based upon an unwarranted and pejorative extrapolation from currently disputed practices. Some experts maintain that, while it is conceivable that the express laws may be applicable to

---

[58] U.S. Congress, House, 124 *Congressional Record,* April 6, 1978, pp. H2548–49 (remarks of Representative Trent Lott).

[59] Postal Rate Case no. R74–1, Opinion of Chief Administrative Law Judge Seymour Wenner, vol. 1, p. 164 (May 28, 1975).

[60] See 124 *Congressional Record,* March 21, 1978, p. H2280 (remarks of Representative Paul Simon).

certain generations of electronic mail, it is difficult to conceive of these elastic laws designed to safeguard gross postal revenues being success-fully extended to encompass the ultimate in foreseeable systems—electronic source-to-source services. It has also been pointed out that at least some of the potential targets of any such expansionary activity are hardly commercial or, for that matter, political eunuchs. Large and very sophisticated corporations, including AT&T, Exxon, Xerox, and IBM, are demonstrably capable of safeguarding and furthering their commercial interests. In this respect, firm incentives may differ depending upon whether the Postal Service is an independent competitor or a joint venturer. Past experience in both the ocean-shipping and regulated airline businesses teaches that very efficient firms may tolerate, indeed foster, regulatory systems and restraints on competition that allow them to earn substantial monopoly rents by pegging regulations of price and service availability at levels sufficiently high to shelter much less efficient and putatively "competitive" operators. Finally, it should be borne in mind that the Postal Service maintains that it has the authority to suspend the application of the express laws on an ad hoc basis, arguments to the contrary notwithstanding.[61] This rather ingenuous tool, as public counsel for the Postal Rate Commission described the suspension theory, would seem to afford the Postal Service a ready means of reaching an accommodation with larger electronic mail competitors. From the public's standpoint, it is not clear that they would be better served by a shared monopoly than by a single electronic mail monopolist.

What Is to Be Done in This Area?

Postal issues ordinarily have a political quotient far higher than their strictly legal component. Not unexpectedly, therefore, most potential solutions are dependent upon political initiatives undertaken by the Congress or the president. Electronic mail services are now developing in what is essentially a regulatory and political vacuum. If there is now any entity with significant control over these developments, it is most likely to be Postal Service management.

It is basically unfair to place the burden of developing and implementing public policy in this field on the Postal Service management. Nor is it clear that the policies the Postal Service may eventually develop governing electronic services will find widespread acceptance.

---

[61] Legal memorandum of the assistant general counsel, Litigation Division, Postal Rate Commission, "Concerning the Role of the Postal Rate Commission in the Exercise of Legal Controls Over the Private Carriage of Mail and the Postal Monopoly," July 31, 1974, filed in Docket MC73-1, *Mail Classification Schedule, 1973.*

The best course of action at this time seems to be for the political leadership, whether legislative or executive, to take the initiative and develop some comprehensive plan, and in the process resolve many of the current legal issues and general uncertainties that pervade this whole field. Politicians are not necessarily required to provide perfectly correct answers every time. But it is appropriate to insist that they provide some kind of answer and thus at a minimum alleviate needless uncertainties. Even a "wrong" answer can be desirable if it lessens unnecessary consumer and business-sector confusion. As Candidate Carter explained,

> The Bible says: "If the trumpet gives an uncertain sound, who shall prepare himself to the battle?" [I Corinthians 14:8.] As a planner and a businessman, and a chief executive, I know from experience that uncertainty is also a devastating affliction in private life and in government. Coordination of different programs is impossible. There is no clear vision of what is to be accomplished, everyone struggles for temporary advantage, and there is no way to monitor how effectively services are delivered. [62]

Reasonably clear signals from the government are especially important in high-technology areas. Jordan Baruch, assistant secretary of commerce for science and technology, recently began an inquiry into the alleged absence of recent innovation by American industry. As a White House statement noted, "In recent years, private sector research and development has concentrated on low-risk, short-term projects directed at improving existing products. Emphasis on the long-term research that could lead to new products and services has decreased." [63] Improving the climate for innovation is especially important, since traditionally the United States has been internationally preeminent in this area. [64]

Experience in telecommunications suggests that the absence of innovation in parts of the industry has been the result of eclectic, frequently hostile policies of the regulatory agency which must often render ad hoc decisions because of congressional reluctance to amend an ancient law to accommodate changed commercial circumstances. In the cable television industry, for example, unguided and erratic FCC policies toward this capital-intensive industry had at least two obvious effects. First, the investment community was reluctant to participate in the development of the business or did so only at extremely high rates

[62] Jimmy Carter, *Why Not the Best?* (New York: Bantam Books, 1976), p. 173.

[63] Arlen J. Large, "Carter Will Turn to Executives for Advice on Ways to Foster Innovation by Industry," *Wall Street Journal,* September 14, 1978, p. 8.

[64] Zbigniew Brzezinski, *Between Two Ages: America's Role in the Technetronic Era* (New York: Penguin Books, 1976), pp. 24–34.

of interest. Second, the climate of uncertainty tended to foster short-term, profit-maximizing managements that sometimes proved too willing to employ undesirable or illegal practices. This should not have been surprising; high-risk environments tend to encourage activities not found so often in more stable industries.

Specialized common carriers seeking to compete with the Bell System companies have also been the victims of regulatory uncertainties. Regulators have criticized these firms for failing to provide the new and innovative services the bureaucracy initially expected. The most reasonable explanation for this shortfall, however, is that the regulators themselves created a climate of needless uncertainty. Under such conditions, even the most innovative of managements will tend to focus on offering conventional services with known sales potential. New offerings will tend to be deferred when there is considerable regulatory uncertainty. Moreover, such uncertainty tends to inhibit demand; major customers generally are unwilling to commit themselves to a supplier, no matter how new and innovative the offering, if because of confused government signals it is unclear that the supplier will be in business tomorrow.

At this stage in development, it seems that the government has an opportunity to clarify the electronic mail—indeed, the overall Postal Service—situation and to do so fairly easily. The following three-part program has been advanced and seems reasonably worthy of consideration.

First, the Postal Service would be permitted to continue to diversify into the electronic mail field through some separate corporate entity. The Postal Service itself would continue to be subject to the regulation of the Postal Rate Commission, which would have authority over the allocation of resources to electronics. Those services, whether provided by the separate entity directly or via joint venture, would be subject to very minimal, legislatively prescribed Federal Communications Commission regulation. This separation of traditional and electronic undertakings presumably would reduce, if not eliminate, "moving target" cost allocation problems. It would also seem desirable generally to impose on this separate entity an "open-market" obligation. That is, it (or its joint-venture partners, if used) would be generally required to purchase a substantial portion of any component goods and services competitively and from nonaffiliated suppliers. Such an open-market obligation would have the effect of using Postal Service demand to draw new and more suppliers into what may become the dominant part of the electronic communications market.

Second, the private express laws and their coverage would be clarified and, over stages, completely repealed. Legislation such as passed by the House of Representatives or considered by Senate subcommittees this year would have made clear that the express laws do not apply to electronic messages. It should be made clear that messages transmitted in whole or in part electronically are exempt from these statutes. The preponderant view appears to favor continuation of the policy, reflected in the 1970 Reorganization Act, that the Postal Service remain independent and aim toward self-sufficiency. As the Postal Service progressively becomes, by virtue of electronics, more of a business and less of a public service, it would therefore seem appropriate to lift the special statutory monopoly the organization currently enjoys. If the organization is simply one of several communications companies, there would not seem to be substantial justification for according it special statutory protection from competition. The current monopoly could be phased out over several years, beginning with the exemption for "time-sensitive mail" that has been proposed.

Third, to assure that service, particularly to rural areas, is not adversely affected, some general "tax" on all document delivery and electronic firms could be considered. At present, the costs of providing service to less well-populated regions represent only a small fraction of the overall Postal Service budget. A considerable portion of rural delivery services, indeed, is funded through the Postal Service but in fact provided by contract or star-route carriers. With the revenues derived from a general assessment on all carriers, service to rural areas could be maintained. In this respect, it may be desirable to charge the Postal Rate Commission with the obligation to subsidize rural delivery services, much as for many years the Civil Aeronautics Board has been responsible for assuring that adequate air service to rural areas is maintained.

Legislation would be necessary to implement much of any program such as this. Indeed, legislation and political guidance in this field would be desirable regardless of whether electronic mail developments and regulatory adjustments and changes in the coverage of the express laws might be achieved administratively. In the 95th Congress, both the House and the Senate made serious efforts to provide the political framework generally considered desirable to accommodate changes in this area. It is hoped that the next Congress will further consider such measures.

Commentary

Roy A. Nierenberg

Kenneth Robinson's discussion of electronic diversification by the Postal Service is intelligent and informed. While I agree with much that he says, I will focus here on points of disagreement and areas where the analysis does not go far enough.

Robinson's speculations as to the motivations of the Postal Service in utilizing this new technology form the backdrop for much of his analysis. In my judgment, the sinister motivations he perceives are not very realistic. He speculates that a major motivation of the Postal Service is to provide work for its employees, of which there are over half a million. Were mail volume to drop precipitously, there would be a surplus of workers to handle the mail. Because the no-layoff clause in the service's contract with the postal unions, even as recently modified, limits laying off postal workers, the service would be unable to adjust the size of the work force to handle economically the drastically reduced mail volume. These circumstances, Robinson suggests, result in an "employment imperative" that encourages the Postal Service to take uneconomic actions to ensure that postal workers will be kept busy. I cannot really agree with this thesis. The postal work force is already declining. The recent modification of the no-layoff clause limiting its protection to members of the present work force and future employees with more than six years' experience will allow greater flexibility in making further reductions.

More important, I do not think that postal management approaches major new product decisions such as electronic diversification on that basis. My experience at the Postal Service and my study of postal affairs indicate that there is a genuine sense of public responsibility to fulfill a mission—to provide mail service. Entry into the electronics field is probably viewed by postal management as a substitute for or an extension of current services of the type traditionally provided by the Postal Service. We should not, therefore, allow the ogre of an "employment

190

imperative" or similar sinister motives to color our thinking about electronic diversification by the Postal Service.

Postal Service entry into electronic mail may take place, as Robinson suggests, through joint ventures with electronic communications firms. Thus, the Postal Service would not do the whole job itself but would team up with a company such as Western Union to provide electronic mail service. In this regard, several joint ventures and development contracts signed recently by the Postal Service, and extending beyond the now-familiar Mailgram service, are worth noting. The Postal Service has signed a preliminary contract with Comsat to examine aspects of an international electronic message service called INTELPOST. Another service to be provided jointly with Western Union called ECOM (electronic computer-originated mail), which is analogous to a bulk Mailgram, is now before the Postal Rate Commission. In addition, in the research and development stage, RCA is evaluating for the Postal Service a comprehensive electronic message service system (EMSS).

Robinson argues that in the case of a joint venture the FCC would then have jurisdiction over the action of the Postal Service. This is not at all clear to me because the FCC jurisdiction may attach to and stop at the regulated electronic communication company rather than extend to the Postal Service. This may depend, furthermore, upon the contractual relationship between the service and the joint venturer.

The heart of Robinson's paper is a discussion of the private express statutes and their relevance to the issue of electronic diversification. (The private express statutes, of course, are the series of federal laws that preclude competitors of the Postal Service from providing lucrative first-class mail service; they even prohibit the use of home mailboxes by other than Postal Service carriers.) The relationship of these statutes to the issue of electronic mail is, as Robinson notes, not so much a legal question as a political question. Nevertheless, I shall focus upon the legal aspects and their treatment in Robinson's paper.

In my view, Robinson inadequately acknowledges the policy reasons behind the private express statutes. These statutes were intended to facilitate universal mail service. That is, the private express statutes protect the Postal Service's revenues to enable the service to provide universal mail service at moderate rates. It is my view that this policy justification should be reexamined. The same goals might be achieved by more efficient and less expensive means—for example, by an explicit subsidy for high-cost, first-class rural mail.

In a filing before the Postal Rate Commission in January 1976, the Council on Wage and Price Stability urged such a reexamination and suggested an agenda for further discussion. The following issues and subissues, among others, were identified.

1. Impact on society of repeal or relaxation of the private express statutes
   a. How would the consumer be affected (in terms of rates paid and quality of service)?
   b. How would postal workers be affected (in terms of wages, fringe benefits, and working conditions)?
   c. What would be the impact on businesses, nonprofit organizations, and state and local governments (especially with respect to differential impacts by geographic area)?
2. Effects of the private express statutes on the efficient allocation of the nation's resources
   a. Is the Postal Service truly a natural monopoly?
   b. What are the effects on the Postal Service's operational efficiency?
3. Policy issues to consider
   a. Should the private express statutes be repealed or simply relaxed?
   b. Could many of the same goals be achieved through improved Postal Service performance?
   c. In the event competition developed, should it be regulated?
   d. What mechanisms could be devised to enable private firms to offer service in rural and other low-density areas?
   e. What interconnection problems might arise, and how could they best be resolved?

Robinson expresses concern with the Postal Service's interpretation of the private express statutes and with the power that the Postal Service has claimed to suspend the private express statues in certain circumstances. Suspension can have benefits, particularly in times of mail stoppages, as well as costs imposed by furthering the postal monopoly. For example, in anticipation of a possible mail strike last summer, the Postal Service drew up contingency plans, one of which involved relaxing the private express statutes. Nonetheless, were the private express statutes used to forbid private initiatives in the electronic communications area, this would clearly be against the public interest.

One rationale for not allowing the Postal Service entry into electronic communications was not raised in Robinson's discussion but is worth considering. When a private company enters a new field, the stockholders assume the risks. If the venture is a success, the stockholders will benefit; if the venture is a failure, the stockholders will suffer any losses. The Postal Service has no stockholders, however. Therefore, the risks of improvident entry by the Postal Service into the electronic communications field would be borne by postal rate payers and, possibly, by taxpayers. Since these groups do not have an opportunity to vote on the provision of electronic mail service, a policy judgment should be exercised before the service is permitted to embark in these areas.

To support this policy judgment, there should be a thorough analysis of the financial risks inherent in major investment to enable the Postal Service to provide electronic communications services, particularly in light of earlier experience surrounding the billion-dollar investment in the bulk mail system. Moreover, this analysis should include an evaluation of the probable costs and benefits of alternative postal investments, which quite possibly could result in equivalent social benefits at lower costs. In my judgment, several major issues should be resolved:

• Would precluding the Postal Service from providing electronic communications services result in greater or lesser inefficiencies compared with the possible stifling of private initiatives that could result from Postal Service involvement?

• How important are the usual postal policy considerations, such as the provision of universal access to service, in considering Postal Service's provision of electronic communications services?

• Is electronic mail service merely an extension of customary mail service, or is it a precursor of fully electronic service and therefore a major encroachment on private vendors of similar services?

• What would be the effect of Postal Service involvement in electronic communications on innovation in this area?

Until any final policy decisions are taken, I believe that the Postal Service should be able to explore the provison of electronic communications services, and even to test services that would complement services already provided. However, the Postal Service should not take steps that would discourage private initiatives in this area. Finally, since the Postal Service is, for better or worse, the principal delivery system in the nation, private vendors of electronic communications services should be allowed to interconnect with any eventual postal transmission and delivery systems.

10

Politics and the Future of Postal Services

James I. Campbell, Jr.

Throughout its long history, the federal Post Office has owed its existence and prosperity more to its political pull than to its mastery of the arts of law or economics.

The Post Office Department was born in 1782 as an executive department of the central government, which was then organized under the Articles of Confederation; it was continued in the same form by the present federal government in one of its first acts, the Act of September 22, 1789.[1] The president managed the Post Office Department directly through his lieutenant, the postmaster general. Each year Congress not only approved the postal budget but also determined the categories and prices of various postal services and mandated the performance of certain noncompensatory services required by congressional concepts of the public interest.

Under the Postal Reorganization Act of 1970, the Post Office was born again as the U.S. Postal Service, an independent federal agency.[2] This independence is imperfect, however, since the Postal Service must go to Congress annually for an appropriation that means all the difference between making a profit and breaking even, and every move toward more economically rational management invokes congressional threats to resume control. The Postal Service is also forced to abide by various procedures and criteria for setting prices and costs not shared

Note: The views expressed in this paper are those of the author and do not necessarily reflect the position of his client, a domestic and international private carrier of time-sensitive commercial papers and business records.

[1] See George L. Priest, "The History of the Postal Monopoly in the United States," *Journal of Law and Economics*, vol. 13 (1973), pp. 45–51.
[2] P.L. 91–375, 85 Stat. 719.

by private companies who are somewhat more truly independent. All in all, the Postal Service is still dependent upon Congress's favors and its willingness to invest the post office—legally and spiritually—with the mantle of "the government."

This paper briefly summarizes the current game of postal politics, describes the major actors and players, and offers some thoughts on how postal politics will be likely to affect the general shape of future postal services.[3]

Central Political Issue: Protection from Competition

Postal politics are characterized by a bewildering complexity of issues: Who will name the postmaster general? What fraction of costs must be attributed to which class of mail? Who is to be allowed reduced rates? Is the Postal Service a public service, or should it be "put on a businesslike basis"? What is the proper role of the Postal Rate Commission? And so on. Most of these issues, however, are minor or of secondary importance to the issue that will determine the basic shape of the post office of the future.

The main fact of postal life is that, to an increasing degree, the Postal Service cannot compete with private industry and will be even less able to do so in the foreseeable future (ten to twenty years). In September 1978 the Senate postal subcommittee summed up the situation as follows:

> The Postal Service faces a future fraught with potentially greater economic pressures than so far experienced. Techno- logical developments pose a major threat to the volume of first-class mail, which is the Service's bread and butter, its primary raison d'être. Third-class bulk mail, another mainstay of the Postal Service's financial base, has declined in use as advertisers, faced with higher postal rates, have sought more cost-efficient media. . . . Second-class mail users, too, are in- creasingly turning to alternative means of distribution, as are book publishers and others. Long gone is the typical business

---

[3] In this paper, which is merely a primer on postal politics, only the level of appropriations and the postal monopoly are discussed in any detail. More fundamentally, only three legislative forums are discussed, the administration and the postal committees in both houses of Congress. This is, of course, merely a simplification. A more complete picture would require a discussion of the congressional committees that rule upon legislation concerning the alternatives to postal delivery, such as telecommunications, airline express services, and surface carriers (especially the first). One should also take into account the attitudes of the postal appropriations committees in both chambers, the Senate Budget Committee, the House Rules Committee, and even the members of the old Senate Post Office Committee. To understand each of these additional congressional forums one must, in turn, understand the "players" and the pressures that shape their decisions.

195

user of parcel delivery service, who has found more specialized
service at competitive rates to his advantage.[4]

The major reasons for this dismal outlook in the Postal Service's competitive position have been well described by others. The basic facts are
simple. The postal business is labor-intensive, and the Postal Service
has agreed to pay its employees more than private industry pays its
employees (average postal wage in July 1978 was about $18,700). Fur-
thermore, the Postal Service has agreed to a guarantee of lifetime jobs
for all current workers. In short, the Postal Service's costs are noncom-
petitive and out of control.[5] Lifetime guarantees for current employees
will fade in significance as the current employees retire. About half will
retire in the next decade (see n. 20, below). Since the 1978 contract
provides that only future employees with six years' service will get
lifetime guarantees, the Postal Service can, at least theoretically, regain
control of its labor costs at some time in the future. However, the Postal
Service has little control over other cost factors that are also increasing,
such as the number of delivery points it must serve or the price of
gasoline.

On top of this, the Postal Service faces new competition from forms
of communications in which the Postal Service is not especially adept—
air express delivery and electronic message systems. The use of air
express delivery services as a communications medium has grown very
rapidly over the last decade. Changing technology and the increased
scale of business have contributed to this development, as has the increase in postal rates. The real price of air transportation has declined
with the introduction of jumbo jets, and the cost of delayed communications would appear to have risen as the modern business tries to
coordinate the activities of more and more offices within increasingly
tight schedules. For example, a delayed report, inventory record, or
blueprint might today hold up the work of ten "downstream" offices
instead of the one or two of fifteen years ago.

In response to these changes, the Postal Service began express mail

---

[4] U.S. Congress, Senate, Subcommittee on Energy, Nuclear Proliferation, and Federal
Services, *Postal Service Amendments Act of 1978: Report to Accompany H.R. 7700*, S.
Rept. no. 95–1191, 95th Congress, 2nd session, September 13, 1978, p. 5.

[5] See U.S. Congress, General Accounting Office, "A Summary of Observations on Postal
Service Operations from July 1971 to January 1976," in U.S. Congress, Senate, Committee
on Post Office and Civil Service, *Problems of the U.S. Postal Service: Compendium of
Studies, Articles, and Statements on the Postal Service*, 94th Congress, 2nd session, March
1976, pp. 65–66 (description of the contracts of 1971, 1973, and 1975); *Wall Street Journal*,
September 18, 1978, p. 7 (description of the 1978 contract). See generally Douglas K.
Adie, *An Evaluation of Postal Service Wage Rates* (Washington, D.C.: American Enterprise Institute, 1977); U.S. Postal Service, *The Necessity for Change*, staff study (1975;
rpt. ed., U.S. Congress, House, Committee on Post Office and Civil Service, 94th Congress, 2nd session, December 1976).

in 1970. While express mail revenues have grown tremendously in the last seven years—from $18,000 in 1970 to over $46 million in 1977—most of this new business seems to have been captured by private companies such as Federal Express, Purolator Courier Services, Emery Air Freight, and the various airline small-parcel express services. At this point, it appears improbable that the Postal Service will outcompete these air express delivery companies in the foreseeable future.[6]

Even assuming the Postal Service is able to equip itself to offer electronic communications, most observers expect that private competitors using these technologies will be able to outcompete the post office for a significant proportion of first-class mail.[7]

Because the Postal Service is becoming increasingly less competitive with private industry, it seems to me that it will flourish only in areas where it is protected from competition. And such protection can be gained only from the game of postal politics. Traditionally, the postal laws have employed two forms of protection sufficient to shield the Postal Service from competition. One method has been to tax the citizenry and give the money to the Postal Service so it can afford to price so far below its inflated costs that postal rates are set below the prices of unsubsidized private competitors. (Of course, such tax appropriations also permit the Postal Service to provide services that the private sector would not supply at all.) The other method is to prohibit private carriers from engaging in competition with the post office.

As a preliminary matter, therefore, to discover the major effects that postal politics will have on postal services, one should orient one's review of the postal political game to look for clues about how and how much the political forces will attempt to shield the Postal Service from competition. What amount of public appropriations will the Postal Service be granted? How much protection will be granted by means of legal penalties against competition?

---

[6] See U.S. Congress, Senate, Subcommittee on Energy, Nuclear Proliferation, and Federal Services of the Committee on Government Affairs, *Hearings on [S. 3229 and H.R. 7700]*, 95th Congress, 2nd session, 1978, pp. 2–407 (statements of William J. Anderson, deputy director, General Accounting Office; Melvin E. Bailet, executive vice president and general counsel, Loomis Corporation; and DHL Corporation).

The potential diversion of first-class mail to express delivery systems (both air express and surface express) has been estimated very roughly by the Congressional Budget Office at $200 to $400 million. U.S. Congress, Senate, Committee on the Budget, *Waiver of Section 402(a) of the Congressional Budget Act with Respect to Consideration of H.R. 7700*, S. Rept. no. 95–1244, 95th Congress, 2nd session, September 26, 1978, p. 2.

[7] See generally U.S. Commission on Postal Service, *Report*, vol. 2, pp. 425–617 (study of A. D. Little, Inc.) and 861–957 (study by Program of Policy Studies, George Washington University). Common sense suggests that the diversion by air express and electronic message systems will not be additive. That is, telecommunications will divert from air express delivery services as well as postal services.

The Legislators: Congressional Committees and the President

A new postal law is essentially an amalgam of decisions made by three groups of legislators: (1) the House subcommittees on Postal Operations and Services and on Postal Personnel and Modernization; (2) the Senate Subcommittee on Energy, Nuclear Proliferation, and Federal Services; and (3) the executive branch (primarily the Domestic Council, the Office of Management and Budget, and the National Telecommunications and Information Administration).[8]

The House Committee on Post Office and Civil Service has two subcommittees with concurrent jurisdiction over fundamental changes in the postal laws. The Subcommittee on Postal Operations and Services has been chaired by James Hanley of Syracuse, New York, for the past three Congresses. The Subcommittee on Postal Personnel and Modernization is chaired by Charles Wilson of Los Angeles. The two subcommittee chairmen seem to agree on most postal issues and frequently hold joint hearings, although Hanley generally takes the lead.

The House postal subcommittees embody the old school of thought on postal matters. The old school was talked into the creation of an independent, businesslike post office in 1970, and they seem still to harbor doubts about the present independent Postal Service perhaps because its creation repudiated their stewardship over the old political Post Office Department. In a revealing address to a witness from the Postal Service, Chairman Wilson voiced his feelings as follows:

> The thing that continually disturbs me is when you people, who don't know what you are talking about, talk about the Post Office Department. These statements that it was ready to go bankrupt and there was low morale and it was in a quagmire are convenient exaggerations. Where in the world did you pick up that sort of stuff? This Postal Reform Act of 1970 was sold to the Congress by a couple of good salesmen, Larry O'Brien and Red Blout. We were conned very frankly.[9]

When the Postal Service initially foundered, the old school was quick to declare a disaster and propose that Congress take back control over postal affairs, straighten out the mess, and reassume supervisory au-

---

[8] Of course, important amendments are occasionally accepted from the floor in congressional debate, but such amendments are rarely enacted into law without the support of at least one of the committees of jurisdiction. Sometimes a member of one body will add an amendment over the wishes of his committee, but such a floor amendment almost necessarily needs the support of the legislative committee of the other body in conference.
[9] U.S. Congress, House, Subcommittee on Postal Operations and Services and the Subcommittee on Postal Personnel and Modernization of the Committee on Post Office and Civil Service, *Joint Hearings on H.R. 7700: Postal Service Act of 1977,* 95th Congress, 1st session, September 1977, pp. 220–21.

thority over postal affairs. A cynic might suggest that the old school identifies with the post office as though it were their own creation and sometimes favors whatever will aid the post office without regard for the larger, perhaps contrary, interests of the public. A more charitable and perhaps more accurate view would be that the old school sees postal services as a basic governmental function, like defense or highway building, which always has been and always will be necessary to the well-being of the nation. Either way, for the old school the idea that the Postal Service must pay for itself seems as arbitrary as the notion that the Coast Guard should charge for its search and rescue operations.

The attitudes of the old school were nicely summarized in a 1974 report by the now defunct Senate Post Office Committee:

> In February, 1973, two years and four months after the enactment of the wide-ranging Postal Reorganization Act, abolishing the Postal Service's role as a Federal Department, taking away the Congressional rate-making function, establishing the Board of Governors to direct the new postal establishment, and endowing the Postmaster with unprecedented powers and authority, the Postal Service was in serious trouble. . . . Complaints poured at an unprecedented rate into Congressional offices; businessmen complained of lost documents and agreements wrecked by late deliveries . . . truckloads of massed immobile mail were reported. . . . Service nationwide was slow and unpredictable. . . . The goals of [the reorganization] clearly had not been approached; and neither then nor now [March 1974] has there been anything like victory in the race with catastrophe. [10]

The old school has been very "political" in its approach to postal legislation in both a good and a bad sense. It has been close to interest groups such as the postal unions and publishers and skillful in obtaining legislative results. For example, the Postal Reorganization Act amendments of 1976 established a congressional study group, the Commission on Postal Service, to review the record of the Postal Service and recommend new legislation. Both the Senate and House bills and their legislative history made clear that this study was to be unrestricted. In the words of the Senate bill, "The Commission shall not be limited to any subject areas for consideration." Nonetheless, the conference report contains an oblique sentence, "The conferees agree that the Commission should not study areas relating to matters covered under chapter 12 of title 39, United States Code." The reference is to the labor relations chapter of the postal code. Whether as a result of this sentence or not,

---

[10] U.S. Congress, Senate, Committee on Post Office and Civil Service, *Investigation of the Postal Service*, S. Rept. no. 95–727, 93d Congress, 2nd session, March 1974, p. 2.

the Postal Service Commission had very little criticism of postal wages or basic labor-management policy despite the fact that labor accounts for 86 percent of postal costs.[11] Chairman John Glenn of the Senate postal subcommittee subsequently commented upon this omission with some incredulity, "How can you run a business and not have a major study cover 86 percent of the costs? . . . All of these [postal policy] options are so tied up in the type of labor and the wage scales . . . that I don't see how we could consider them while completely ignoring the work source factor."[12]

In 1977 the House Post Office Committee's ideas on postal policy were embodied in its version of H.R. 7700. This bill would increase congressional scrutiny of rates and service changes, abolish the Board of Governors, make the president directly responsible for the postmaster general, require the Postal Service to begin developing an electronic message system, and increase the standing appropriations for the Postal Service from $0.92 billion to $2.52 billion (fiscal year 1978). The House committee bill was strongly supported by postal unions.

(H.R. 7700 was amended in important respects by the full House and then overwhelmingly approved in April 1978. The Senate postal subcommittee completely rewrote the bill and reported it to the Senate on September 18, 1978. On October 15, 1978, the 95th Congress adjourned without completing action on H.R. 7700.)

The Carter administration's position and approach are the polar opposite of the old school's. The Carter administration's position was initially stated, apparently without prior consultation with Congress, in testimony to the House committee on September 20, 1977. Bowman Cutter summarized the executive's evaluation of the Postal Service as follows:

> We believe that the efforts begun in 1970 to overcome the problems which faced the old Post Office Department—mounting deficits, low morale and poor working conditions, and a lack of modern techniques for handling the mail—should be continued. . . . Progress has been made to accomplish these

---

[11] U.S. Congress, House, Committee on Post Office and Civil Service, *H.R. 8603, Postal Reorganization Act Amendments of 1976: Legislative History,* 94th Congress, 2nd session, October 1976, pp. 55–57, 503, 537. In a similar manner the conference committee reported a bill directing the Postal Rate Commission to report on "new electronic fund transfers and communication techniques . . . and the feasibility of the Postal Service operating such systems." Neither the House bill nor the Senate bill had mentioned such a review, but postal participation in telecommunications has long been advocated by Chairman Hanley (ibid., pp. 7, 231–38, 280–83).

[12] U.S. Congress, Senate, Subcommittee on Energy, Nuclear Proliferation, and Federal Services of the Committee on Government Affairs, *Hearings: Evaluation of the Report of the Commission on Postal Service,* 95th Congress, 1st session, 1977, p. 50.

goals. The average postal worker's wages and fringe benefits now average $17,300, and working conditions in postal facilities have been greatly improved. The Postal Service continues to provide a wide range of services, delivering mail in most instances, on a timely basis. . . .

We believe that the most equitable way for meeting these challenges [of declining mail volume and electronic technology] is to retain a Postal Service that is essentially independent and able to balance the needs of mail users against the cost of the services provided. In our view, a postal system having the flexibility and freedom to conduct its operations according to market demand and public need is a desirable system to retain. [13]

The position of the Carter administration has not changed significantly since this testimony.

Statements of the administration position are heavily laden with catchwords of free-market rhetoric. The administration speaks of "operations according to market demand" and of an "independent" Postal Service able "to balance the needs of mail users against the cost of the services provided." Before the Senate subcommittee, the administration opposed even a temporary freeze in first-class rates for individuals, despite the obvious political advantages of such a measure. [14]

So strongly does the administration's position smack of free-market terms that it seems odd that the Carter administration has not picked up on the hints of the Ford administration and recommended the repeal, or at least the reexamination, of the postal monopoly. The answer cannot be the Republican origin of this idea, for such did not prevent President Carter from championing airline regulatory reform. Nor would a concern for labor's displeasure seem decisive, since the postal unions could not abide by any of the other administration positions on the postal laws. The answer lies, perhaps, in the White House's announced determination to balance the budget by 1982 and the fear of having to bail out the Postal Service.

In postal politics, the House committee and the Carter administration present a remarkable contrast. While the House committee seems attentive to the needs of various interest groups, the Carter administration seems to be oblivious to them. Rather, the administration position seems more a combination of two conflicting, a priori goals

---

[13] House, Subcommittee on Postal Operations and Services and Subcommittee on Postal Personnel and Modernization of the Committee on Post Office and Civil Service, *Joint Hearings on H.R. 7700*, pp. 179–80.

[14] Senate, Subcommittee on Energy, Nuclear Proliferation, and Federal Services of the Committee on Government Affairs, *Hearings on [S. 3229 and H.R. 7700]*, pp. 21 to 35 (statement of Bowman Cutter, Office of Management and Budget).

worked out in a back room of the old Executive Office Building: balance the budget and operate the Postal Service like a business. Similarly, if the old school is strikingly savvy in old-fashioned politics, then the Carter administration is remarkably innocent. The language of the administration's testimony before the House committee could hardly have been better chosen to rile the veteran congressmen who, after all, have been working on postal issues for many years prior to the advent of the new administration. The old school's crises are greeted cheerfully as challenges. The products of congressional deliberations are termed "subsidies" instead of "authorizations" and "appropriations." The committee chairmen were amazed that the administration people did not consult with them informally and extensively on postal legislation prior to testimony, and the administration's representative was amazed at their amazement.

The approach of the third group of postal legislators, the Senate postal subcommittee, is somewhere between that of the House subcommittee and the Carter administration, a middle position that befits its recent origin and politically attuned members. In 1976 the Senate abolished the Senate Post Office Committee and transferred jurisdiction over the Postal Service to the Subcommittee on Energy, Nuclear Proliferation, and Federal Services of the Government Affairs Committee. Chaired by Senator John Glenn, the seven-member subcommittee has only one member (Senator Ted Stevens) who had been on the old postal committee.

The Senate postal subcommittee's general position is embodied in its first report on postal legislation, the report on H.R. 7700, issued on September 18, 1978. Like the White House, the Senate subcommittee endorsed the basic independence of the Postal Service, indicated reluctance to raise substantially federal appropriations for the Postal Service, and implied that, to some extent at least, the Postal Service must succeed or fail on its own merits. On the other hand, like the House committee, the Senate subcommittee felt the political pressure of general and specific cries for rate relief. The subcommittee bill thus would freeze the first-class rate for individuals for four years and provide extra low rates for children's magazines, political parties' mailings, small-circulation magazines, and certain library materials. The subcommittee's bill would also provide a limited exemption from the postal monopoly for time-sensitive letters, thereby responding to pleas from businessmen that have been building for several years. Finally, the Senate subcommittee version of H.R. 7700 strikes a third theme:

> The committee does not believe that . . . a final long-term "solution" is feasible at this time, given the fast pace of change in the total communications market, of which the Postal Serv-

ice is but a part. And it believes an improved level of information and data to be necessary before the Congress undertakes to make public policy decisions that could be a significant new departure for the Nation.[15]

Accordingly, the bill provides for various reports over the next four years and necessitates congressional reexamination of the postal laws before then by terminating many of the provisions of the bill, including appropriations, at the end of fiscal year 1982.

The Senate postal subcommittee appears to hold the "swing vote" between the opposing views of the House committee and the Carter administration. The subcommittee's report on H.R. 7700 seems to me, at least, to have been a sound first attempt to strike a workable middle ground on these issues, and it therefore probably points to the general direction of the next round of postal legislation.[16]

The Players

Before these three legislative forums, various parties, including the other legislators, strive to win statutory reification of their positions. Those influential in postal politics include the Postal Service, the postal unions, the beneficiaries of below-cost postal rates, the businessmen who use private carriers, and the general public.

The Postal Service itself is the group of top and middle managers represented by the postmaster general. In April 1978, a thirty-seven-year veteran of the postal service, William Bolger, became the postmaster general. Bolger's promotion completed the career employees' take-over of the top administrative jobs at the Postal Service and their ousting of the outside political appointees who had held such jobs when the Post Office was an executive department.

The dominant political goal of this group appears to be survival, that is, avoidance of a reassertion of presidential appointment power

---

[15] Senate, Subcommittee on Energy, Nuclear Proliferation, and Federal Services, *Report to Accompany H.R. 7700*, p. 4.

[16] It was rumored that H.R. 7700 as reported by the Senate Government Affairs Committee was unpopular with the administration, the Postal Service, and the postal unions. If so, this lack of support seems to me to reflect not so much the lack of political soundness of the committee's bill as the extreme difficulty of finding common ground between widely divergent views. It was also rumored that the House committee was willing to negotiate with the Senate as a step in the process of getting some bill enacted. If true, such an attitude by the politically astute House group would tend to confirm this assessment.

As the description of the "players" in the text suggests, however, there does seem to be one glaring omission in the Senate committee bill. That is a lack of any statutory assurances for rural postal delivery. Past postal political history strongly suggests that the support of rural groups will be necessary to obtain postal legislation, especially if the postal unions are in opposition.

or detailed management direction from Congress. Presented with the possibility of presidential appointment of the postmaster general in the House-passed version of H.R. 7700, the Postal Service wrote to the Senate committee that "the most drastic alteration" worked by the bill was a "resounding rejection of career-oriented management of the postal system." A second objection was to a provision for an open-ended subsidy to be appropriated each year by Congress. Such a provision would take the basic control of the budget out of the hands of the Postal Service and place it back in the hands of the congressional legislative and appropriations committees. Indeed, the Postal Service generally favors an eventual end to congressional appropriations altogether. The Postal Service, however, supports laws that provide it with competitive advantages without attendant outside scrutiny. Thus, the Postal Service strongly supports an expansive postal monopoly and specific authority to price its products without regard to fully allocated costs. [17]

If "postal independence" is the watchword of the Postal Service, then "public service" is the battle cry of the postal workers. The postal workers argue strongly that the free-market approach of the 1970 Postal Reorganization Act failed to recognize that the post office is a public service, not a private enterprise. As such, the postal laws should commit whatever appropriations are necessary to fund the biggest, most broadly available, most technologically sophisticated postal service that is possible (within the general constraints of lifetime guarantees of all workers, prohibitions against part-time workers, and high average wage levels). The postal unions therefore support increased congressional appropriations for the Postal Service and resumption of the political control that such large appropriations would necessarily entail. Indeed, postal unions have testified to Congress that they believe postal officials are trying to "do away with" the Postal Service. Like the Postal Service, however, the unions strongly favor the broadest possible postal monopoly and wide latitude for postal pricing policies. [18]

The political strength of the postal unions—a key political variable in the future of the Postal Service—seems to me to be headed for sharp

---

[17] Senate, Subcommittee on Energy, Nuclear Proliferation, and Federal Services of the Committee on Government Affairs, *Hearings on [S. 3229 and H.R. 7700]*, (statement of Postmaster General William F. Bolger and letter from Bolger to Abraham Ribicoff, July 19, 1978).

[18] Ibid. (Statement of American Postal Workers Union); Senate, Subcommittee on Energy, Nuclear Proliferation, and Federal Services of the Committee on Government Affairs, *Evaluation of the Report of the Commission on Postal Service*, pp. 128–207; House, Subcommittee on Postal Operations and Services and Subcommittee on Postal Personnel and Modernization of the Committee on Post Office and Civil Service, *Joint Hearings on H.R. 7700*, pp. 82–90.

decline. The numbers of postal employees has dropped over the last eight years from approximately 750,000 to approximately 650,000.[19] As postal wages continue to increase and new techology reduces the need for postal workers, it can be expected that union membership will continue to decrease rapidly as more than 300,000 postal workers will reach retirement age before 1986.[20] More important, perhaps, since the 1978 postal contract gives current employees a guarantee of lifetime employment, it has removed much of their personal incentive to fight the political battles for new postal legislation in their few remaining years of service.

A third important group of participants in postal politics is the businesses who receive reduced rates for the delivery of their publications and other products. This group includes publishers, advertisers, and parcel shippers. Of course, these businesses have historically defended their reduced rates with great vigor and, as a corollary, they have favored increases in the federal appropriations for the Postal Service. The steep increases in postal rates, however, seem to be gradually driving these historic postal allies to private carriage.[21] If so, then their interest in large postal appropriations and other means of shoring up the Postal Service will inevitably decline.

Rural mailers do not have a lobbying organization, but they have traditionally been very well represented in Congress. For example, in 1975 when the General Accounting Office suggested closing a number

[19] Senate, Subcommittee on Energy, Nuclear Proliferation, and Federal Services of the Committee on Government Affairs, *Hearings on [S. 3229 and H.R. 7700]*, p. 7 (statement of William J. Anderson, deputy director, General Government Division, General Accounting Office).

[20] John F. McLaughlin, "The National Commission on Postal Service: An Opportunity to Rethink the Traditional Role of Postal Services in a Changing World," October 18, 1976, mimeographed. McLaughlin was a staff member of the Office of Strategic Planning, U.S. Postal Service, at the time he presented this paper.

[21] Second-class mailings are decreasing because, as the Magazine Publishers Association indicated, "alternate delivery through the private sector is feasible for a substantial portion of [magazines and newspapers]." A large group of direct mail advertisers is now suing for a declaratory judgment that the postal monopoly does not apply to their third-class matter. *Associated Third Class Mail Users* v. *U.S. Postal Service*, 440 F. Supp. 1211 (D.D.C. 1977), appeal pending, D.C. Cir. no. 78–1065. And the Postal Service's fourth-class service for parcels handled only 300 million parcels in 1976, compared with 900 million parcels in 1959 (during the same period, United Parcel Service's business increased from 100 million to 1 billion parcels). This abandonment of parcel post seems likely to continue since the American Association of Publishers, for example, testified to the Senate postal subcommittee that book publishers would soon begin "large-scale diversion" to private carriers. See Senate, Subcommittee on Energy, Nuclear Proliferation, and Federal Services of the Committee on Government Affairs, *Hearings on [S. 3229 and H.R. 7700]*, pp. 668–70 (statement of Chapin Carpenter, Jr., senior vice-president/Washington, Magazine Publishers Association; statement of Leo Albert, president, Association of American Publishers).

of rural post offices to save money, congressional hearings were immediately called in which thirty-seven congressmen and three senators filed statements in opposition to the cutbacks. [22] In 1976 Congress enacted a statutory moratorium on the closing of small-town post offices. [23] The rural interests have always supported a well-financed Postal Service, and concerns for small-town service have long been used to justify a strong postal monopoly. Unlike the commercial users of second-, third-, and fourth-class postal services, these groups have little alternative to a federally supported Postal Service, and there seems to be little reason to believe their interest or influence in postal politics has diminished.

In the last few years, the business community generally has emerged as a participant in the postal politics. Their interest is primarily the rapid and reliable delivery of time-sensitive documents such as financial instruments, shipping papers, construction plans and specifications, real estate listings, intracorporate memoranda, and so on. Because satisfactory service is not available from the Postal Service and because the Postal Service has been expanding its claim of monopoly, these companies have sought a clear congressional declaration that the postal monopoly does not cover such documents. During summer of 1978, the private carriers themselves joined in this effort. [24] So far, this group has been successful in obtaining an amendment to the Senate committee version of H.R. 7700 and getting a similar amendment added to H.R. 7700 on the floor of the House.

Finally, the general public influences the game of postal politics, and there are many signs that it is losing some sympathy for the Postal Service. Since 1970 Congress has apparently received a large and steady stream of complaints. As the Senate postal committee reported last month, "Service is widely perceived as having deteriorated." [25] In 1976 Ford administration figures began to hint at the need to repeal the postal

[22] U.S. Congress, House, Subcommittee on Postal Service and Subcommittee on Postal Facilities, Mail, and Labor Management of the Committee on Post Office and Civil Service, *Joint Hearings on GAO's Recommendation That 12,000 Small Post Offices Be Closed,* 94th Congress, 1st session, 1975.

[23] Postal Reorganization Act Amendments of 1976, P.L. 94–421, section 9, 90 Stat. 1310–11.

[24] Senate, Subcommittee on Energy, Nuclear Proliferation, and Federal Services of the Committee on Government Affairs, *Hearings on [S. 3229 and H.R. 7700],* pp. 355–436 (statement of the National Association of Manufacturers; statement of Melvin E. Bailet, executive vice-president and general counsel, Loomis Corporation). The House provision was the amendment sponsored by Trent Lott, 124 *Congressional Record,* p. H2549, April 6, 1978. The Senate committee version is described in Senate, Subcommittee on Energy, Nuclear Proliferation, and Federal Services, *Report to Accompany H.R. 7700,* pp. 17–21.

[25] Senate, Subcommittee on Energy, Nuclear Proliferation, and Federal Services, *Report to Accompany H.R. 7700,* p. 5.

JAMES I. CAMPBELL, JR.

monopoly, [26] hints that were echoed by such prominent senators as Democrat Alan Cranston and Republican Jesse Helms. [27] More recently, a poll of mail users gave the Postal Service only a "somewhat favorable" rating, with 46 percent of people registering "major complaints" about the postal service. [28]

Prospects for Higher Appropriations

Given these legislative forums and participants, how will postal politics resolve the question most basic to the future of postal services: How much protection from competition, through either appropriation or monopoly, will be granted the Postal Service?

The report of the President's Commission on Postal Organization, which led directly to the 1970 Reorganization Act, squarely stated the fundamental constraint on increasing public appropriations to the Postal Service:

> Theoretically, any subsidy voted by Congress should be paid from tax funds. The practice, however, presents serious difficulties for the postal service. . . . Because so many postal activities have common costs, it is impossible to isolate the costs of subsidized services from those of ordinary mail services. *If subsidies were funded by appropriation, therefore, it would be extremely difficult to avoid detailed Congressional and Executive involvement with all postal management matters.* [29]

The use of large appropriations to shield the Postal Service from competition would be tantamount to reversing the national policy in favor of an independent Postal Service adopted in the 1970 act. For the reasons described above, this reversal of policy is strongly opposed by the Postal Service and the president. On the other hand, the end of the independent Postal Service is strongly favored by the House committee, the postal unions, and the rural interests. Judging from the disillusionment with big government evinced by the public over the last several years, how-

---

[26] Secretary of the Treasury William E. Simon, Chairman of the Federal Reserve Board Arthur F. Burns, and a representative of the Council on Wage and Price Stability all spoke in favor of reexamining the need for a postal monopoly. Senate, Committee on Post Office and Civil Service, *Problems of the U.S. Postal Service,* pp. 149–50.

[27] U.S. Congress, Senate, Committee on Post Office and Civil Service, *Hearings on S. 2844: Postal Amendments,* 94th Congress, 2d session, April 20, 1976, p. 149; see also S. 3025, 94th Congress, 2nd session, 122 *Congressional Record,* pp. S2174–76, February 24, 1976.

[28] Commission on Postal Service, *Report,* vol. 2, p. 54.

[29] President's Commission on Postal Organization, *Towards Postal Excellence* (June 1968; rpt. ed., U.S. Congress, House, Committee on Post Office and Civil Service, 94th Congress, 2nd session, November 24, 1976), p. 142 (emphasis added).

ever, I would suspect that the public as a whole prefers an independent, self-sustaining post office to higher taxes to pay for ever-higher wages for federal employees with guaranteed lifetime jobs. Despite their well-rehearsed pleas for more funds and lower rates, I do not think that the various second-, third-, and fourth-class users constitute a strong political force for reversion to higher appropriations. The Senate subcommittee's postal bill, although sensitive to political considerations, seems to share this last assessment, since it does not give substantial rate relief to these groups generally.

A year ago the balance of political power on the question of the fiscal independence of the Postal Service may have been fairly even. But the continuation of long-standing political and technological trends has changed the cast and relative strength of the players in postal politics. The Senate committee seems to reflect the practicalities of postal politics better than either the House committee or the administration. Its decision to support an independent Postal Service and to oppose large public appropriations appears to be the deciding vote that will foreclose the possibility of a return to the massive postal subsidies of former years.

One glaring loose end in this analysis, however, is the fate of postal services to small towns. The losses incurred in service to rural America can only increase. Congressmen sympathetic to the needs of small-town inhabitants appear to have the political strength (perhaps because of the justness of their cause) to obtain some guarantee of postal service despite any financial losses. To oblige the Postal Service to serve unprofitable points, of course, means public appropriations and political control, notwithstanding the reasoning above. The most likely resolution of these contrary policies would be the establishment of a means of separately financing small-town postal service in a more or less automatic fashion. One method would be to provide for an annual appropriation for rural postal service equal to a given percentage of the Postal Service's budget. Another method would be to establish a fund for rural postal service financed by a tax on postal services (or, to take changing technology into account, a tax on all public and private transportation of documents, or all public and private communications). Such separate funding of the postal service to small communities would roughly parallel the way in which Congress handled a similar problem of small-town service in its deregulation of the Civil Aeronautics Board.

Prospects for the Postal Monopoly

The prospects for the Postal Service's receiving some sort of political protection from competition by means of the postal monopoly laws are more complex.

Today, the postal monopoly laws provide imperfect protection against competition because they consist of statutes more than 100 years old which, on their face at least, do not protect the Postal Service against very much. Actually, the postal monopoly only prohibits the regular private carriage of "letters and packets" over post routes or between places the post offices regularly serve. By the Postal Service's reckoning, personal letters and business letters account for only 14 percent of first-class mail revenues, and all other correspondence adds only another 16 percent, a total of 30 percent of first-class revenues, or about 15 percent of total postal revenues.

In short, the cloak of the 1782 postal monopoly covers the body of the massive 1978 Postal Service like a string bikini. Furthermore, obtaining congressional enactment of a broader statutory monopoly seems politically infeasible. During the last century, the Post Office has mounted unsuccessful campaigns to persuade Congress to expand its monopoly to telegrams, parcel post, and special delivery service. It would appear even more difficult to obtain an expansion of the postal monopoly today from a Congress and president who are undoing the statutory monopolies of the airlines and considering similar deregulation of other regulated industries.

The Postal Service seems to agree. In the 1970 Reorganization Act, Congress virtually invited the Postal Service to ask for a more expansive monopoly and to recommend other changes in the private express statutes. But, in its report to Congress in 1973, the Postal Service declined in the following fashion:

> The Private Express prohibitions have historically centered on letter mail. They have been held not to extend to the private carriage of periodicals and unaddressed circulars. Economic analysis indicates that retaining prohibitions on the private carriage of letters would be sufficient to ensure the continued capability of the Postal Service to meet its national service objectives. In these circumstances, extension of the monopoly to periodicals or unaddressed circulars—which would surely displace existing private enterprises—seems unnecessary. [30]

In retrospect, this 1973 report seems to mark an institutional decision to abandon attempts to expand the postal monopoly by statutory amendment and to seek instead de facto expansion by more indirect, but still political, means. Current attempts by the Postal Service to enlarge its monopoly seem derived, consciously or unconsciously, from two fun-

---

[30] U.S. Postal Service, *The Private Express Statutes and Their Administration* (June 29, 1973), p. 10.

damental premises. First, the postal monopoly is valuable to the Postal Service not so much for its literal meaning as for the degree to which it allows the Postal Service to intimidate persons into using the mail. Second, the postal monopoly can most easily be expanded by convincing enough people that the monopoly already includes all sorts of items and then obtaining congressional or court ratification of this position.

Over the last few years, the Postal Service's renewed efforts to persuade persons to comply with the postal monopoly have taken the form of visits and letters to customers of private carriers rather than to the carriers themselves.[31] This approach seems to reflect the fact that it is easier to persuade a customer to increase his costs by a small fraction than to convince a private carrier to get out of business.

Technically, the club with which the Postal Service threatens a private carrier's customer is the possibility that the local U.S. attorney might prosecute him and, if he is found guilty, that he might be liable for a fifty-dollar fine.[32] The Postal Service suggests that this might be fifty dollars per illegal letter, although in fact no one seems to know for sure whether this fine is fifty dollars per letter or fifty dollars per prosecution since no one has ever been prosecuted under this statute. The Postal Service also tells customers that they are liable for back postage for items shipped by illegal carriers, a very considerable amount of money in many cases.[33] However, legal opinions of both the Postal Service solicitor and the U.S. attorney general reject the possibility of such liability.[34] By such methods, at least some shippers are persuaded to use the Postal Service (or to pay postage for items shipped privately), especially firms who are dependent upon federal contracts and are wary of headlines such as "ABC Company Cheats Fed out of Postage!"

The Postal Service appears to be moving now to strengthen this club. By virtue of a few lines on page 240 of the 333-page "technical and conforming" amendment to the Senate's 382-page revision of the U.S. Criminal Code (S. 1437), the Senate passed a bill that would increase the fine for customers of private carriers from $50 to $10,000 (and the fine for carriers from $500 to $100,000). Largely unnoticed by shippers or carriers, this "technical and conforming" amendment could only have been the work of the Postal Service. (This bill became stalled in the House committee and so was never approved by the 95th Congress.)

---

[31] This conclusion is drawn from personal experience in dealing with many shippers and private carriers.

[32] 18 *U.S. Code* 1696(*b*).

[33] 39 C.F.R. 310.2(*a*), 310.5.

[34] 4 Ops. A.G. 349 (1844); 6 Ops. Sol. POD 619 (1918).

Similar tactics by the Postal Service were evidenced on August 16, 1978. A few minutes before the Senate Government Affairs Committee was about to give final approval to a new exemption from the postal monopoly for time-sensitive letters, the Postal Service persuaded Chairman Glenn to offer an enforcement amendment that would allow the Postal Service itself to assess "civil" fines for abuse of the new exemption. Under this last-minute amendment, instead of bothering the U.S. attorney and the district court judge, the new enforcement procedures would allow the Postal Service to serve as prosecutor, judge, and jury. Significantly, the enforcement mechanism proposed by the Postal Service is directed only against customers, not carriers.

In addition to enhancing its enforcement authority, the Postal Service has also been attempting to gain general acceptance for an expansive interpretation of the current postal monopoly laws. As proposed in the Board of Governor's 1973 report on the private express statutes, broad new postal monopoly regulations were formally adopted by the Postal Service in September 1974 (39 C.F.R. 310, 320). These regulations proclaim that the statutory monopoly over the carriage of "letters" in fact extends to virtually any tangible object bearing information to an identifiable person or address. As many observers, including counsel for the Interstate Commerce Commission and the Postal Rate Commission, pointed out, these 1974 regulations promote a far broader view of the postal monopoly than was generally accepted previously, even by the Post Office.[35] Suddenly, blueprints, data processing, packages of merchandise containing advertising, and many other items were declared by the Postal Service to be within the postal monopoly.[36]

A politically necessary concomitant of the Postal Service's expansive claims of monopoly authority has been the assumption by the Postal Service of a newly discovered power to suspend the postal monopoly in selected instances (a power, it seems quite clear, that the Congress has never granted the Postal Service).[37] With this power, the Postal Service mollifies powerful users of private carriers by "suspending" the monopoly with respect to their particular documents.[38]

---

[35] Interstate Commerce Commission, "Comments on Proposed Restrictions on Private Carriage of Letters," August 23, 1973; legal memorandum of the assistant general counsel, Litigation Division, Postal Rate Commission, "Concerning the Role of the Postal Rate Commission in the Exercise of the Legal Controls over the Private Carriage of Mail and the Postal Monopoly," U.S. Postal Rate Commission Docket MC73-1 (July 31, 1974), pp. 2–3.

[36] U.S. Postal Service, *PES 74–14,* 1974; *PES 78–11,* 1976; *PES 75–9,* 1975.

[37] Postal Rate Commission Docket MC73-1, pp. 33–42; Priest, "Postal Monopoly," pp. 79–80, nn. 229–30. These two references review the statutory content and legislative history of the claimed suspension power in great detail and make absolutely clear that the Postal Service has no power to suspend operation of the postal monopoly.

[38] Several "suspensions" appear politically inspired. For example, checks are outside the

The obvious purpose of these expansive claims of monopoly and careful suspensions is to create an impression of a long-established tradition of a very broad postal monopoly, thus placing any proposed statute to the contrary in the politically difficult posture of being an attack on the Postal Service. The public counsel for the Postal Rate Commission explained this technique as follows:

> The suspension technique is a rather ingenious tool for achieving what appears to be the Postal Service's goal, i.e., gathering under its exclusive domain nearly all mailable matter. It permits the immediate adoption of a broad definition of the scope of its monopoly while keeping potential ire of mailers under control. No mailer can really complain so long as there is a suspension in force. If Postal Service were to withdraw its suspension some years hence, it should cause no surprise when Postal Service argues in court that the long standing administrative interpretation of the scope of the postal monopoly should be given great weight.[39]

Although the Postal Rate Commission counsel was thinking in terms of the courts, such an approach is, of course, well suited to obtaining a ratification of an expansive postal monopoly from the legislature as well.

These efforts by the Postal Service to obtain a broader monopoly by indirection are essentially political in nature. That is, they are aimed at affecting the product of congressional and executive deliberations. So far, they have met with some success but no new laws. As noted above, bills to increase the Postal Service's ability to intimidate persons into abiding by its interpretation of the postal monopoly have been approved without much dissent, although none has yet been enacted. The Postal Service's attempts to shift the political debate to the view that anything less than the postal regulations is perceived as a reduction of the monopoly likewise seems to have gained ground. For example, Representative Trent Lott's amendment to H.R. 7700, which exempts time-sensitive intracorporate letters and other items from the postal monopoly, was based upon the 1974 postal regulations as though they were indeed the law. Similarly, the Senate postal subcommittee was discouraged from clarifying the definition of "letter" in the postal monopoly laws apparently because of the aura of complexity and mystery that the Postal Service had succeeded in weaving about this statutory

---

monopoly when sent to or from banks but inside the monopoly when sent between individuals. 39 C.F.R. 3101(a)(7)(ii). Data processing is not within the monopoly if delivered within certain time limits, but otherwise it is in the monopoly—thereby tending to exempt the payroll and accounting information of larger companies but not the smaller firms without sophisticated computers. 39 C.F.R. 320.

[39] Postal Rate Commission Docket MC73–1, p. 33, n. 1.

term. Groups of users who have been granted a suspension by the Postal Service do seem less willing to push for a clearer statute.

The eventual effect that these Postal Service machinations will have on the postal monopoly is very difficult to predict. It seems that the Postal Service has, in real terms, expanded its de facto monopoly by convincing many businessmen and congressmen that the postal monopoly includes far more than mere letters (as that term is used in ordinary speech). Nonetheless, until this enlargement of the monopoly is ratified by a major court case or a congressional statute, it appears entirely possible that some judge will declare that the emperor's postal monopoly robe is mostly holes.

Summary

The most important effect that politics will have on the future of postal services will be the degree to which the political game grants the overpriced and increasingly obsolete Postal Service protection from competition. This protection would probably be in the form of higher appropriations or increased postal monopoly.

Meanwhile, postal politics has changed a great deal in the last few years. The political importance of old interest groups, such as the postal unions and the beneficiaries of reduced postal rates, is slowly declining (although they are still very important players in the game). New interest groups, such as the business community, the private carriers, and, eventually, the telecommunications companies, are becoming active participants. And the roles played by traditional groups, such as the Postal Service, the president, and the Senate committee, have altered dramatically.

The new postal political game seems very unlikely to grant the Postal Service substantially higher appropriations or a forthright increase in its statutory monopoly. This has left the hard-pressed Postal Service with little alternative but to seek from the political game laws that provide an enlargement of the de facto postal monopoly but do not have the appearance of an outright expansion. The Postal Service has pursued this strategy with cleverness and some success, but this campaign has also created a demand for new exemptions from the claimed monopoly. At this point, it is very unclear how much more monopoly protection the Postal Service can gain from this indirect political process.

Commentary

Timothy J. May

I have difficulty agreeing with James Campbell's main thesis: that the principal determinant of the post office of the future will be the fact that the Postal Service cannot compete with private industry. In making this judgment, Campbell sweeps aside as of minor or secondary importance such issues as whether the Postal Service is to be run as a public service or a business, and the method by which costs are attributed to the various classes of mail. I believe that, to the extent that traditional postal products continue to have a usefulness to consumers in the future, the ability of the Postal Service to compete with private industry will in large measure be determined by the so-called minor or secondary issues of whether the Postal Service is viewed as a public service or a business, and whether a rational cost attribution system can be designed for the fixing of the prices that consumers will have to pay for various postal services.

Campbell emphasizes the substantial increases in postal rates since postal reorganization as a fundamental cause of the erosion of the Postal Service's competitive position. He also—correctly, I think—puts his finger on the principal cause of those increases, namely, the three wage contracts negotiated under the collective bargaining powers created in the Postal Reorganization Act. It is difficult to weigh the legitimacy of these wage increases because of the noncomparability of postal work with that performed by workers in other industries. These contracts were, after all, the result of the collective bargaining process, although lurking in the background was the veiled threat of an illegal postal strike that would have had a crippling effect upon the economy. We do know, at least, that postal wages have exceeded, by a very large percentage, increases granted to all other government employees, and have exceeded by a substantial margin increases granted in the private sector. On the other hand, postal wages were, by all informed persons, believed to be substantially depressed in 1970.

214

Campbell also foresees vast diversions of business from the Postal Service to the express carriers and to the electronic message media, forms of service that the Postal Service, even if it makes the attempt, will not effectively be able to provide competitively. I suspect he is correct in his belief that the Postal Service will never be a dominant figure in the express service or in the electronic communications service, although I do believe it will have its proper role in supplying those services as well.

Campbell concludes that the Postal Service will become increasingly dependent upon business it captures solely because it is protected from competition through the postal monopoly laws or through tax subsidies that will enable it to provide services below cost.

Campbell defines the important governmental influences on postal affairs. Without subscribing to his characterizations of the old guard represented by the House subcommittees, the fresh view provided by the brand-new Senate subcommittee charged with postal affairs, or the budget consciousness of the White House, I cannot really disagree with his analysis of the basic positions or attitudes of any of the three. It is accurate to suggest that the House Postal Service subcommittees believe that postal reform was a mistake; that they bought a pig in a poke when they approved postal reform; and that, by and large, they give great attention to the wishes of the postal unions—whereas the Senate subcommittee, with all fresh faces save one, comes to the subject without any preconceived notions; but, alas, at the same time they come to the subject without any experience or learning. Campbell is correct when he says that the legislation produced by the different bodies is reflective of the experience they have had in postal affairs and the voices that influence them. He is just as unerringly accurate in his characterization of the public posture of the White House on postal matters, as reflected in testimony submitted on the Hill, primarily through the Office of Management and Budget. That testimony, which blinks at all the problems, is clearly reflective of the position Campbell ascribes to the White House: a belief that the Postal Service should be run primarily as a business with everyone paying his own way; an exceptional concern that Mr. Carter's budget might, in any way, be burdened with having to absorb postal costs; and a total insensitivity to the political realities of the many different special interests who will either gain or lose depending upon the legislative output—a posture unconstrained by any of the politics of the situation.

I was amused that Campbell cited as an example of the political naiveté of the White House position their opposition to a freeze on first-class postal rates for citizens whereby, until 1982, there would be no increase in the amount of postage paid by the ordinary citizen. Campbell notes that, while there would appear to be obvious political advantages in supporting such a proposal, the White House nevertheless opposed it, either because of political naiveté or because of concern about having to pay for this proposal out of the administration's budget. What he neglects to point out, however, is that the whole concept of a lower citizen rate was dreamed up by this very White House and at the president's insistence was proposed by the Post Office in the most recently concluded rate proceeding. Significantly, the proposal, as advanced by the White House via the Postal Service, was that there would be a freeze on the postage paid by citizens at the old thirteen-cent level, the cost of this lower rate to be subsidized by business users of the mails. Fortunately, the Postal Rate Commission saw this proposal for what it was—a naked political grab that could not be justified on either pricing or costing grounds—and disapproved the proposal. Senator Glenn, perhaps misled by the administration's prior advocacy of this tenderhearted view of the plight of the ordinary citizen and his postage bill, sought to create the same preferential rate for citizens legislatively, except that this time the taxpayers, rather than business mailers, would have to subsidize the cost. The White House vehemently opposed this approach to helping out the ordinary citizen. This does suggest, even to the untutored mind, that not only is there political ineptitude among the White House staff but there is an overweaning concern about encumbering the federal budget with any of the costs of running a viable Postal Service.

Campbell's exegesis of the Senate bill divines therein some political sagacity which I, for one, do not perceive. It is perfectly obvious that the Senate subcommittee began the drafting of the bill with the firm purpose in mind of crafting legislation that the White House, although perhaps not inclined to embrace the product totally, would find acceptable. That purpose necessarily dictated that, at least for the near term, there would be no significant burden placed upon the budget by the provisions of the legislation. Campbell credits the Senate subcommittee with a certain susceptibility to political nuance; that characteristic is perhaps too subtle to have come to my attention. Merely because the Senate subcommittee agreed that there would be some subsidy for small opinion journals and classroom publications, and merely because the Senate subcommittee, through the amendment process, agreed to some minor relief from the private express statutes, is not, to my mind, an example of political acumen. We should bear in mind that the subsidy for small second-class publications was identical to a provision contained in the House-passed bill. Even this administration, which wants to be known for its stinginess in spending federal monies, agreed that it would be better to continue the voices of the small magazines than to have to stand convicted of extinguishing those voices by increasing postage rates. In other words, to the best of my knowledge, no human voice was ever raised against the payment of these few dollars to keep alive these small but intellectually, culturally, and educationally important magazines.

The acceptance by the Senate subcommittee of language affording some relief for time-sensitive communications again was a response to the fact that the House bill contained an invasion of the private express statutes that was, by comparison, extremely wide-ranging. The Senate subcommittee attempted primarily to narrow the differences to the point where the postal unions, while not agreeing to any lapse in the monopoly, would believe that they did not need to marshal all their forces to defeat the bill.

Finally, Campbell perceives that the Senate subcommittee's bill implies a certain tentativeness about the direction in which legislation should steer the Postal Service because of an inadequacy of studies and data. Consequently, the Senate bill is honeycombed with requirements for a variety of studies to be conducted over the next four years, with sunset provisions for a number of the features of the legislation. With all due respect to the value of having more studies about a well-studied subject, I must enter a dissenting note; I believe that we know more about the Postal Service, its method of operations, the costs of those operations, how well it performs, and the degree of consumer acceptance of the services supplied than we do about any governmental operation in the world. Further studies, I suggest, will not add materially to the sum total of our knowledge about the Postal Service and whither it tends. It is, on the other hand, the time-honored device by which those charged with the responsibility for directing public affairs manage to pass on, perhaps to some succeeding administration, the responsibility for making decisions that will in fact foreclose the future, good or bad, for the enterprise.

Campbell has managed to give a thumbnail sketch of the principal parties who have an interest in the future of the Postal Service in about as accurate a way as I have ever seen done, in either a brief or a lengthy treatment. I commend its reading to all students of the subject. The players, according to Campbell, include, first of all, postal management, which he says consists of a group of surviving careerists who have succeeded after many years in getting rid of outsiders, both political appointees and, under the most recent experiment, recruits from private industry who sought to apply the techniques of business to the running of the Postal Service. It is true that, to an extent unimagined by any government careerist in any other agency in 200 years, this vast enterprise is now totally controlled by those who have been nurtured through the system. I do think, however, that Campbell is short on charity when he suggests that the principal objective of postal management is to make sure that its members survive.

The instinct for survival is, of course, a human trait that we all, to a greater or lesser degree, share. I do believe, however, that many of the top people in postal management, despite the fact that they have spent most of their lives there, do have a broader view of their duties and their hopes for the Postal Service than a mean preoccupation with the guarantee of their own jobs. In fairness, Campbell does translate survival into a retention by careerists of the plotting of their own destiny unfettered by congressional or executive control in any important elements. It is hard to tell whether he believes that this is good or bad. I believe that it is an unfortunate development, which was necessarily ordained by the Postal Reorganization Act in setting up an independent Postal Service that functions largely free from the usual constraints. I submit that there is no other enterprise in the world with a budget verging on $18 billion a year, employing almost 1 percent of the national work force, affecting the daily lives of every citizen, that reports to no one and is answerable to no one in the final analysis. The market is no substitute regulator because the service is a monopoly.

The next most important participants in postal affairs, according to Campbell, are the unions, a force he perceives as having an increasingly declining influence on postal matters, for reasons to which I do not necessarily subscribe. It is obvious that the political strength of the postal unions has been on the decline and that all public employee unions are heading into tough weather. I suspect that the public is becoming somewhat fed up with the antics of public employees and what is perceived as their disregard for the public interest. The political strength of the public employee unions must derive in large part from the support and sympathy of the public.

Campbell would agree that one union in particular, the National Association of Letter Carriers, maintains a very aggressive posture, particularly when it comes to any weakening of the postal monopoly. Indeed, the letter carriers initiated the first lawsuit in modern times to enforce the postal monopoly. It is interesting that it was the National Association of Letter Carriers rather than the Postal Service that brought this lawsuit, which was to enjoin the so-called Independent Postal System of America (IPSA) from functioning as a private postal system. (I handled the IPSA case in the Tenth Circuit Court of Appeals.) In that case the court had before it a complete record of the 100-year expansion, well beyond any statutory authority, of the Postal Service monopoly. And the court appeared to be shocked, during oral argument, to learn how far the Postal Service had gone beyond what appeared to be a rather limited grant of monopoly. The court was equally annoyed at the inability of counsel for the Postal Service and letter carriers to justify or defend this vast extension of coverage. The court went so far as to chastise both counsel. Notwithstanding, the opinion ultimately issued by the Tenth Circuit Court of Appeals made no mention whatsoever of any of these difficulties or of any of the expressed opinions advanced by the court in oral argument, finding, rather, that this expansion of the monopoly power had been acquiesced in over a period of 100 years by the Congress; finding moreover that the Postal Reorganization Act itself vested large powers in the Postal Service to expand and define the limits of the postal monopoly.

I dwell on this case at some length only because I think it is important to disabuse people of the idea that the courts are somehow going to prevent the Postal Service from gobbling up terrain in the private express area. I for one do not believe that will happen.

Campbell's next important category of participants on the postal scene includes what he calls "subsidized users." Campbell seems to have succumbed to the kind of propaganda and misinformation that newspapers and economists at American Enterprise Institute forums are fond of perpetuating. There is no subsidy whatsoever to either advertisers, who are primarily third-class mailers, or to parcel shippers. Publishers—that is, those holding second-class mailing privileges—have, since 1970, had their rates subsidized. Much to their regret, however, this is the final year of that subsidy. Beginning next July, they will no longer receive so much as one penny of subsidy. Nonprofit organizations—colleges, hospitals, the Easter Seal Society, the blind, and others—have been and will continue to be subsidized. I presume that Campbell does not have reference to those groups.

Campbell is correct, however, in noting that magazines, no doubt in part because their subsidized rates are coming to an end, have been seriously exploring the possibilities of alternate delivery. In several parts of the country there are very successful alternate delivery operations, although the amount of carriage by private delivery still represents less than 1 percent of the total. But the Postal Service must be aware of and concerned about the fact that, with the end of subsidy, and with the kind of rate increases visited upon magazines and newspapers (almost 500 percent) over the last eight years, this effort to find an alternate competitive medium for delivery will be increased.

Advertisers, primarily third-class mailers, have also figured out that they can help keep their own postal rates lower by threatening the Postal Service with the possibility of using an alternative method of delivering their messages. Unfortunately for them, however, the Postal Service's interpretations of the postal monopoly would appear to prohibit most of the materials they send from being sent outside the Postal Service. For that reason, as Campbell notes, third-class users have filed a lawsuit seeking, essentially, to have the courts declare that the postal monopoly does not apply to third-class mail. The federal district court has already ruled against the advertisers, and I predict that the court of appeals will affirm.

Campbell also notes that parcel shippers have deserted the Postal Service for private carriers in droves; whereas postal volumes for parcels have declined from 900 million in 1959 to 300 million in 1976, United Parcel Service, the sole national private parcel carrier, increased its volumes in the same period from 100 million to 1 billion. Without so saying, Campbell implies that the loss of postal volume is due to management inefficiency or poor service. In fact, the vast amount of this volume left the Post Office and was driven into the hands of United Parcel Service only since the Postal Reorganization Act. This act, according to court decisions, requires rates to be made in a way that removes any pricing discretion from the Postal Service. Quite simply, parcel post has been compelled through court decisions to bear an artificially high price, which the private carrier, United Parcel Service, is very effectively able to undercut. There are numerous reasons for UPS's ability to undercut the Post Office's parcel price, not the least being that United Parcel Service is not burdened with the obligation of handling single-parcel shipments from householders but can focus its efforts on large-volume business shipments that are far more economical to handle.

Campbell notes evidence that book publishers intend to desert the Postal Service. Despite testimony to that effect given by the Association of American Publishers, the cost of shipping books by private systems is still substantially in excess of the price charged by the Postal Service; consequently, the day of large-scale diversions of books from the postal system to private carriers is some time off.

Another important group mentioned by Campbell are those living in rural areas. This group has no organization, but they have always managed to fare well; the postal laws are honeycombed with prohibitions against reductions in service that would have an impact on rural areas. Rural mailers do not need to organize into a lobby because their congressional representatives are keenly sensitive to their needs and, without prompting, tend to those needs.

I was pleased to note that Campbell has given equal billing to United Parcel Service, the sole national private parcel carrier. United Parcel Service, because of its rate structure and because the Postal

Service is bound by law to charge artificially high postal rates, has a virtual monopoly on business parcels and a rate of return on investment that is the envy of the *Fortune* 500. Campbell is all too correct when he says United Parcel Service has enormous political clout and is a force that must be reckoned with. The most recent example of its muscle is the contest between the postal unions and UPS on the adoption of the floor amendment offered by Representative Paul Simon, which was strenuously opposed by the postal unions and which United Parcel Service succeeded in having overwhelmingly adopted by the House. Of course, the fact that the International Brotherhood of Teamsters is a close ally of UPS may simply be another illustration of the fact that some unions have far more clout than others.

A recent entrant, noted by Campbell, into the ranks of those who influence postal affairs is the so-called time-sensitive group, composed primarily of private carriers such as Purolator, Federal Express, and their principal customers. This amalgamation of carriers and customers had some limited success, at least within the Senate subcommittee, in gaining acceptance of some minor relief from the postal monopoly laws. Suffice it to say that the provision they succeeded in including in the Senate legislation was in part responsible for the fact that the legislation was not permitted to reach the Senate floor for a vote. It was one of the key provisions of the legislation that the Senate Budget Committee said would have ruinous revenue consequences to the Postal Service and for which reason the Senate Budget Committee refused to grant a waiver from the budget ceiling requirements.

The last important group mentioned by Campbell is the public. Obviously the public is not organized in any formal sense; however, the public has let its various representatives know of its concern about Postal Service, and it appears to be quite effectively represented in the Congress at large. Campbell has cited statistics indicating that in fact the public is becoming increasingly dissatisfied with both the Postal Service and postal rates. The depth of this resentment, however, is something that is not known.

It is Campbell's principal thesis that because of the substantial wage increases that resulted in much higher rates, and because of technological change and substitution of communication means, the Postal Service is in danger of becoming extinct unless it can, through one of two devices, insulate itself from private competition. Those devices are: (1) substantial appropriations from tax revenues that will permit the Postal Service to charge rates lower than the competition; or (2) an insulation of high postal rates from competition because of the reservation of the business to the Postal Service under the postal monopoly. It is Campbell's conclusion, with which I find it difficult to disagree, that the Congress probably will be unwilling to vote large appropriations to the Postal Service in the future. At the same time, I cannot agree that appropriation from taxes to the Postal Service is tantamount to reversing the national policy in favor of an independent Postal Service expressed in the 1970 Postal Reorganization Act. While appropriations could be used by the Postal Service to shield itself from competition, the Postal Service itself is opposed to such appropriations; and those users who have advocated increased appropriations have not advocated them because they wish to shield the Postal Service from competition. Rather, they have found that the Postal Service supplies to the public vast amounts of services not needed by business users of the Postal Service, which the public, or at the very least, the public's representatives, have continued to insist be supplied, and which must be paid for by the business users of the Postal Service even though these services are not required or used by these businesses.

Campbell also ventures to guess that the public would prefer an independent, self-sustaining Postal Service to the increased taxes that would be needed to continue to pay higher wages to postal employees. If, of course, the issue were presented in that way in any public opinion poll, Campbell would be found to be correct. I believe, however, that, if the public is told they must either pay higher taxes or face a discontinuance of delivery to their homes six days a week, closure of their local post office, and curtailment of numerous other public services performed by the Postal Service, the public's answer would be quite different than that intuited by Campbell.

By way of buttressing his belief that large appropriations will not be voted by the Congress in the future, Campbell essays his judgment that second-, third-, and fourth-class users do not constitute a strong political force for reversion of national policy to higher appropriations for the Postal Service. I would like to be able to disagree with that conclusion, but given the failure of these users to succeed in the enactment of either the House or the Senate version of H.R. 7700 over the last two years, I am afraid I must agree. And I must agree with Campbell's larger conclusion that the Congress will not give appropriations to the Postal Service sufficient, in his words, to form a substantial degree of protection to the Postal Service from private competition. Campbell neglects to mention the remaining option, the substantial curtailment of services to the public that are neither needed nor desired by the vast bulk of the business users of the system. If the Postal Service were to opt for that alternative, the same low rates could prevail without the need for large amounts of subsidy from the Congress.

222

This brings Campbell to the real meat of his paper, the fact that the only real alternative left to the Postal Service to maintain itself as a viable system is to insulate itself from future competition through an exertion of the postal monopoly laws. He describes the literal meaning of the existing postal monopoly, which has been intact in virtually the same language for some 100 years, as a very thin shield. He believes that the literal rendering of that language would protect from competition only personal letters, business letters, and other correspondence, which constitute only 30 percent of first-class revenues or some 15 percent of total revenues. I do not really understand why he wants to dwell upon a literal reading of the statute, which the Postal Service has avoided since the turn of the century and which the courts and the Congress have long since abandoned. The harsh reality is that the Postal Service construes that postal monopoly language in such a comprehensive way that it covers not only virtually all first-class mail but practically all third-class mail as well. We are now talking about monopoly protection for close to 75 percent of total postal revenues.

In a rather puzzling section, Campbell discusses the curious behavior of the Postal Service in not attempting to get Congress to enact a stronger monopoly law, even though he believes the 1970 Postal Reorganization Act was an invitiation to the Postal Service to ask for more monopoly powers. Frankly, I do not read the 1970 act in that light, although I am aware that the Postal Service deliberately misconstrued the act as holding out that option. Quite clearly, the legislative history of that act and the Kappel commission report that provided the underpinnings of that legislation envisioned that the Postal Service, after studying the exercise of its monopoly, would come to the Congress with suggestions for a reduction of the degree of its monopoly control over mail. Nevertheless, the Postal Service is content with the statute as it exists and certainly has no intention of trying to expand its breadth legislatively. The Postal Service, historically, as Campbell has noted, has sought the expansion through administrative devices.

Campbell's thesis is that the Postal Service finds the present statute sufficiently useful because it is employed to intimidate postal customers into believing that their materials are covered by the monopoly. Through threats of fines and demands for back payment of postage, many mailers are coerced into compliance. I know that kind of excess has in fact taken place. It is, however, not nearly so pervasive as Campbell would lead us to believe.

He does point out an ominous development for those who utilize private carriers in the belief they are doing so without violating the law. The Postal Service has been active in seeking legislation to translate its present enforcement powers into what amounts to increased penalties for violation of the monopoly. The Postal Service has been extremely reluctant (although some postal inspectors have not been) to threaten people with criminal prosecution. That threat is the service's only real bargaining tool in coercing customer compliance with its version of the monopoly. These legislative efforts seem to have died with the imminent adjournment of Congress; but there is no reason to believe that those efforts will not be revived.

Campbell's principal thesis is that, confronted with technological change, an irrefutably high wage base that results in extremely high prices for postal products, and an unwillingness to accept the complications and invasion of authority that would accompany increased appropriations to assist in maintaining competitive prices, the Postal Service has constructed a strategy of maintaining their competitive posture through expansion of the postal monopoly. Campbell points to the service's 1974 regulations on the private express as a clear instance of this expansionist approach. Those regulations do nail down a number of gray areas by proclaiming that any tangible object bearing information to be communicated to an identifiable person or address is, with quite few exceptions, subject to the monopoly. Campbell overstates the matter, however, when he lists examples of materials that are now covered but were not heretofore, specifically blueprints and data-processing materials. One solicitor's opinion in 1960 did rule that blueprints were not "letters," but that opinion was not subsequently followed. I would have to agree with the present Postal Service ruling: Blueprints fit even a narrow definition of the term "letter," as used in the statutes. Data-processing materials have, under most circumstances, been held subject to the monopoly for two decades. As another example, Campbell cites advertising materials that are included in merchandise packages sent by private delivery. This truly is an innovation of the Postal Service, although for its own reasons the Postal Service, while proclaiming that these materials are covered by the monopoly, is not presently enforcing this construction.

Campbell notes that the strategy of the Postal Service embraces a concept of suspension of the monopoly so that it can politically appease powerful antagonists. His examples include the appeasement of the banks through the ruling that checks when sent in bulk between banks are not subject to the monopoly, whereas checks when sent between individuals are. Under some circumstances, checks were not regarded as letters prior to the 1974 regulations but are now regarded as letters when sent between individuals. This would clearly seem to be a discrimination in favor of the banks. Another example cited by Campbell to demonstrate this point is that data-processing materials have been exempted from the monopoly when those materials must be processed within certain time limits—a benefit only to big companies with processing equipment. Actually, this example argues against Campbell's position. Rather than being an expansion of the Postal Service's powers, this represents a retraction, since the Postal Service's position for at least twenty years has been that data-processing materials were subject to the monopoly if any use was made of the materials by the addressee, irrespective of the time limits within which they had to be processed.

The Postal Service might very well choose to suspend the monopoly in a number of circumstances, and that decision may be prompted by political reasons. Should that prove to be the case, I for one believe that the Postal Service should be applauded for that sagacity. After all, it is a very harsh government that tells the American people that, notwithstanding the fact that the government does not choose to provide the service that the American people need, this government will nevertheless compel them to use the Postal Service or pay a penalty for using a private delivery service. The Postal Service is to be applauded if it utilizes its suspension powers to correct those kinds of situations.

Discussion

BERNARD SOBIN, Civil Aeronautics Board: I want to make some comments on the Postal Service's expanding into electronic communications, whether with or without a monopoly. I would favor its entry into that area if a real complementarity could be demonstrated between what the Postal Service has to do and electronic communications. This has also been called an economy of scope. If the Postal Service is in some peculiarly advantageous position to provide these services officially and economically, it ought to do so, with or without the protection of a monopoly. The only time I see the possibility of an advantage is when the electronics services deliver hard copy, which the Postal Service presumably does well.

I see nothing that gives the Postal Service any advantage whatever over any other company in the electronic communications area. As a government agency not known for its rate innovations, ingenuity, expertise in technological fields, and so on, the Postal Service would perhaps be better advised to leave this area to private industry, with or without regulation.

MR. TIBETT: Timothy May seemed to believe that there was a postal monopoly in the hard-copy area. Would he clarify why the exception for telegrams in the hard-copy area would not exclude from monopoly similar kinds of hard copy?

TIMOTHY J. MAY: This is only hearsay, but I understand that Western Union went to the White House—before my time—and got that exception. I think that is why it does not apply to anything else.

MR. TIBETT: Then the exception is not written in the statutes somewhere?

MR. MAY: The 1974 regulations expressly exclude telegrams.

MR. TIBETT: By company name or by generic description?

MR. MAY: As telegrams. My predecessors at the Post Office told me that at one point they were going to move against Western Union, and the issue was resolved in the White House. I do not remember which administration it was.

MR. TIBETT: Since anybody can sell under the name "aspirin," why can't anybody call such messages telegrams? That seems to be a generic term now, too.

MR. MAY: I have had some clients who tried to use the term "telegram," and they heard very quickly from Western Union about it; the Federal Trade Commission also complained.

CHARLES L. JACKSON: To what extent can the Federal Communications Commission go after any Postal Service operation that is being provided by a private carrier or after the Postal Service itself if it provides any category 1, 2, or 3 electronic mail service? In other words, to what extent can the FCC extend its regulatory authority to the Postal Service, either directly or indirectly, if the Postal Service contracts out to the private sector?

KENNETH ROBINSON: My guess would be that the FCC, if it chose to extend its regulatory authority, could probably sustain that in the courts. This question arose very recently in the reselling and brokerage decision: Does the commission have the authority to regulate a person who leases bulk capacity from another well-known monopolist, AT&T, and then resells that capacity in either a conditioned form or a pure form to others? Logically, one would not think that a party reselling a communications service would be subject to Title II regulation by the FCC. The commission already regulates the underlying carrier. If there are objections to what the broker is doing, there already are many alternatives.

The FCC managed to find a regulatory imperative in the statute that says the commission shall grant certificate. The commission asserted the authority over the objection of IBM and a number of others, including the Department of Justice. That case was taken to the Second Circuit Court, which affirmed the commission's decision. IBM, the Department of Commerce, and the Justice Department petitioned the Supreme Court for certification, and the Supreme Court declined to review the case. So I do think that if the FCC chose to extend its authority it could quite easily do so.

A classic example is provided by the cable television industry. In 1965 the FCC appeared before its Senate oversight subcommittee pleading an inability to regulate the cable television business and asking for enabling legislation. I do not know where they found the authority, but many people in the cable television industry will tell you that it is quite real.

DR. JACKSON: What about placing conditions on the authorizations of the radio licenses given to any common carriers of some service to the public?

MR. ROBINSON: The FCC statute is unusual in placing conditions on so-called 214 certificates, because the statute was carried over from the Interstate Commerce Commission, which certificates carriers as to route, commodity, time—a host of variables. When the FCC carried its statute over in 1934, that kind of ornate regulatory cartel management really was not necessary because there was only one company to manage.

I assume that was one reason the explicit authority to put conditions on all these little variables was more or less deleted. The FCC has asserted its authority to place conditions on 214 certificates, and in fact it does. Quite frequently, it conditions entry—one can get involved in a business only if various incorporation procedures are undertaken, one can serve only certain groups, and so on. Again, I think there is very little that a full-fledged regulatory agency, such as the FCC, cannot do, if it so chooses.

Selected AEI Publications

AEI Associates Program